Beyond Scenography

Focused on the Anglophone adoption from the 1960s onwards, *Beyond Scenography* explores the porous state of contemporary theatre-making to argue a critical distinction between scenography (as a crafting of place orientation) and scenographics (that which orientate acts of worlding). With sections on installation art and gardening as well as marketing and placemaking, this book is an argument for what scenography does: how assemblages of scenographic traits orientate, situate, and shape staged events. Established stage orthodoxies are revisited – including the symbiosis of stage and scene and the aesthetic ideology of 'the scenic' – to propose how scenographics are formative to staged atmospheres. Consequently, one of the conclusions of this book is that there is no theatre practice without scenography, no stages without scenographics. *Beyond Scenography* offers a manifesto for a renewed theory of scenographic practice.

Dr Rachel Hann is Lecturer in Scenography at the University of Surrey, UK.

Beyond Scenography

Rachel Hann

LONDON AND NEW YORK

First published 2019
by Routledge
2 Park Square, Milton Park, Abingdon, Oxon OX14 4RN

and by Routledge
711 Third Avenue, New York, NY 10017

Routledge is an imprint of the Taylor & Francis Group, an informa business

© 2019 Rachel Hann

The right of Rachel Hann to be identified as the author of this work has been asserted by her in accordance with sections 77 and 78 of the Copyright, Designs and Patents Act 1988.

All rights reserved. No part of this book may be reprinted or reproduced or utilised in any form or by any electronic, mechanical, or other means, now known or hereafter invented, including photocopying and recording, or in any information storage or retrieval system, without permission in writing from the publishers.

Trademark notice: Product or corporate names may be trademarks or registered trademarks, and are used only for identification and explanation without intent to infringe.

British Library Cataloguing-in-Publication Data
A catalogue record for this book is available from the British Library

Library of Congress Cataloging-in-Publication Data
Names: Hann, Rachel, author.
Title: Beyond scenography / Rachel Hann.
Description: New York : Routledge, Taylor & Francis Group, 2018.
Identifiers: LCCN 2018003731 | ISBN 9781138785052 (hardback) |
    ISBN 9781138785069 (pbk.) | ISBN 9780429489136 (ebk.)
Subjects: LCSH: Theaters—Stage-setting and scenery. | Motion pictures—Setting and scenery.
Classification: LCC PN2091.S8 H2525 2018 | DDC 792.02/5—dc23
LC record available at https://lccn.loc.gov/2018003731

ISBN: 978-1-138-78505-2 (hbk)
ISBN: 978-1-138-78506-9 (pbk)
ISBN: 978-0-429-48913-6 (ebk)

Typeset in Adobe Caslon
by Apex CoVantage, LLC

Printed and bound in Great Britain by
TJ International Ltd, Padstow, Cornwall

Contents

Acknowledgements — vii

Introduction — 1
Scenography as theatre-making 5
Theatre, performance and scenography 8
Research questions and chapters 14

1 Place orientation, scenic politics and scenographics — 19
Scenes and scenic politics 24
Scenographics 28
Othering tactics 32

2 Scenography and the Anglophone theatres — 39
The first adoption of scenography 40
Continental differences pre-1960 41
The second adoption of scenography 42
Sound and costume as scenography 46

3 Scenography beyond scenographers — 51
Mise en scène and scenography 52
Whose scenography? 56
Beyond dramaturgy and choreography 58
Expanded scene design? 61

4 Scenography happens — 67
The time of scenography 68
Scenography beyond set 71
Gecko's MISSING set 73

5 Scenographic worlding — 79
Stage geographies 81
Stage ideologies 84
Scenography beyond stages? 86
Stage-scenes beyond vision 92

6 Scenographic cultures — 99
Installation art and scenographic scale 101
Interior design and scenographic behaviours 104
Marketing and scenographic seduction 108

Gardening and scenographic curation 111
Protest and scenographic activism 113

7 Scenographic architecture   119

Fast architecture 120
Trompe l'oeil *and scenographic propaganda 125*
Potemkin villages and scenographic placemaking 127

Conclusion   133

Bibliography   137
Index   147

Acknowledgements

First and foremost I wish to thank those colleagues who have supported my academic development. I acknowledge the influence, advice and provocations of Christopher Baugh and Scott Palmer as being foundational to all my research. I also remain indebted to Sidsel Bech for listening and debating my positions on scenography, along with all the colleagues and students at Edge Hill University who gave encouragement and focus to my critical thinking. Many of the ideas featured here first converged as part of those student discussions. I have written this book in the same challenging, yet supportive, spirit that I conducted those workshops and seminars.

Since arriving at the University of Surrey in 2015, I have been deeply inspired by the level of debate and thoughtful critique that my colleagues cultivate. In particular, I wish to recognize the detailed feedback from Adam Alston, Patrick Duggan and Shantel Ehrenberg. Your generosity and challenging questions have shaped my research process. You are all stars.

The manifesto that features within this book was first shared at the 2nd International Performance Design Symposium in Rome and Fara Sabina, January 2014. I acknowledge the feedback and encouragement from colleagues received at that event as being formative to the ideas that feature in this book. These include Dorita Hannah, Kathleen Irwin, Anna Birch, Reija Hirvikoski and Mónica Raya, who suggested that I publish the manifesto.

I wish to acknowledge colleagues from the Theatre & Performance Research Association who have reviewed, commented and challenged me on the arguments included within my presentations featured as part of the Scenography working group (at Glasgow, 2013), Dramaturgy and Directing (Worcester, 2015) and Performance and the Body (Salford, 2017).

There are also the many discussions that I have had with colleagues and peers on the topic of scenography that, while often informal, have been crucial to the development of this book. These include Emily Orley, Elizabeth Wright, Joslin McKinney, Nick Hunt, Rodrigo Tisi, Juliet Rufford, David Shearing, Angrette McCloskey, Andy Lavender, Luis Campos and Siobhán O'Gorman.

I am indebted to the following colleagues who have offered explicit comments on translations, interdisciplinary usages, aligned content and histories of terminologies – thanks to Sofia Pantouvaki, Kirsty Lohman, Pamela Howard, Arnold Aronson, Thea Brejzek and Christin Essin.

Research is always a porous process and filters into all aspects of debate and discussion. In that regard, I wish to thank the PhD researchers I am fortunate enough to supervise for their searching questions – specifically: Michelle Man for prompting discussions on 'witness'; Ele Slade for debating orientation; Meg Cunningham for querying worlding; Susannah Henry for approaches to landscape and embodiment; Will Osmond for discussions on auto-ethnographic writing; and Melissa Addey for world-building in literature.

I wish to thank Talia Rodgers for commissioning the book and Stacey Walker for her support in its completion. There are also those nameless colleagues who acted as reviewers for the proposal and drafts. Your comments and encouragement have been a guide throughout.

Lastly, I am hugely thankful to my beautiful partner, Nicola, for her support and love while I was squirrelled away writing this book. I am also grateful that she convinced me to take weekend breaks with our friends Martin and Chris. To celebrate the importance of a work–life balance, I have included accounts of our experiences within the pages of this book. It seemed a fitting tribute.

Scenographics irritate the disciplined orders of world.

Introduction

Scenographer and architect Frederick Kiesler's (1890–1965) manifesto 'The Theatre is Dead' (1926, see Figure 1) offers a point of departure for this book. The crux of my argument begins from the provocation that, to paraphrase Kiesler, *we are working for a scenography that has survived scenography*. I trace how in the twentieth and early twenty-first centuries there have been numerous cases for succeeding, transgressing, de-centring away from the institutional orthodoxies of theatre. Anticipating the taxonomies of performance as well as the postdramatic, Kiesler's proposition of a theatre beyond theatre informs my reappraisal of scenography in response to intermedial and immersive practices. It also frames my argument for how scenographic traits operate within diverse material cultures such as installation art or gardening. Accordingly, this book is a study in scenographic excess; of going *beyond* scenography.

The title is influenced by Hans-Thies Lehmann's usage of 'beyond' in his argument for postdramatic theatre, where the 'adjective "postdramatic" denotes a theatre that feels bound to operate beyond drama, at a time "after" the authority of the dramatic paradigm in theatre' (Lehmann 2006: 27). However, this book does not aim to offer a departure from the term 'scenography'. It is not an argument for ideas of post-scenography *per se*. Instead, I am concerned with the crucial returns that an investigation of the beyond entails. Cultural theorist Homi Bhabha outlines how the term 'signifies spatial distance, marks progress, promises the future; but our intimations of exceeding the barrier or boundary – the very act of going beyond – are unknowable, unrepresentable, without a return to the "present" which, in the process of repetition, becomes disjunct and displaced' (Bhabha 1994: 4). Bhabha considers how the task of going beyond 'is neither a new

FOREWORD

THE THEATRE IS DEAD.

WE ARE NOT WORKING FOR NEW DECORATION.

WE ARE NOT WORKING FOR NEW LITERATURE.

WE ARE NOT WORKING FOR NEW LIGHTING SYSTEMS.

WE ARE NOT WORKING FOR NEW MASKS.

WE ARE NOT WORKING FOR NEW STAGES.

WE ARE NOT WORKING FOR NEW COSTUMES.

WE ARE NOT WORKING FOR NEW ACTORS.

WE ARE NOT WORKING FOR NEW THEATRES.

WE ARE WORKING FOR THE THEATRE THAT HAS SURVIVED THE THEATRE.

WE ARE WORKING FOR THE SOUND BODY OF A NEW SOCIETY.

AND WE HAVE CONFIDENCE IN THE STRENGTH OF NEWER GENERATIONS THAT ARE AWARE OF THEIR PROBLEMS.

THE THEATRE IS DEAD.

WE WANT TO GIVE IT A SPLENDID BURIAL.

ADMISSION 75 CENTS.

KIESLER

Figure 1 'The Theatre is Dead' by Frederick Kiesler was a manifesto for the 'International Theatre Exposition' in New York, 1926. It was published as a one-page preface to a special issue on the exhibition for *The Little Review*.
Source: Kiesler (1926: 1)

horizon, nor a leaving behind of the past', but rather a 'here and there, on all sides, fort/da, hither and thither, back and forth' (Bhabha 1994: 1). In framing this study in terms of the beyond, I seek to recognize how concepts and practices of scenography are in a state of toing and froing, of moving between learned certitudes and potentials of practice. I argue that scenography sustains a feeling of the beyond where the crafting of a 'scene' – inclusive of the orientating qualities of light and sound as well as costume and scenery – encompasses a range of distinct methods for atmospheric transformation that score how encounters of 'world' are conceptualized and rendered attentive.

Evidenced with accounts of my own experiences, I outline how the idiosyncratic practices of contemporary scenography have exceeded the old certitudes of scene painting and set design. I argue that scenography isolates how an accumulation of material and technological methods 'score' ongoing processes of 'worlding'. A combination of *Welten* and *Weltet* were employed by Martin Heidegger (1927) to stress how the ongoing active qualities of 'the world' are irreducible and can only be conceptualized in terms of worlding. Anthropologist Kathleen Stewart (2007, 2011, 2014) expands upon this position to argue how multiple thresholds of worlding are negotiated as part of everyday life. Stewart frames this notion of worlding in terms of compositional theory:

> Here, compositional theory takes the form of a sharply impassive attunement to the ways in which an assemblage of elements comes to hang together as a thing that has qualities, sensory aesthetics and lines of force and how such things come into sense already composed and generative and pulling matter and mind into a making: a worlding.
>
> (Stewart 2014: 119)

The attunement that Stewart describes is predicated on how a worlding assemblage operates as a generative force that orientates moments of action, reflection, and worldly experience. In relation to scenography, Stewart argues that these multiple perceptual worldings are encountered as momentary 'scenes', where 'Scenes becoming worlds are singularities of rhythm and attachment. They require and initiate the kind of attention that both thinks through matter and accords it a life of its own' (Stewart 2014: 119). Consequently, the scene as an attentive singularity *scores* – irritates, highlights, reveals – orders of world; a scoring that is equally evident at land borders between nations, the attentiveness of stage geographies, or the imposition of a crime scene. In that regard, I propose that scenographic traits score ongoing processes of worlding through discrete interventional acts of 'place orientation', where orientation is inclusive of haptic proxemics and orders of knowledge. My argument for place orientation situates scenography's intellectual and practical concerns as complementary to the established lexicon of theatrical design whether stage design or *mise en scène*. While also a mediator for spatial figuring, I outline how scenography happens as a temporal assemblage that is linguistically more akin to notions of 'staging' than 'set'. I argue that a renewed differentiation affords scenography a platform from which to invite intellectual bridges with other academic disciplines beyond theatre. To study scenography in the early twenty-first century is to study a practice that is always seeking, always implicated, within a transgression of borders, whether disciplinary, linguistic, geographic or practical. It is, however, Bhabha and Kiesler's promise of a return that informs the overall shape of this book's argument. I contend that the holistic implications of the contemporary approach render scenography a trait of *all* theatre. I summarize this argument by revisiting the deterministic assumption that has defined conceptions of scenography. Specifically, that there is no theatre practice without scenography.

My proposal for scenography's centrality to all acts of theatre is evidenced through a re-reading of the 'stage-scene' symbiosis. I argue that the Ancient Greek σκηνή (*skēnē*), a tent or hut, was an act of place orientation. Before any etchings on the surface, the placement of the *skēnē* changed how the θέατρον (*theatron*, a place for seeing) was conceived, understood and experienced. As Marvin Carlson observes, 'The skene house, in addition to its practical service, provided a tangible sign for the hidden "other" world of the actor, the place of appearance and disappearance, the realm of events not seen but whose effects condition the visible world of the stage' (Carlson 1989: 131). The very act of introducing a temporary structure onto the ὀρχήστρα (*orchēstra*), the place for dancing, radically changed the conceptual and material circumstances of staging henceforth. While Carlson focuses on how the *skēnē* gave material and symbolic credence to 'off-stage' worlds, this intervention also confirms how scenography scores perceptual encounters of 'world' more broadly construed.

'Stage' as a discrete concept arguably began with the notion of the *proskenion* (a platform constructed 'in front of the scene'). Centuries later the stage concept would be rendered discrete from scene forming the basis for the perspective stages of the Renaissance, which sought to isolate stage from world, scene from spectators. Nevertheless, I argue that stages and scenes are symbiotic in conception and execution – where all stages are also scenes. This reading is evident in the etymology of many continental European languages (such as French and Norwegian) where variants on the term *skēnē* translate as 'stage'. The 'skene house', as Carlson terms it, reshaped the spatial orientations of the *orchēstra* and, over time, would flatten the conceptual distinction between a place for dancing with the orientating qualities of the s*kēnē*. I express this tension through the hybrid term 'stage-scene'.

Furthermore, I confront the assumption that a singular legacy emerged from σκηνογραφία (*skenographia*) and instead argue how each linguistic variation is conditioned by distinct theatrical cultures of place orientation. From *skenographia* to *scénographie*, *escenografia* to *szenografie*, I recognize these linguistic variations and their associated conventions by consciously applying the Anglophone scenography (with a 'y') throughout this book. When discussing a continental variant, the Latinized spelling of the variant in question is employed in recognition of these distinct histories. Beyond the politics of the term's usage, the overall aim is to map how the orientating qualities of the *skēnē*, and its symbiosis with the stage concept, have become fundamental to all conceptions of theatre.

Contrary to my argument on the centrality of scenography to contemporary theatre-making, I write this book at a time when the English-language appropriation is being actively contested and challenged. Whether its lacklustre adoption by the professional Anglophone theatres or its removal from the subtitle for the Prague Quadrennial (PQ), scenography is in a state of uncertainty that has been magnified by an expansion of its practical remit in the last few decades. Arguments for scenography's application beyond the institutional orthodoxies of theatre has rendered the term politically loaded and, in certain quarters, been supplanted by 'Performance Design'. Correspondingly, the idea of scenography is often ignored by English-speaking theatre communities, with accusations of academic pretension. This association partly stems from the adoption of scenography as a critical argument for why 'designers' should have creative and conceptual parity with directors, performers, choreographers, dramaturgs, etc. The notion that scenography is conceptually *for* designers has been an underlying feature of this argument. Yet, I contend that scenography is formative to all theatre-making and is, therefore, implicated within the labours of directors and performers, as well as choreographers and dramaturgs. I am arguing for the recognition of scenography as a holistic strategy of theatre-making. Therefore, when introducing an example or case study I apply a form of thick description (Geertz 1973) rather than images to describe the experience. These are typically written in the first person and recount my own encounter with a scenography or scenographic culture. My aim is to capture a sense of the multiplicities involved within the bodily act of place orientation. From masks to costume, light to sound, architecture to bodies, these discrete stimuli are connected through the act of scenography. Each stimulus acts upon performers and spectators as part of a wider encounter of place orientation. I argue that, within the collaborative context of theatre-making, scenography exceeds the defined role of a singular scenographer.

While many of the interdisciplinary relationships I describe have been conceptualized as part of an expanded ethos, *Beyond Scenography* operates as my critique of 'expanded scenography' – a terminology that has come to account for scenographic ideas or practices that exceed the ideologies and orthodoxies of the institutionalized theatres. Whether in terms of the spatial configuration of a public garden or the staged quality of interior design, I argue that the expanded ethos reflects a wider politics that seeks to de-centre the practice of scenography away from theatre. The argument for Performance Design stems from a similar position. The borderless concept of performance offers a framework for transgressing the professional hierarchies (of supporting a director or playtext) along with an anti-theatrical negative charge (of conventional or inauthentic). As an act of dissociation and transgression, an expanded remit promotes an expanded ownership of scenography and invites those beyond conventional design roles to critique and argue the case for scenography. This approach also affords those within conventional roles to exceed defined design crafts. In light of this critical expansion, the plural condition of an expanded field has arguably rendered scenography an inclusive material practice that is potentially borderless in its scope and intention. The term 'scenography' is now applied to the design of a parliament building (Filmer 2013) as well as the experience of mountaineering (Carver 2013). Scenography is *potentially* everywhere. However, this post-disciplinary positioning sustains a counterargument on the critical usefulness of scenography for other disciplines that already sustain established critiques on theatricality and performativity. My response centres on the critical capacity of a scenographic 'potential'. I isolate this trait within the distinction between the terms 'scenography' and 'scenographic'.

I contend that the potentiality of a scenographic trait is one of the driving forces behind scenography's current state of excess. I argue that the proposal for an expanded scenography is founded on the assumption that a scenographic trait exceeds the artistic and professional orthodoxies of the institutional theatres: where scenography and scenographers are often partitioned as additional and illustrative, rather than formative and critical. My call to consider the critical implications of scenographic traits aligns with art critic Dorothea von Hantelmann's critique on the overuse of the term 'performative' in art cultures. Indeed, von Hantelmann isolates this relationship directly:

> Today it is widely believed that 'performative' can be understood as 'performance-like'. Understood in this false sense it has become a ubiquitous catchword for a broad range of contemporary art phenomena that, in the widest sense, show an affinity to forms of staging, theatricality and mise-en-scene.
> (von Hantelmann 2010: 17)

The affinity that von Hantelmann describes – with staging, theatricality and *mise en scène* – are, I argue, directed towards how art practices evoke the scenographic traits of theatre. Furthermore, I complicate how the application of *mise en scène* in art cultures is typically in reference to the 'stage-like' or 'set-like' qualities of the work. Instead, I position *mise en scène* as a distinct system of interpretation and translation that frames the situational orientations of scenography.

Scenographer Thea Brejzek argues that, with the expansion of scenographic traits beyond theatre orthodoxies, 'the scenographer emerges not as the spatial organizer of scripted narratives but as the author of constructed situations and as an agent of interaction and communication' (Brejzek 2010: 112). I adopt Brejzek's focus on 'constructed situations' to consider how certain art or social practices evoke an affinity with situational acts of staging. Crucially, if scenography happens as an interventional situation, then the orientations of scenographic traits are inclusive of all human and non-human agents that render a place as eventful, attentive.

To capture the multiple and porous orientations that render place attentive, I employ the notion of 'scenographics' as a collective term for how the methods of costume, stage geography, light and sound orientate interventional encounters of place. Moreover, I argue that the term 'scenographic' is critically distinct to scenography, with the implication being that an object or event can impart a scenographic trait without necessarily being considered scenography. This conceptual distinction is akin to the relationship between performance and performativity, theatre and theatricality, choreography and choreographic. As part of this differentiation, I approach a scenographic trait as *orientating* and scenography as a *crafting*. My intention is to map how these evidently related concepts apply to artistic and social scenarios beyond institutional conceptions of theatre. I attempt to dissuade the reader from understanding notions of scenographic as singular and monolithic. My adoption of scenographics stresses the inherent plurality and multiplicities that sustain a scenographic encounter. Consequently, scenographic traits result from a combination of orientating stimuli that exceed strict ontologies of empiricism and complicate the neat separation of theatrical crafts.

The scenographer Darwin Reid Payne employed the term 'scenographics' within the opening paragraph of *Computer Scenographics* (1994): 'While the first word of the title – *computer* – is ubiquitous in the present-day world, the second – *scenographics* – is not found in any dictionary to date' (Reid Payne 1994: xi; emphasis in original). Reid Payne continues to note that:

> scenographics has yet to find a place … And yet, I can think of no better word – coined or not – to describe the subject of the book that follows. *Scenographics* seems to me to be an apt description of the kinds of drawings scenographers make.
> (Reid Payne 1994: xi; emphasis in original)

While Reid Payne's adoption stems from the 'graphics' of drawing or plurality of 'computer graphics', my own usage moves beyond perspectival rendering methods to consider how broader conceptions of place orientation are enacted by situational acts of staging. I also eschew terms such as 'scenographically' or 'scenographical' for matters of comparative ease, although I would argue that these terms proceed from scenographic orientations rather than the crafting of scenography. While my arguments on place orientation remain significant to my argument on the potentialities of a scenographic trait, the concept is presented as a lens through which to critique the historicity and peculiarity of staging techniques within interdisciplinary critical territories. In this regard, I propose that the orientating potentials of scenographics occupy a similar critical territory to performatives or dramaturgies in performance theory and afford a renewed lens on how material cultures evoke scenographic methods more generally.

While the critical potential of scenographics drives the through-line of this book, there is an underlying concern that with the expansion of scenography beyond theatre the particularities of scenography as conditioned by theatrical orthodoxies may become obscured or lost. Interestingly, Czech scholars of scenography were aware of the possible issues that a holistic approach poses when applied beyond the institutional theatre. Scenography historian Barbara Příhodová outlines how theatre theorist Růžena Vacková (1901–82) was wary of how scenography may struggle to retain its distinctiveness within a wider interdisciplinary context:

> Although Vacková considers the visual components of theatrical production to be a kind of visual art, she vigorously draws attention to their specificity, which she argues rests in their service to deliberate theatricality and to the sense of temporality they evoke.
>
> (Příhodová 2011: 256)

Theatre historian and scenographer Christopher Baugh (2013: 224) shares this concern, as he argues that the lack of a centralizing practice, such as the conditioning factors of theatre, may necessitate that scenography loses its distinctiveness before that distinctiveness has been appropriately accounted for within academic circles. In focusing on the methods of scenography as 'of the theatre', I argue that this affords a means of articulating scenography's 'specificity', to employ Příhodová's term. However, this position does not account for situations that may employ, or appear to employ, these methods that exceed the institutional contexts of theatre. My argument for scenographics isolates how the place-orientating methods of scenography shape other social and art practices beyond the institutional theatres.

Scenography as theatre-making

My overall methodological focus for this book is to consider what scenography *does*; how it orientates, situates and shapes theatre practice. This is a departure from other studies that have begun by asking what scenography *is* (Howard 2002, 2009; McKinney and Butterworth 2009). To achieve this aim, I draw upon a range of critical frameworks; including 'queer phenomenology' (Ahmed 2006), 'new materialism' (Bennett 2009), 'worlding' (Stewart 2014), 'affective atmospheres' (Anderson 2009; Böhme 2013) and 'assemblage' (Deleuze 2006). My intention is to argue why the intangible affective qualities, or 'affects', of scenography are formative to all contemporary theatre-making to consider how scenographies *move* spectators and performers emotionally as well as physically.

Edward Gordon Craig (1872–1966) is often cited as a decisive influence on scenography within academic studies (Howard 2002; Baugh 2005), having worked as an actor, director and designer. While he would not have used the term, Craig's association is partly due to his instance in 1908 that theatre would remain literary and kinaesthetically restricted in its artistic focus 'until the painter shows a little more fight' (Craig 2009: 65). Craig proposed that the theatre artist of the future would be versed in all manner of stagecrafts, which blurred the division between 'creative' practices (movement, gesture, direction, poetry) and 'technical' practices (stage management, scenery, costume, lighting, sound). The legacy of this position is evident in Duška Radosavljević's (2013) argument that the collaborative contexts of contemporary theatre have sustained the idea of a 'theatre-maker' that collapses the hierarchal roles of author, director, designer, performer, etc. Interestingly, Radosavljević cites the notion of 'theatre-making' as an Anglophone innovation that complicates pre-defined roles into a holistic approach: 'theatre-making anticipates an all-inclusive collaborative process whether the outcome is a solo show or an ensemble piece, a new play or a performance installation' (Radosavljević 2013: 23). Consequently, the notion of scenography as technical or supplementary to other practices (such as acting or dance) is challenged within the blurred models of collaboration that theatre-making sustains. No one aspect of theatre-making is any more or less integral to the creative process than any other. Within this context, scenography emerges as a distinct strategy for how theatre happens that extends to the movement and placement of performers, as well as the affective qualities of light and sound.

The provocation of scenography *as* theatre-making aligns with how the Czech scenographer Josef Svoboda (1920–2002) sought to argue the case for scenography. This position is aptly summarized by Jarka Burian, who argued that Svoboda's 'urge toward creativity based on synthesis rather than exclusiveness [rejected] narrow connotations of stage "design" in favor of the more inclusive demands of "scenography"' (Burian 1974: xxii). As evident within Burian's assessment, since the 1960s scenography within the Anglophone has operated as a provocation in a similar model of Kiesler's call (1926) for a theatre that has survived the theatre. Scenography asks individuals to revisit the established concepts and practices of 'design' in theatre-making, while also promising theatrical designers a means of creative liberation and recognition. This tension is at the crux of scenography's current state of excess. Svoboda's argument for scenography as synthesis has afforded a conceptual plurality that sustains projects from architecture to live art. Yet this inclusive approach has confused established orthodoxies, as scenography's practical reference points contradict the neat separation of theatre crafts and tasks that partition creatives from technicians, directing from design, or costume from set. Accordingly, the linguistic and practical boundaries of what is, and is not, scenography remain contested in the early twenty-first century.

I argue that the uncertainty associated with the Anglophone usage of scenography has led to it being positioned as an academic surrogate (for stage design), misapplied (as set design) and, in interdisciplinary contexts, often avoided (in favour of staging or *mise en scène*). Likewise, without a recognized critical framework applicable beyond the immediate contexts of a theatre event, in the manner of the dramaturgical or choreographic, the analysis of a scenographic perspective as a cultural trait has been negligible. Concurrently, in the first decades of the twenty-first century, contemporary theatre has seen a renewed focus on spatial and material affordances. Immersive and intermedial practices employ a range of scenographic approaches that invite an explicit emphasis on the assemblages that orientate a staged encounter – whether situated in a theatre, gallery, on the street or distributed via digital processes. Baugh summarizes the current status of scenography within contemporary theatre:

> One might argue that scenography has become the principlal dramaturgy of performance-making – perhaps close to a direct translation of *scaena* and *graphos* 'drawing with the scene' – where all aspect of 'the scene' (scenic space, embodied action, material, clothes, light and sound) may become the materials laid out on the performance-maker's 'palette'.
> (Baugh 2013: 240)

In light of these practices and the holistic reading indicated by Baugh, scenography has grown in scope and confidence. This newfound assertiveness is articulated by the former artistic director of the PQ, Sodja Zupanc Lotker, and performance scholar Richard Gough, who propose that multiple scenographies are encountered in daily life:

> Notions of expanded scenography such as environments that we perform in – our home, a restaurant, a cruise ship, a parking lot, a public square, a theatre venue, a parliamentary building and Everest – make us rethink scenography as a system. Scenography is not a setting that illustrates our actions any more – it is a body (a discipline, a method, a foundation) in its own right. It is a discipline that has its own logic, its own distinctive rules.
> (Lotker and Gough 2013: 3)

Beyond the interpretation of stage figurations, Lotker and Gough's provocation positions scenography as a system for conceiving and encountering environments – whether designed or found. The notion of a scenography that exists beyond the crafts of scene painting and set construction challenges the orthodoxies of theatrical design. The allied practices of set design or scenic art are rendered historic or diminished in relationship to the theoretical and practical implications of, what curator Hans Peter Schwarz (2011: xix) has termed the 'new scenography'. What is more, Lotker and Gough's phraseology situates scenography as a distinct discipline of study, independent of theatre and performance studies. Whereas Baugh's description of scenography as a holistic theatrical practice is one cause for debate, the conception of a new or expanded scenography invites an altogether different challenge – one that operates beyond the established crafts and disciplinary situation of theatre design.

The idea of an expanded scenography is a subject that Brejzek defines as a 'transdisciplinary practice [that can] no longer be assigned to a singular genre – set design comes to mind – and a singular author' (Brejzek 2011a: 8). Performance designers Dorita Hannah and Olav Harsløf also evoke the expanded context of scenography, as they ask: 'But what happens when design leaves the confines of the stage and begins to wander?' (Hannah and Harsløf 2008: 12). Scenography as an expanded field is contextualized as a distinct strategy or approach to artistic practice that focuses on how design *performs*: from intermedial graphics to dance architecture. This argument has been summarized within the heading of Performance Design, which allows artists to emphasize the 'performative nature of their creative work as both the speculative and projective act of *designing performance* and the embodied and ongoing practice of *performing design*' (Hannah and Harsløf 2008: 14; emphasis in original). Hannah and Harsløf stress that, unlike the established orthodoxies of theatrical production, the practice of performance design can exist in isolation; it is not a means of designing *for* performance. With the wider communities of architecture and fine art now apply the language of performativity on a regular basis, the banner of Performance Design also aims to account for the diverse range of practices that investigate how objects, environments and assemblages also perform. With an intentionally broad remit, Performance Design is, at least in part, a redefining of the methods of scenography as a critical and artistic practice that operates beyond the institutional remit of theatre.

Intrinsic to these new tensions between allied terms and communities of practice is that scenography operates as a radical proposition. Yet, within Europe this situation is linguistically almost unique to the Anglophone (and Germanic) contexts given the apparent 'introduction' of scenography. This linguistic obstacle is not present in the majority of continental European languages, which already host variants on the ancient Greek in place of the variation that comes with notions of 'stage design', 'theatre design', 'scenic design', etc. The theatre scholar Kenneth Macgowan (1888–1963) and stage designer Robert Edmond Jones (1887–1954) summarized how a new and, importantly for this book, 'Continental Stagecraft' emerged across Europe in the 1910s that also challenged theatrical design orthodoxies. Macgowan and Jones cite how individuals such as Adolphe Appia (1862–1928) and Craig confronted the presumptions of the 'realistic theatre' that had become a dominant theatrical form in this period. A New Stagecraft would demand a new theatrical rhetoric of place orientation, where artists are:

> constantly at work upon plans for breaking down the proscenium-frame type of production, and for reaching a simple platform stage or podium ... This means, curiously enough, that the designers of scenery are trying to eliminate scenery, to abolish their vocation.
>
> (Macgowan and Jones 1923: 126)

Similarly, the stage designer Joseph Urban (1872–1933) argued that this 'new art is a fusion of the pictorial with the dramatic [demanding] not only new designers of scenery, but new [directors] who understand how to train actors in speech, gesture and movement, harmonizing with the scenery' (Urban 1913 cited in Aronson 2005: 137). The theatre-maker Tadeusz Kantor (1915–90) forty-eight years after Urban echoes this position, arguing that

> [the] terms 'the stage set,' 'scenery' or 'stage design' become useless and unnecessary in the new theatre. They imply a distinction. What is understood by

these terms ought to be integrated with the theatrical whole so strongly as to melt into the entire stage matter. It should not be discernible.

(Kantor 1961: 212)

Approached as a conceptually inclusive and holistic strategy of theatre-making, scenography in English has been strongly associated with the legacy of the New Stagecraft's non-representational approach to theatre-making, an approach that has also been thought of as 'continental' in conception. The provocation of scenography is, therefore, often qualified in certain quarters by a political lens that implies a historic distinction between 'continental' and 'Anglophone' theatrical orthodoxies. While this is more contextual than critical in its relevance to this study, the perception that scenography operates as a challenge to Anglophone theatrical orthodoxies frames its adoption and current status.

The notion of scenography as theatre-making features throughout this book and is, in part, a provocation and a challenge to argue otherwise. With notions of dramaturgy and choreography now being considered formative to theatre-making, scenography, too, must make a claim for its centrality if it is to take its place as an equal partner within this triad. The chapters that follow plot a framework for arguing scenography's centrality to theatre-making. The critical and political potential for scenography is unmistakable when considering the ubiquity of the term 'staging' within academic scholarship, artistic practice and everyday life. Used as a verb, 'to stage' is to 'put on an event' that stresses a sense of situational temporality *and* material placement. This, I argue, is to isolate the orientating traits that scenography enacts within theatre. Svoboda's legacy in arguing scenography as synthesis – of light, sound, movement and materiality – is that the concept and practice now applies to all manner of staged events. Scenography exceeds a strict focus on model boxes, scenery and perspective stages as well as the logistical remit of a solo scenographer. Consequently, the challenge is to argue why scenography is to staging as choreography is to movement, as dramaturgy is to sequencing. In doing so, I argue that scenography will emerge as a vital and formative strategy of theatre-making and lay the groundwork for realizing its capacity as critical framework for how 'scenes' render 'place' attentive more generally. Yet, my focus on theatre-making affirms scenography as 'of the theatre'. This position is reflective of a number of practical and conceptual challenges in the twentieth century that questioned the very need for theatre at all.

Theatre, performance and scenography

Kiesler's provocation that 'we are working for the theatre that has survived the theatre' (1926: 1) summarized a number of tensions that defined and framed theatrical experimentation in the twentieth century. The call for a theatre beyond theatre became a familiar trope within experimental practice and theory. The expanded remit of scenography echoes how the idea of theatre was transformed in the last century – with the increase in site-specific practices or performer-less theatres, as well as the formation of performance theory, challenging previous positions on what constituted theatre-making. Paradoxically, theatre as a familiar concept has arguably remained stable within the popular domain.

In his 1968 manifesto on the state of theatre, the first line of Peter Brook's *The Empty Space* has been cited countless times. While Brook's first line defines theatre as an actor on a 'bare stage' while 'someone else is watching', it is the rest of that same opening paragraph that has remained dominant to how theatre is perceived in popular culture:

> Yet, when we talk about theatre this is not quite what we mean. Red curtains, spotlights, blank verse, laughter, darkness, these are all confusedly superimposed in a messy image covered by one all-purpose word. We talk of cinema killing the theatre, and in that phrase we refer to the theatre as it was when the cinema was born, a theatre of box office, foyer, tip-up seats, footlights, scene changes, intervals, music, as though the theatre was by very definition these and little more.
>
> (Brook 1968: 11)

Cited significantly less than the bare stage idea, the rest of Brook's opening paragraph articulates an understanding of theatre that, beyond those aligned with the academic study of theatre and performance studies, remains largely intact. Central to Brook's argument is that, when cinematic methods challenged theatre's cultural place as a predominant leisure activity, this shifted theatre as an experimental art form beyond the gaze of popular consumption. High schools and community groups often enact theatrical conventions reminiscent of theatre before modernism and the twentieth century, for the same reasons that many commercial producers still produce work that speaks to this understanding: because it is recognizably theatre. There is no need to become familiar with the form or methods. The rest of Brook's paragraph *is* theatre for many within our shared global cultures. The forebears of our contemporary usage of scenography – namely Appia, Craig and Svoboda – worked in theatre forms and mediums that operated beyond the popular Anglophone orthodoxies that Brook outlines. To understand scenography's provocation is also to understand how theatre – both as a practice and concept – was changed by a series of intellectual and practical challenges in the twentieth century.

While the advent of cinema challenged theatre as a primary leisure activity, theatre scholarship was confronted with the concept of 'performance'. Diane Taylor states that performance 'is not always about art' (Taylor 2016: 6). While noting that it relates to the work of actors or the actions of dancers, Taylor stresses that the term 'performance' does not denote that the 'actions are not "real" or have no long term consequences' (Taylor 2016: 25). Marina Abramović has also emphasized the actuality of her performance art works, which she compares to the artificiality of theatre. 'Theatre was an absolute enemy. It was something bad, it was something we should not deal with. It was artificial … We refused the theatrical structure' (Abramović in Kaye 1996: 180). Abramović conflates wider sociological readings of performance, as refined by Erving Goffman (1958), to position her work as an artist who creates events that are 'real' and 'authentic'. The anthropologist Victor Turner approaches the distinction between performance and theatre – the politically real and the contrived – from an altogether different perspective. 'Theatre is, indeed, a hypertrophy, an exaggeration, of jural and ritual processes; it is not a simple replication of the "natural" total processual pattern of the social drama' (Turner 1982: 12). Turner's reading of theatre as a 'hypertrophy' – as a state of excess that emerges from its surroundings and yet is peculiar to it – aligns with Eugenio Barba's observations on the 'extra-daily' actions of performers. Barba argues that extra daily techniques 'move away from daily techniques creating tension, a difference in potential … which appear to be based on the reality with which everyone is familiar, but which follow a logic which is not immediately recognisable' (Barba and Savarese 1991: 18). As distinct from the daily techniques of appearance and behaviour, the extra-daily is a hypertrophic act that exceeds and demarcates itself from the disciplined expectations of day-to-day normativity.

Alan Read in *Theatre in the Expanded Field* (2013) echoes Barba's conception of theatre as extra-daily when arguing that 'a capacity for performance is a capacity to irritate, and to be irritated' (Read 2013: xviii). As with Turner's hypertrophy, Read argues that performance 'could be said to act as a foreign body, as a third person, always at odds with those things upon which it does its work' (Read 2013: xix). Likewise, performance scholar Cathy Turner applies Barba's term to differentiate 'theatre dramaturgy' from everyday dramaturgies, observing that 'if we are not able to separate conceptually the dramaturgy of the artwork from that of the everyday, at least temporarily, the effect will be to dismiss the transformative potential of theatre's alternative worlds' (Turner 2015: 4). Accordingly, I argue that scenes operate as worlding irritants. Framed by Stewart's (2007, 2011, 2014) implied position that 'worlding' accounts for the ongoing negotiations of worlds aside worlds (as discrete from an essentialist conception of 'the world'), I propose that the scene concept isolates how the constituent elements of place are rendered attentive through a hypertrophic act that intervenes, others, and scores normative experiences of human-centric worlding. Moreover, a stage-scene operates as an enacted land border that demarcates the thresholds between perceptual worlds. The operational situations of dance, opera, live art, and theatre are all extra-daily forms of staging – acts of human-centric worlding. Each sustains a particular situation of viewing, of watching, or participation. These situations are, in scenographic terms, tantamount to the same situational practice of staging.

Abramović's criticisms of theatre are directed towards a politics of theatricality rather than operational situations of staging. Carlson has described how the duality of theatricality, in that it is simultaneously a thing and a representation of a thing, has provided a distinct challenge to wider ontological binaries of real and not real for centuries: 'From Plato onward one of the most predictable attacks on theater has been precisely that it provided empty representations that if unchallenged threatened the authenticity of the real self' (Carlson 2002: 240–41). Nevertheless, Carlson argues that the codified and eventual act of theatre can be viewed under different terms:

> Theatricality can be and has been regarded in a far more positive manner if we regard theater not as its detractors from Plato onward have done – as a pale, inadequate, or artificially abstract copy of the life process – but if we view it as a heightened celebration of that process and its possibilities.
>
> (Carlson 2002: 244)

In considering how theatre and theatricality presents extra-daily acts of communication beyond the disciplined systems of normativity, Carlson proposed that the positive attributes of theatricality's politics might be considered more directly. As Tracy C. Davis points out, the tensions between self and role, authentic and contrived, is theatricality's 'virtue, recognizing the gap between signifier and signified, truth and effect' (Davis 2003: 142). Jill Dolan extends this position to argue that the 'affective consequences of theatre and performance are indeed real and useful, whether or not we can measure them empirically' (cited in Essin 2012: 98). Performance has, nevertheless, sustained a distinct critical territory from theatre when considering questions of 'reality'. J. L. Austin (1962) defines performatives as linguistic 'doings' that exceed the binaries of constative statements that affirm an idea as either 'true' or 'false'. Similarly, Judith Butler (1990) stresses that the performativity of contrived learned social traits – such as the enactment of gender characteristics – are rendered normative due to their very repetition and reinforcement by systems of power (such as language). In both Austin and Butler's frameworks, performatives and performativity focus on acts that in and of themselves are agnostic to questions of 'truth'. Yet, these same traits and acts are 'reality-producing' in that they affirm experiences as 'true' through their very repetition, their normativity.

In light of the politics of theatricality and the assumed authenticity of performance, Richard Schechner has argued that the conceptual and practical concerns of performance relegate theatre to the 'string quartet of the twenty-first century: a beloved but extremely limited genre' (Schechner 1992: 8). While he later retracts this statement (2000), Schechner's observation stems from a modelling of a feedback loop where the social dramas of life are informed, yet distinct from, the aesthetic dramas of theatre (see Figure 2). Citing Victor Turner's notion of 'social dramas' as moments of conflict that can be eventful (Watergate, migrations) or institutional (school, church), Schechner's underlying argument is that it is 'performance' not 'theatre' that connects the social and aesthetic dramas of life. Lehmann, while recognizing theatre as a sub-area of performance, has offered a useful counterargument to Schechner's positioning of theatre as historic. The German scholar argues that 'the decline of the dramatic is by no means synonymous with the decline of the theatrical. On the contrary: theatricalization permeates the entire social life' (Lehmann 2006: 183). Honing in on the significance of aesthetic works (broadly defined as art) within any art–life loop, Lehmann suggests that 'the real of our experiential worlds is to a large extent created by art in the first place … Human sentiment imitates art, as much as the other way around, art imitates life' (Lehmann 2006: 37). Andy Lavender agrees with Lehmann and cites that, after postmodernism and the increased focus on how cultures are performed, 'theatre' became a verb. 'The processes of theatring were all around us, as cultural production staged individuals (actual and fictional) across diverse platforms, presenting them for spectatorship' (Lavender 2016: 197). Lehmann's expanded notion of theatre as a theatricalization of social life, and Lavender's notion of 'theatring', encompass the critical perspectives of performance while also focusing on the representational questions exposed through a politics of theatricality. Crucially, the notion of theatring isolates the orientating potentials of staged acts (whether framed as art or life) as an activity that transcends institutional concepts of theatre as a finite medium.

If we concede that to *do* theatre is to stage events, then the affective qualities of theatre are no less real

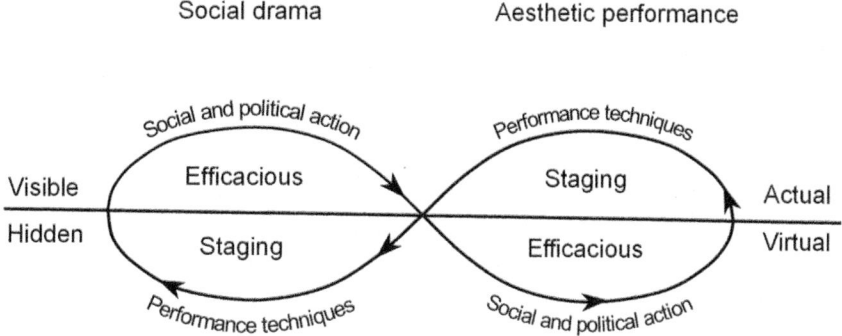

Figure 2 Schechner's mutual feedback loop of performance between Turner's social drama and aesthetic performances
Source: Schechner (2013: 77)

than the ever-present repetitions of performance. Though framed and situated by different ideological frameworks, theatre and performance are equally concerned with how actions are conceived, performed and understood. In terms of this book, performance relates to acts of display or communication that typically recede into normativity. Theatre is a conscious or heightened act of performance. One is an extra-daily hypertrophic act; the other is rendered transparent by repetition and normativity. This seemingly radical repositioning of theatre adopts the expanse of performance studies, while focusing on extra-daily acts. Performance is daily. Theatre is extra-daily.

Given that this book considers scenographic acts beyond institutional theatres, I employ an expanded reading of theatre coupled with a focused understanding of performance. To navigate this distinction, I employ two readings of 'theatre': institutional and operational. The first relates to the historically and legally defined tradition of theatre as a practice of artistic expression, employment and civic identity. The second focuses on how the concept of theatring is evident within wider cultures of staging. In this instance, staging relates to a deployment of particular material–spatial strategies (stage–spectator), as well as how places are rendered attentive as discrete acts of worlding (place orientation). It is notable that Schechner's feedback loop positions staging as a central caveat to both processes. Schechner argues that the techniques of staging are hidden in the social dramas of life and visible in the aesthetic dramas of theatre. Likewise, I argue that an operational understanding of theatring applies the stage orthodoxies of the institutional theatres, without being disciplinary and politically tied to 'The Theatre' as a cultural practice. The visibility of these techniques as contrived systems for 'seeing' is heightened in an institutional theatre and, more often than not, rendered invisible through an ideological nullification that frames operational acts of theatring. The term 'theatre' is, nevertheless, applied in both distinctions where the notion of theatring is collapsed into the operational usage for linguistic ease. 'Theatricality' is reserved for discussions on the ideological structures of (re)presentation within art and social behaviours, which is distinct from staging as a situated material practice.

On a whim, I decide to attend the Royal Academy of Art's exhibition on 'Sensing Spaces: Architecture Reimagined' in March 2014. Upon entering the entrance hall and purchasing my ticket I find myself within an atrium with projections of citations upon calico-like hangings on the walls. To my surprise, a citation by Appia appears. I'm surprised because Appia was not an architect. I'm surprised because he was a scenographer. I'm reminded of the conversations I have had with colleagues who lackadaisically term 'bad' architecture as 'scenographic': as inauthentic or physically flimsy. As I traverse the installations evidently hosted within the broader architecture of the Royal Academy (RA), I cannot help but view these in terms of scenography. They exist as temporary structures that have been constructed for the purpose of evoking an experience of architecture: of a particular studio's principles or working methods. While I spend some time with all of the exhibits, it is the last installation by Grafton Architects that drew my attention. In particular, upon first entering the final room of their section I looked up at the grey cuboid structures that hung form the RA's ceiling. The bottom edges of these structures were just at arm's length. The greyish tones of the hung structures appeared tarnished and weathered in an uneven texture scored by the shadows from the light sources high above. I reach up and knock the surface in the full expectation of it being solid and rendered in a metallic or solid material. I'm surprised for the second time. My knock makes no noise. The structures are constructed from fabric with a (possibly) wooden internal frame, which reminds me of the techniques applied to theatrical scenery: stretched material over a frame that has been textured with a dye or paint. I cannot avoid the association and sit to consider this thought. I watch numerous other patrons enter the room, look up, and knock the structures just as I had done. Each time there is a moment of surprise. I realize that Grafton Architects are examining architecture through means of scenography. I realize that these structures are scenographic in conception and experience. Yet, they are removed (or protected) from the negative politics of theatre as disingenuous. While these structures might be termed 'theatrical' in their material surrogacy, the installation itself is ideologically removed from the institution of theatre. I remember Appia's inclusion at the start. I realize that, while this is not scenography in an institutional sense, it is also not not scenography.

The moment of surprise that occurred when knocking upon the fabric surface at the RA's *Sensing Spaces* exhibition is also a moment of ideology in action: it invites the question 'Is this architecture or scenography?'. Schechner applies the double negative of 'not not' to argue how actors perform within an anti-structure, where an actor 'no longer has a "me" but has a "not not me"' (Schechner 1985: 112). This double negative of performing character, while still being a recognizable individual, stresses an inherent duality, a duality that is symptomatic of the act of staging. The institutional framing of the gallery situates the experience in terms of installation art. While not institutionally theatre, the spatial and material interventions of installation art share many of the same place orientating affects of scenography. Furthermore, the ideological framing of the exhibition in terms of architecture enforces an ideological distance from scenography by matter of the two practices' critical histories. The philosopher Gernot Böhme summarized this relationship by citing a version of the poet Friedrich Schiller's phrase '*art serene*, life is serious', arguing that this asymmetry of art and life 'continues to distinguish architecture from stage design. Architecture does not build for the sake of the engaged or detached spectator watching a play, but rather for the people who experience, in space, the seriousness of life' (Böhme 2006: 406). In this instance, the seriousness and imposed 'realness' of architecture is privileged over the speculative conditions of theatre. Yet, the situational and temporary contexts of this exhibition render it scenographic. The explicit crafting of how spectators attend to and interact with the attentive objects as a speculative act (of architecture) positions the situation as operationally theatre. The installation has spectators and a scene of action; it is an extra-daily temporary staging within the gallery; it moves people in terms of the choreographic; it orders participation in terms of the dramaturgical; it orientates a feeling of place in terms of scenographics. The experience of the installation is operationally an act of theatring. Consequently, the 'performance' of installation art is, I propose, intrinsically bound to the scenographic (as well as the choreographic and dramaturgical) traits that orientate and situate the encounter as an act of staging, of theatring.

Performance, as both a concept and genre of art-making, is readily applied to all manner of cultural and art contexts (see Diamond 1996; Fischer-Lichte 2008). The interdisciplinarity afforded by this familiarity has led to notions of the performative and performance occupying the critical territory of the scenographic and scenography. One of the signposts for this tension has been the renaming of PQ's subtitle for the 2011 festival, from 'Scenography and Theatre Architecture' to 'Performance Design and Space'. This is mirrored within recent debates surrounding *l'Organisation Internationale des Scénographes, Techniciens et Architectes de Théâtre's* (OISTAT's) 'Performance Design' commission, which changed its name from 'Scenography' in 2013. These changes are symptomatic of the tensions that have emerged within continental Europe concerning the usage of 'scenography'. The increased status of performance within art institutions over the last twenty years (i.e. MoMA's retrospective of Abramović in 2010 or the opening of The Tanks devoted to live art at Tate Modern in 2012) has seemingly lent itself to the critical expansion of scenography given its focus on the ephemeral agency of material and design.

Emerging as a new disciplinary heading, Performance Design was originally applied in support of undergraduate programmes in Denmark and New Zealand that combined the study of architecture/spatial design and theatrical design. The convenors of these degree programmes, Hannah and Harsløf, define this heading thusly:

> As a loose and inclusive term Performance Design asserts the role of artists/designers in the conception and realization of events, as well as their awareness of how design elements not only actively extend the performing body, but also perform without and in spite of the human body.
>
> (Hannah and Harsløf 2008: 18)

The usage of the term 'performance' within this heading intentionally echoes the remit of Performance Studies, which Barbara Kirshenblatt-Gimblett describes as a 'post-discipline of inclusions' (2004: 43). This post-disciplinary remit informs Brejzek's reading of an expanded scenography as a transdisciplinary practice. While scenography has a particular history with the emergence of Performance Studies through *TDR: The Drama Review*, there is a danger that a slippage has begun to occur between Performance Design and scenography: an implied surrogacy that is reminiscent of how scenography has been conflated with notions of set design in English. In order to avoid this linguistic and disciplinary confusion, the particularities of each terminology require outlining in relation to its partner.

Performance Design, argue Hannah and Harsløf, offers theatrical designers a means of emancipation from the established hierarchies of the production team within many Anglophone and continental theatres: 'the contemporary scenographer is generally expected to serve and supplement the theatre director's imagination rather than initiate projects or experiments with their spatial realm' (Hannah and Harsløf 2008: 12). Interestingly, Hannah and Harsløf's usage of the term 'scenographer' implies the Danish *scenograf*, what in English would typically be translated as 'stage designer'. Notably, the idea of servitude is aligned with the notion of a *scenograf*, which is counter to the liberating vision as outlined by Svoboda, Howard and other Czech-influenced readings. The two groups are discussing two different forms of liberation: from the hierarchical structure of theatrical production and from theatre itself. Svoboda's scenography is a means of collaboration within the institutionalized theatre, while Performance Design is an argument for emancipation from the theatre institution. Moreover, the emergence of this shift in focus is scored by an increase in theatre work taking place beyond a theatre building.

In a publication by the Victoria & Albert Museum (London) on twentieth- and twenty-first-century plays in the United Kingdom, actor Simon Callow labels the first decade of the new century as 'the decade of the site-specific show' (cited in Dorney and Gray 2014). Theatre beyond the theatre challenges the disciplinary conditions of theatre design and has invited the expanded territory of Performance Design. Scenographer Kathleen Irwin relates this shift to the new approaches demanded from these 'found' environments: 'The impulse to experiment with found space redefined the scenographic function; the scenographer's focus shifted from interpreting text within prescribed stage space to deconstructing found space within a critical context' (Irwin 2008: 44). This blurring of theatrical and non-theatrical environments has led to a number of academic enquiries into how 'space' performs (see McKinney and Palmer 2017). In line with this surge in academic scholarship on the performance place/space, the remit of Performance Design recognizes the expansive range of scenographic practices undertaken within and beyond the theatre, both as a professional institution and disciplinary remit. Consequently, Performance Design sustains a post-disciplinary heading that is not aligned with any one institutionalized arts practice. It is a borderless grouping of a range of topological, anthropological and political approaches to spatial/material design. Scenography is a practice of theatrical place orientation, indicative of the methods and encounter of theatrical environments. Performance Design is the post-disciplinary context of scenography. In turn, scenography is one possible strategy of Performance Design.

My usage of scenography is qualified by the post-disciplinary framing of Performance Design. Yet, I contend that scenography remains a distinct strategy within this critical landscape. In this regard, I argue that Svoboda's inclusive and holistic approach to theatrical design is a 'radical' departure from the prescriptive qualities of the pre-1960s French *décorateur* and the English 'set designer'. Indeed, Svoboda was conscious of this radical differentiation, as Burian outlines:

> He does not believe the English-American term 'designer' to be adequate, and other general terms such as '*bühnenbilder*' or '*décorateur*' are even less satisfactory because, according to him, they all imply a person who conceives a setting for a play, renders it two-dimensionally on paper – perhaps stunningly – and then in effect retires from the field, having fulfilled his commission. Svoboda's concept of his work involves much more than this; hence his preference for the term 'scenography'.
>
> (Burian 1974: 15)

In rejecting the terminologies of other theatre cultures (whether Germanic, Francophone or Anglophone), Svoboda argued that scenography operated as a form of 'psycho-plasticity', where '[d]ramatic space is psycho-plastic space, which means that it is elastic in its scope and alterable in its quality' (cited in Burian 1974: 30). The intangible qualities of movement and rhythm, as exposed by the experience of material in time, were for Svoboda the fundamental materials of scenography. Indeed, the history of scenography's holistic usage in English has been intertwined with conceptual ideas on unity and balance that emerged with the New Stagecraft of the 1910s and 1920s.

Histories on early twentieth-century theatrical experimentation often present the ideas of scenography and the New Stagecraft as being interchangeable and deterministic – with the assumption that one is merely a precursor for the other. Theatre scholar Dennis Kennedy (1993, 2001) describes this period as a 'scenographic revolution'. Indeed, the influence of the French understanding that positions *scénographie* as a predominantly visual exercise can be seen in Kennedy's definition: 'Scenography can profitably be thought of as a visual counterpart to text; while the spoken dialogue of the play creates the verbal sphere of the production, the scenography creates the visual' (Kennedy 2001: 12). This is a significant distinction from the radical Czech approach, as defined by Svoboda, that embraces sound, and other temporal non-visual elements, as concerns of scenography. Aside from German and English, all other continental variants of the Greek *skenographia* are institutionally tied to the theatre and typically translate as either 'theatre design', 'stage design', 'set design' or 'scenic design'.

The term 'theatre design' is taken to signal a distinct alignment with a particular institutionalized practice. While theatre now occupies a broad conceptual territory, the connotation of an institutionalized understanding of theatre (as theatre building or theatre orthodoxy) positions theatre design as institutionally specific. Theatrical design, within this context, does offer a useful means of recognizing the extension of theatre-based stagecrafts and design techniques beyond institutional theatres, such as music festivals and sports stadiums. Subsequently, 'theatrical design' is employed within this book to denote a collection of material and technological staging techniques that have been developed in response to theatrical orthodoxies. These orthodoxies include stage delineation, scenery, costume, sound design, and all forms of stage lighting (from footlights to spotlights). Other terms to have emerged within the higher education environment include 'design for performance' and 'design for the stage'. While these phraseologies embrace multiple platforms of practice, they also retain an alignment with the established orthodoxies of theatre practice, such as scenography's symbiosis with stage and design as a servicing *for* performance. Performance Design, in this regard, sustains multiple readings without any focus on theatre as a central practice, and is approached as a post-disciplinary field of practice with no allegiance to an established set of disciplinary orthodoxies or techniques.

Research questions and chapters

Focused on the Anglophone adoption from the 1960s onwards, this book explores the porous state of contemporary theatre-making to argue a critical distinction between scenography (as place orientation) and scenographics (that which orientate interventional acts of worlding, of staging). Therefore, *Beyond Scenography* is less an investigation into how to make scenography or even why make scenography, but rather an argument for what scenography does. The following research questions inform the overall structure and sequence of the chapters:

- What is the status of the term scenography in the English language?

- How has a holistic reading of scenography influenced the study and practice of staging?
- What is the critical distinction between scenography and scenographic?
- How does a scenographic trait apply beyond theatre practice?

Prompted by Kiesler's manifesto, the key ideas and positions that feature as part of these investigations are summarized within statements placed on insert pages throughout the book. These operate as a manifesto on scenography and scenographics that focuses on the principal arguments and critiques that inform the overall conclusions.

Chapter 1, 'Place orientation, scenic politics and scenographics', details the theoretical framework that underpins my approach on scenography and scenographics. To argue this point, I review distinct approaches from human geography and performance theory to conceptions of space, place, material and body with a particular focus on the dual implications of 'orientation', which accounts for haptic proximities (distance, scale, etc.) and social perceptions (normativity, otherness, etc.). I contend that in approaching scenography as place orientation this considers how staged acts are understood from a holistic-bodily perspective. I also consider how 'the scenic' operates as a distinct aesthetic ideology that co-opts experiential encounters *as-if-it-were* a quantifiable painted image: as a fixed commodified object. This method of quantifying experience is, I propose, aligned with the aesthetic politics of the 'picturesque'. This aesthetic position is discrete from the interventional and situational affects of scenographics. Taking the position that the terms performative and theatricality are often overused within art criticism and practice, I outline how the argument for scenographics augments these established concepts to provide a more precise framework for how staged atmospheres and situations affect materials and bodies alike. Last, this chapter concludes by introducing how scenographics enact the othering tactics of queering and surrogacy.

Chapter 2, 'Scenography and the Anglophone theatres', provides a historiography of scenography in the English language and how this has shifted in response to changes in theory and practice. I outline why a radical Czech-influenced scenography emerged within English-speaking theatrical cultures and how this holistic approach (inclusive of sound, stage geography, objects, light, costume) challenges the established linguistic variations across continental Europe. This chapter concludes by considering the hierarchies of scenography. Specifically, I review the inclusion of costume and sound within this holistic remit and how this has challenged established orthodoxies on scenography, principally that scenography is neither exclusively visual nor spatial.

Chapter 3, 'Scenography beyond scenographers', investigates how the English language adoption of scenography confronts base assumptions on the interrelationships between directing and design. Beyond universities and art schools, I trace how the term is often ignored or distrusted due to its apparent resistance to the Anglophone theatrical hierarchies (of playwright, director, designer, performer). I relate this explicitly to scenography's ill-defined relationship with *mise en scène*. As part of a renewed lexicon of scenographic practice, I review the history of *mise en scène* in English and how this concept relates to contemporary approaches to staging. Scenography's potential to emerge as a key concept within the English language theatres is furthered by the histories of two other continental practices and terminologies that met initial resistance, but were later adopted – namely choreography and dramaturgy. I review how the steady adoption of choreography in the 1930s and now dramaturgy in the last twenty years emerged out of the need to better define and articulate the complex acts of theatre-making; to offer new directions of practice and shared authorship, as well as further refining the established lexicon. One of the conclusions of this book is that, while the Anglophone adoption of scenography is formative to all theatre practice, this holistic approach has exceeded the strict capacity of the scenographer role. As choreography has exceeded the choreographer and dramaturgy has exceeded the dramaturg, I argue that the blurred conditions of contemporary theatre-making render scenography a shared undertaking whose authorship is not typically exclusive to any one named individual. When scenography exceeded the conventions of scenery, I propose that scenography also exceeded the exclusive role of the scenographer.

Chapter 4, 'Scenography happens', consolidates my argument for scenography to stand alongside its sister continental European theatre-making strategies, both conceptually and practically. Informed by new materialist notions of atmosphere and assemblage, this chapter argues that the linguistic associations of the term 'set' do not fully stress the temporal qualities that are intrinsic to the experience of place orientation. In particular, this chapter examines how Gilles Deleuze's (1925–95) articulation of an assemblage offers a framework for arguing the peculiarities of scenography. Deleuze approaches an assemblage as a coalition of components that are qualified by a shared association, which is ad hoc or informal. As Deleuze argues, in 'assemblages you find states of things, bodies, various combinations of bodies, hodgepodges; but you also find utterances, modes of expression, and whole regimes of signs' (Deleuze 2006: 177). Accordingly, new materialist Jane Bennett stresses an assemblage 'not only has a distinctive history of formation but a finite life span' (Bennett 2009: 24). The 'finite life' of an assemblage is to observe that the relationships, or coherence, of a network of things become manifest within a particular moment, at a particular time. Evidenced by a case study on the Gecko Physical Theatre's re-staging of *MISSING* (2012), I propose that in isolating how scenography happens this confronts an underlying misconception about scenography within the Anglophone theatres: that it is an academic surrogate for set design, as distinct from a strategy for how theatre is manifested in time. I conclude this chapter by confronting the linguistic bias that positions scenography as the introduction of visual objects into the 'stage space'.

Chapter 5, 'Scenographic worlding', reviews the symbiosis between stage and scenography. In particular, scenographics are considered in relation to their potential to render 'worlds' attentive and defined. As Jean-Luc Nancy puts it, the 'world is always the plurality of worlds' (Nancy 1997: 155). Worlding is approached as a series of ongoing and irreducible processes that qualify the porous and interconnected manifestation of worldly encounter. Accordingly, I argue how scenographics score perceptual orientations of world. The hybrid concept of a 'stage-scene' is proposed to stress how scenographics score the process of worlding in the same manner as land borders. Stages-scenes simultaneously reveal and affirm how worlds are felt, whether politically speculative or 'real'.

In this regard, I consider how stage geographies are rendered attentive through material interventions and ideologies. I revisit the assumption that stages precede scenography as an 'empty space'. I contend that stages are manifested through the orientating qualities of scenographics. This is inclusive of how stages occur within the mixed reality events of Blast Theory as well as the immersive practices of Punchdrunk. I conclude by mapping the conceptual importance of conceiving scenographics beyond vision and how stages are bound to situational stage-scenes through scenographics.

Chapter 6, 'Scenographic cultures', applies the conclusions of the previous chapters to argue the scenographic qualities of wider art events and social practices. From installation art to gardening, I argue that the communication and encounter of certain cultural practices evoke scenographic orientations. Critical discourse on the status of practices such as marketing and interior design in the twentieth century has presented an alternative canon that rarely acknowledges scenography's shared traits. I argue how a focus on scenographics exposes these tensions and offers a means of reconsidering the conceptual affordances of scenography beyond theatre. I outline how scenographics more appropriately account for the affective qualities of these practices than notions of performativity or theatricality. While not intended as a proxy for these concepts, in applying the principles of scenographics to art events and social practices, my objective is to propose renewed intellectual conversations with other disciplines on what constitutes a scenographic trait. To grow the critical capacity of scenography within theatre, I argue that we must consider how scenographics occur beyond theatre.

In Chapter 7, 'Scenographic architecture', I contemplate how architectural discourse has sought to distance itself from scenography. Adopting the position that scenographics are ontologically agnostic, I argue for a renewed reassessment of the role of a scenographic perspective within architectural criticism. In particular, I consider how notions of fast architecture score the slow architectures of monumentality. From scaffolding to projected images, I argue how the interventions of fast architecture are scenographic in conception and execution. To further illustrate this point, I return to two examples of 'classical' scenographic architecture; namely French *trompe-l'oeil* (forced perspective art) and Russian Potemkin villages (staged towns). My aim is to outline how these practices sustain scenographic orientations *alongside-and-with* slow architectures.

In summary, this book plots how the contemporary adoption of scenography in the 1960s arises out of an academic and artistic interest in innovative European design practices. If the legacies of Aristotle's *skenographia* are multiple, then the Anglophone usage has a distinctly Czech flavour in its scope and intent. The history of this contemporary adoption also positions scenography, at least in part, within an academic context – with the term's disciplinary familiarity growing out its usage within the higher education environment alongside experimental artistic practice. Overall, I propose that there is a distinct advantage to recognizing the critical distinction between scenography (as place orientation) and scenographics (that which orientate interventional acts of worlding). Consequently, I propose that the expanded disciplinary contexts of scenography that have emerged in the last decade dictate that our current linguistic conventions for articulating scenography are no longer adequate. Equally, in order to investigate the blurred boundaries between scenography and other disciplinary contexts – be that practices of interior design or protest – it is productive to consider the critical potentials of scenographics beyond scenography.

A scenography of orientation is a scenography of feeling.

CHAPTER 1

Place orientation, scenic politics and scenographics

I approach scenography as an act of place orientation. I argue that the crafting of place orientation situates scenography as a process of material acclimatization that occurs *in time* – a process that can be immediate or durational, intellectual or intuitive. A scenography of place orientation encompasses personal and social decisions, as well as the conditioning affects of physical environments that channel and direct action. Orientations emerge from how bodies relate to objects (body-to-object), relate to other bodies (body-to-body), and how objects relate to objects (object-to-object). Acts of orientation extend to the intangible atmospheric qualities (bright–dim, hot–cold, loud–quiet), along with learned social conventions (familiar–unfamiliar, friend–stranger, safe–risky). In terms of scenography, the processes of place orientation encompass staging formats (arena, end-on, traverse, etc.) as well as the manner in which the stage–spectator relationship is managed (darkened auditorium, seat fabric, speaker positions, etc.). Methods of spectatorship are governed and sustained by methods of place orientation. Equally, theatrical design practices and staging techniques have always sought to exploit the affective qualities of orientation, whether through scale, performer blocking, light colour, sound tempo or the profile of a costume. All are methods of orientating a body–event relationship that alters or crafts an encounter *with* place. To speak of orientation is to recognize the multiplicities of phenomena that situate bodies *within and with place*, oscillating between internal (symbolic, embodied) and external (experiential, proxemic) influences. A scenography of orientation is a scenography of feeling.

Christin Essin (2012) employs the term 'place-orientating' in an analysis of the New Stagecraft and cartography. Essin's usage is focused on how scenography enacts experiential landscapes within theatre practice, where the 'literal stage functions as a canvas for place-orienting representations, the design denoting a specific location for the actions of dramatic characters' (Essin 2012: 7). My own stress on place orientation is part of a wider argument that the affects of scenography are no less real than architecture or national borders. Hannah (2008) describes a similar process within the conception of 'spatial performativity'.

> A theory of spatial performativity is one that insists on exposing the reciprocal relationship between architecture and its inhabitants where both are active elements ... it is intensified in theatre spaces, where every venue contains its own particularities that influence, shape and are in turn shaped by the multiple performances harnessed through the specific spatial program, the social codes of architectural inhabitation, and the *mise-en-scène* of theatrical performance itself.
>
> (Hannah 2008: 42)

Hannah argues that the reciprocity or performativity of architecture sustains and evokes a particular situation of inhabitation and interaction. Architect Bernard Tschumi (1996) similarly speaks of 'event-space' as a principle of how architecture affects, but is equally effected by, human participation. While Hannah and Tschumi have argued the affects of architecture in terms of space, I approach place as intrinsically multi-sensory – or, more directly, I can speak of the smell of a place, but it would seem odd to discuss the smell of abstract space. In this way, place is always multi-sensorial and phenomenological by definition. There is some alignment here with Baz Kershaw's approach to 'an ecology of performance' that explores the 'relationship between humans and the environment' (Kershaw 1999: 214). I extend the emphasis that Kershaw puts on the reciprocity of performance ecologies, to consider how scenography is enacted as a crafted ecology or system of affective materials, atmospheres and orientations – inclusive of the scent of bark or the cold-smooth touch of stone, as well as a tightly focused beam of light or the material assemblage of a surrogate prop object. Conceptions of place sustain an oscillation between human and non-human agents that are equally evident within acts of scenography. Crucially, I stress that scenography is rendered real through its affective interventions that score how place – as a material assemblage *and* social construct – is constituted.

It is 2013 I am attending a performance of The Lion King *at the Liverpool Empire Theatre. As I take my seat, an open stage is waiting. A detailed proscenium frames a deep stage with a lit cyclorama composed of yellows, blues and purples. The light gradient creeping up the cyclorama reminds me of a sun rising, but at a place I have never been. It is gentle, calm. Later, as the action unfolds, that place I have never been, the Serengeti, feels familiar, as the combination of sound, puppetry and choreography situates the action within a colour palette disciplined by documentaries and mass media. Of all the orientation triggers cited within* The Lion King, *the grasslands costume offers possibly the most under-recognized. Designed by director Julie Taymor, the costume is composed chiefly of an ankle-length structural reed skirt with a wide base, a bodice and a large square-based 'grasslands' hat – achieved through a metre-high thicket of imitation grass. Notably, I experience the feeling of grassland solely through the costume's orientations – with no additional elements used to perform this 'place' directly. The performer's rhythmical swaying activates the costume, yet, if isolated from the costume, these movements become arbitrary. While I am watching the performance from afar, the costume was part of a wider ecology of motion and sound that orientated a feeling of grassland. The physical motion of the costume reminds me of wearing an imbalanced tall hat, or when I have held a flag on a tall mast and swayed along. The connection between myself and material, motion and body, is intertwined by the immediacy of a recalled physicality. As I watch the grasslands performer, I also feel the conditions of her costume. Framed by an experiential recall of flag waving, I am orientated by a kinaesthetic awareness of the grasslands place as a felt experience. The grasslands costume enacts an affective relationship with my body and situates me within* The Lion King's *scenographic ecology. I feel the orientation of grasslands.*

While my experience of the grasslands costume occurs through 'kinesthetic empathy' (Reynolds and Reason 2011), it is the manner in which these empathetic relationships orientate my experience of the 'grasslands' atmosphere that situates it as part of a scenographic ecology. A new materialist reading of 'affective atmospheres' captures an articulation of the ephemeral qualities of ecology to which I allude: of scent, light, sound and texture, as well as tempo, aura, familiarity and motion. Geographer Ben Anderson has argued how, 'On the one hand, atmospheres are real phenomena. They "envelop" and thus press on a society "from all sides" with a certain force. On the other, they are not necessarily sensible phenomena' (Anderson 2009: 78). Anderson draws upon the work of Deleuze and the notion of affect, where an affect is 'experienced in a lived duration that involves the difference between two states' (Deleuze 1988: 49). The happening of an atmosphere is, therefore, paramount for it to sustain an affective quality; for it to have an affect. However, Böhme has argued that an atmosphere exceeds the subjective–objective binary and atmospheres are 'indeterminate above all as regards their ontological status' (Böhme 1993: 114). Anderson surmises that this ontological indeterminacy is crucial to how an atmosphere affects, as a folding of counterpoints and learned divisions of matter and air, material and immaterial.

They are indeterminate with regard to the distinction between the subjective and objective. They mix together narrative and signifying elements and nonnarrative and asignifying elements. And they are impersonal in that they belong to collective situations and yet can be felt as intensely personal. On this account atmospheres are spatially discharged affective qualities that are autonomous from the bodies that they emerge from, enable and perish with. As such, to attend to affective atmospheres is to learn to be affected by the ambiguities of affect/emotion, by that which is determinate and indeterminate, present and absent, singular and vague.

(Anderson 2009: 80)

Scenography as a crafting of atmospheres is a distinct line of enquiry taken up by Böhme. 'In general, it can be said that atmospheres are involved wherever something is being staged, wherever design is a factor – and that now means: almost everywhere' (Böhme 2013: 2). Böhme's broad conceptualization of staging echoes the notion of an operational theatre as outlined previously. However, Böhme's focus on how 'stage sets' create atmospheres confirms this position, where it is 'the art of the stage set which rids atmospheres of the odour of the irrational: here, it is a question of producing atmospheres' (Böhme 2013: 3). For Böhme, scenography 'does not want to shape objects, but rather to create phenomena. The manipulation of objects serves only to establish conditions in which these phenomena can emerge' (Böhme 2013: 4). Scenography is a navigation of the immaterial affects of sound and light, as well as the subjectivities of tempo and objective dimensions of physical matter. Understanding scenography as an affective atmosphere that creates phenomena is fundamental to the arguments of this book. Likewise, Böhme argues that scenography has expanded into the 'general art of staging, which has applications, for example, in the decor of discotheques and the design of largescale events such as open-air festivals, opening ceremonies of sports events, etc.' (Böhme 2013: 5). The conclusions of Böhme are that scenography, as staging, is an ideal craft in which to study and conceptualize the ontological thirding of an affective atmosphere.

While the expanded territories of current scenographic scholarship and practice are a distinct departure from the original usage developed in the ancient theatres, I argue that scenographic place orientation transcends this shift. Aristotle's description of σκηνογραφία (skenographia) is, I contend, a means of orientating attention towards a particular encounter *with* place. The *skēnē* was a temporary structure possibly made from wood and/or animal skin that has been described as a rudimentary method of stage concealment. Aristotle (*Poetics* 1449a18; see Aristotle 1966) aligned the emergence of this practice with Sophocles' (c.496–c.406 BCE) introduction of the third ὑποκριτής (*hupokrites*), an answerer or actor, alongside the χορός (*khorós*), the dancing people. While scholars such as A. L. Brown (1984) have contested whether Aristotle actually wrote the line in question (τρεῖς δὲ καὶ σκηνογραφίαν Σοφοκλῆς; literally translated as 'Three and scenography Sophocles'), the account in the surviving Arabic translation of Poetics implies that the *skēnē* enabled the third actor to be concealed from the *orchēstra*. Yet, the very placement of the *skēnē* was also an act of orientation: the *skēnē* reshaped the *orchēstra* and radically altered how theatre was conceived, staged and experienced.

The temporary intervention of what Carlson (1989: 131) describes as a 'skene house' effected the spatial relationships between the *hupokrites*, *khorós* and spectators. The *skēnē* did far more than afford concealment. The *skēnē* introduced a potential to sculpt theatrical encounters through material interventions, which in turn enables new orientations between bodies and spectators. Following these staging innovations, *skenographia* was arguably a process of conceiving action according to a particular crafting of place orientations. One method for achieving this orientation was through depictions rendered on the *skēnē* itself. Later developments in stage technology, such as the *periaktoi* (a three-sided stage truck), exemplified how this process of place orientation became malleable and situated the action within a shifting context of place. While the notion of a scene change as understood today was developed centuries later, the capacity of scenography to orientate the landscape of an open hillside to evoke the atmosphere of an interior palace remains a mainstay of any definition. The core focus of this exercise, I argue, is how the material and immaterial elements of theatre orientate a feeling of place, where the act of placing is an ongoing experiential process (rather than a set object) that recognizes how our bodies acclimatize to, and literately make sense of, an environment. Whether achieved through language or costume, graphic depictions or stage blocking, place orientation is a defining trait of theatre practice.

Place within theatre-making is a topic that has sustained a number of critical enquiries (Chaudhuri 1995; McAuley 1999; Pearson and Shanks 2001; Hill and Paris 2006; Birch and Tompkins 2012 – to name only a few). Sally Mackey presents theatre as a means of critically reflecting on how individuals relate to place, whether literally or emotionally:

> Our relationship to 'place' is critical in contemporary lives. How we are placed or how we place ourselves has changed – and is changing – significantly. Performance-related activities can help the way we relate to place, through reformulating our relationships with the places we know and providing approaches which aid emplacement in new or unfamiliar places.
>
> (Mackey 2016)

My focus on place orientation builds on the social and material relationships that Mackey implies. This position is, nevertheless, counter to how previous scholars have sought to present questions of scenography; preferring to focus on 'space' as an agent of human action (McAuley 1999; Howard 2002; Oddey and White 2006). Place in these accounts is often presented as reductive (finite, descriptive, figurative) or the 'starting block' (typified by site-specific work) from which scenography emerges. Space, on the other hand, is approached as active and open to possibilities. Following this logic, space sustains the notion of a *tabula rasa*: an abstract placeless void from which creativity emerges. Yet, I contend that there is no 'empty space'. Instead, I return to the notion of a 'stage place' to argue how this better articulates the underlying tension between scenography and stage, where scenography as place orientation is a crafting of stage places. Each stage is geographically distinct. Scenography's orienting qualities weave the distinctive conditions of stages into being and sustain the overall navigation of theatre events. Whether explicitly, as with site-specific work, or through negation, as with the ideological conventions associated with a black box studio, I argue that scenography as place orientation amounts to a crafting of stage geographies as felt atmospheres through material and technological interventions.

I approach place orientation, more generally, as a material culture that negotiates the learned and experiential triggers of spatial experience. This is discrete from Michel de Certeau's (1925–86) position that 'space' follows human agency and, consequently, supersedes place as a material construct: 'Space occurs as the effect produced by the operations that orient it, situate it, temporalize it, and make it function in a polyvalent unity of conflictual programs or contractual proximities' (de Certeau 1984: 117). In short, '*space is a practiced place*' (de Certeau 1984: 117; emphasis in the orginal). De Certeau's understanding of place is as a geographic construct, as a fixed point – a point that transcends time. This model proposes that the practising of place exposes how human agency situates a timeless place within a temporal spatial ideology: of near and far, distant and familiar. While de Certeau argues that space is changeable and relative, place 'implies an indication of stability' (de Certeau 1984: 117). However, geographer Doreen Massey argues place is not defined by 'points or areas on maps, but as integrations of space and time; as *spatio-temporal events*' (Massey 2005: 130; emphasis in original). Massey describes place as being 'woven together out of ongoing stories, as a moment within power-geometries, as a particular constellation within the wider topographies of space, and as in process, as unfinished business' (Massey 2005: 131). Massey's understanding of place as 'unfinished business' challenges the binary between space and place as implied by de Certeau. Contrary to de Certeau, Massey sees place as a 'constellation of processes rather than a thing' (Massey 2005: 141). Akin to the new materialist usage of assemblage, Massey stresses how the connectedness of place, as a weaving of stories and spatial topographies, focuses on the ongoing practice of placemaking as a social process.

Place orientation is the means by which places are navigated, rendered attentive and encountered from a holistic perspective. Accordingly, the active processes and human-orientated craft of landscaping is an exercise in place orientation. Yet, landscape and scenography have historically occupied distinct critical positions when considering how place is rendered active. This tension is evident between how notions of landscape are partitioned as 'natural' and conceptualized as a container that disciplines human action. James Corner, a specialist in landscape architecture, argues that the active orientating capacities of landscape are nullified when abstracted as a passive 'setting'.

In particular, Corner argues that landscapes can be crafted – whether through physical intervention or the politics of aesthetics – to serve the needs of the powerful that acts as 'a distancing device' where 'landscape can be used (or deployed) by those in power to conceal, consolidate, and represent certain interests … Landscape is particularly effective in this regard because it so beautifully conceals its artifice, 'naturalizing' or rendering invisible its construction and effects in time' (Corner 1999: 11). David Shearing (2014), however, counterpoints this position within his usage of 'scenographic landscape'. Shearing cites landscape architect Simon Bell (1999) to contend that the level of willing participation *with* a scenography positions it in terms of a bodily holism rather than an ontologically enforced distancing. Arguing that the 'oneness of the experience of landscape is a multisensory immersion that engages the whole body' (Shearing 2014: 11). Shearing concludes that scenography is 'a practice of placing and re-placing the body in the landscape' (Shearing 2014: 13). Whether experienced in terms of oneness or bodily holism, the relationship between space and power is crucial to understanding the interventions of scenography. My focus on place orientation stresses how the practice of scenography exposes the material and immaterial assemblages that are inclusive of ideological frameworks that inform any experience of place. Scenography does not 'make' place, but rather navigates place. While place as a curated social construction captures many similar techniques and methods aligned with scenography, by understanding scenography in terms of place orientation I argue that this accounts for the systems of materiality that tie an event of theatrical placeness together. Scenography is a crafting of place orientation.

I only refer to 'space' in relation to cited theories or positions on spatiality. In particular, I take the position that space denotes the ideological systems of power that demarcate places in terms of the political. While places are constellations of ideology and material circumstance, space is always ideological in its formative conception: as an ordering of materiality. This builds upon Michel Foucault's (1926–84) observation that 'we do not live in a kind of void, inside of which we could place individuals and things' (Foucault 1986: 23). Describing everyday encounters as 'heterogeneous space', Foucault argues that space is ordered in terms of a 'set of relations that delineates sites which are irreducible to one another and absolutely not superimposable on one another' (Foucault 1986: 23). Crucial to this approach is that power and space are intertwined, with Foucault arguing that 'space is fundamental in any exercise of power' (cited in Soja 1989: 19). This position is similarly captured within Henri Lefebvre's (1901–91) *The Production of Space* (1974) that states '(social) space is a (social) product' (Lefebvre 1991b: 26). Lefebvre focused on how space is typically conceived through an 'illusion of transparency' that seeks to present space as 'luminous, as intelligible, as giving action free rein' (Lefebvre 1991b: 27). Geographer Edward Soja outlines how this ideology of spatial transparency is reinforced through language and speech acts, where 'social space comes to be seen entirely as mental space, an "encrypted reality" that is decipherable in thoughts and utterances, speech and writing, in literature and language, in discourses and texts, in logical and epistemological ideation' (Soja 1996: 65). Lefebvre argued that it 'was on the basis of this ideology that people believed for quite a time that a revolutionary social transformation could be brought about by means of communication alone' (Lefebvre 1991b: 29). The notion that systems of power produce space is, Lefebvre argued, nullified through an ideology that presents space as open and ethereal. If the ideology of spatial transparency serves to disguise the orderings of power, then conceptions of abstract or empty space within art practice arguably serve to reinforce the legitimacy of these power relations. This distinction is crucial to the argument that scenography, as an interventional practice, has the capacity to score these systems of power. Scenographies have the potential to reveal and expose how ideologies of space are ordered.

To isolate how these ideologies of power shape spatial experience, Soja refines Lefebvre's triadic model (of conceived, perceived, and lived space) as 'firstspace', 'secondspace', and 'thirdspace'. Soja's modelling draws upon mathematical notions of dimensional space (firstspace) and representations of space (secondspace), such as maps, to argue how these collapse into the thirding of the 'spatial imaginary' (thirdspace).

Everything comes together in Thirdspace: subjectivity and objectivity, the abstract and the concrete, the real and the imagined, the knowable and the unimaginable, the repetitive and the differential, structure and agency, mind and body, consciousness and the unconscious, the disciplined and the trans-disciplinary, everyday life and unending history.

(Soja 1996: 56–7)

Soja employs the notion of the spatial imaginary as an othering – or what he describes as a thirding – principle for problematizing the feedback loop models as employed by scholars such as Schechner. A thirding complicates binary modellings of real and not real, life and art, authentic and inauthentic. Lefebvre recognizes this thirding principle within the notion of the 'imaginary', which 'fills the empty spaces of thought, much like the "unconscious" and "culture"', concluding that a 'third term is the *other*, with all that this term implies' (cited in Soja 1996: 53; emphasis in original). The idea of spatial imaginaries as an othering of material and ideological binaries is paramount to how scenography is approached in this book. Scenography as place orientation is an explicit crafting of spatial imaginaries that scores how place is constituted through a mixture of material circumstance and learned models of place representation. Space as an ideological ordering is, subsequently, felt within a constellation of place. As a departure from previous studies on scenography, in this book place orientation rather than abstract space is presented as the formative locus of scenography.

My framing of scenography as place orientation focuses on how acts of staging reveal how multisensory places are constituted. Massey does, however, argue against the binaries of place/space, local/global. Massey argues that these binaries reinforce the real–imagined divide: where place is typically ascribed to the real and space is imaginary. Massey outlines how this binary is disciplined in daily life:

> In such approaches words such as 'real', 'everyday', 'lived', 'grounded' are constantly deployed and bound together; they intend to invoke security, and implicitly – as a structural necessity of the discourse – they counterpose themselves to a wider 'space' which must be abstract, ungrounded, universal, even threatening.
>
> (Massey 2005: 185)

Massey proposes that space is conceived through the same politics that condition place: 'My argument is not that place is not concrete, ground, real, lived, etc. etc. It is that space is too' (Massey 2005: 185). In abandoning the binary of place/space, Massey instead focuses on the interconnectedness and relational conditions of how material encounters collapse into a spatial imaginary. This assertion acknowledges de Certeau's argument that space is a practiced place, while also recognizing how place is situated within a spatial imaginary. Accordingly, I contend that place orientation binds the real affects of a spatial imaginary to the ordered ideologies of material geography. Scenography scores this dialectic exchange: an exchange that ultimately renders the weaving of place and the spatial imaginary as a condition of worldly encounter rather than a set of symbolic certitudes. Moreover, I argue that notions of *mise en scène* and design dramaturgy better capture a logocentric reading of place. This position is also evident in how conceptions of the 'scenic' and the 'picturesque' are aligned through a distinct aesthetic lens that quantifies the ongoing and experiential qualities of landscape.

Scenes and scenic politics

Scenes are familiar to all quarters of theatrical practice. Craig presents the scene as a core intellectual and practical concern of theatre. Yet, the theatre maker does not equate the scene with 'design' in the typical sense. Instead, Craig argues that: 'First and foremost comes the *scene*. It is idle to talk about the distraction of scenery, because the question here is not how to create some distracting scenery, but rather how to create a place which harmonizes with the thoughts of the poet' (Craig 2009: 10; emphasis in original). Craig continues this line of thought, applying the scene as a means of orientating actors as well as an audience: 'By means of your scene you will be able to mould the movements of the actors' (Craig 2009: 13). The English scenographer and director used the term 'scene' to denote the staging of a felt place that extends to the immaterial qualities of atmosphere. Craig's approach suggests that a scene operates beyond a purely visual interpretation.

Caspar Neher (1897–1962) was also critical of how pictorial worldings were applied to theatre. The German scenographer argued in 1951 that a 'picture is never realistic, the stage is always realistic' (in Willett 1986: 75). For Neher, the notion of a 'stage image' was antithetical to the event of theatre. Robert Edmond

Jones equally argued that a 'drama is not a picture. It is not a symphony, it is not a lecture or a sermon. It is a show of life, lived out in our presence, acted out by players' (cited in Essin 2012: 199–200). Similarly, Appia directed his principal critique of the staging principles of his day at scenic painting. In 1898, Appia argued that the spatial logical of a painterly place had been disrupted with the emergence of electric lighting:

> If we introduce the actor onto the stage, the importance of the painting is suddenly completely subordinated to the lighting and the spatial arrangement, because the living form of the actor can have no contact and consequently no direct rapport with what is represented on the canvas.
> (cited in Baugh 2005: 99)

Whereas previously the low light of candle and then gas lighting had masked the blend between painting and stage, the brighter light of the electric bulb exposed this disjunction of spatial logic. For Appia, the representational secondspace of the painting was no longer appropriate as the 'action' and the 'scene' should be one in the same. They must take place in the same time and space. Painted backcloths offered a representation of place while denying the lived experience of place. Drawing on Heidegger's reading of cartography as a projection of human agency over world, Laura Levin reinforces this observation by arguing that the 'age of the world picture positions the human subject over and against the world in a relation of mastery' (Levin 2014: 7). It is this Cartesian split – between world and human, object and subject, body and mind – that the notion of the picturesque reinforces. Subsequently, the scenic concept is arguably symptomatic of an aesthetic system that seeks to adopt and quantify world as being *for* human subjectivities. In this model, humans are objectively distinct to world and observe from a critical distance.

Often considered in purely visual terms, the Greek *skēnē* was a material intervention that radically changed how the place of drama was conceived and understood. The *skēnē* was an orientating device that exceeded strict definitions of a visual image that irritated worlding thresholds by affording staging possibilities through its very placement, materiality and dimension. While also offering a surface for symbolic representations, the *skēnē* was a staging device that fundamentally altered how *orchēstra* and, in the centuries that followed, stages were encountered. Indeed, with the emergence of the Greek *proskenion* and the vertical structures of the Roman *scaenae frons* the action of drama was elevated beyond the *orchēstra*. In time, this elevated structure would loose its formal relationship to the *skēnē* and become consolidated as 'stage'. Consequently, the stage concept arguably emerges in response to the orientating qualities of the *skēnē*.

Today, a scene is typically understood as a place of action or a fixed moment in time. The English language is littered with phrases and idioms that employ the term 'scene': from 'making a scene' to 'behind the scenes', 'burst onto the scene' and 'set the scene'. In these instances, the scene is a broad concept that relates to dramatic action as well as the logic of a finite stage (of on and off stage). Additionally, the term can also be applied to a place that renders it culturally predominant or highly visible: the 'Hollywood scene' or 'crime scene'. It equally denotes situated experiences of a cultural practice, such as a 'music scene' or 'art scene'. Scenes can signal a spatial politics focused on the convergence of activities that began elsewhere: 'There is a lot of work going on behind the scenes'. Yet, the scene as dramatic action is exaggerated and emotive: 'please don't make a scene'. In this last instance, actions can lead to a demarking of a point in time as distinct or separated out from the disciplined expectations of normativity. In summary, scenes are contextually extra-daily and highly visible, as well as experientially interventional and orientating.

The definition of a crime scene offers a useful summary of how scenes occur through means of intervention. Forensic scientist John Horswell states that '[a]ny place could become a crime scene and it is usually a place where a crime or an incident that may end in legal proceedings has occurred' (Horswell 2004: 32). Horswell stresses that the definition of a crime scene is relational to the criminal incident(s) that have already occurred. A scene is not, however, always defined strictly by a past event. Alan O'Connor (2002) argues that the application of the scene concept to particular social practices, such as the 'punk scene', isolates how an assemblage of places constitute a supportive network: 'When punks use the term 'scene' they mean the active creation of infrastructure to support punk bands and other forms of creative activity. This means finding places to play, building a supportive audience, developing strategies for living cheaply, shared punk houses, and such like' (O'Connor 2002: 226). In this instance, the scene operates as an orientating concept that brings disparate normative contexts together for the purpose of curating a shared practice. O'Connor's usage of scene also stresses how this orientation marks places as special or highly visible within the socio-political lives of that group.

The scene idioms I cite evoke either the politics of theatricality or the operational practices of a scene as a metaphor for something other or extra-daily: an irritant. These idioms do, however, present the notion of a scene as a boundaried concept that focuses on a spatial 'witness' – of being complicit and together, while also distinct and discrete – as well as a structure for action. In light of this observation, I propose that a situational encounter of a stage-scene is critically distinct to the ideological position of the scenic. Whereas a stage-scene is always situationally scenographic, the scenic is a positively charged conceptual framework that sustains the politics of the picturesque.

In an article entitled 'Picturesque' (1997), Dabney Townsend observes:

> The initial impetus toward picturesque theory comes not from some innate love of scenery and nature, as one might expect (though there is no reason to dispute the existence of such an attraction), but from the quite spirited debates over the relation of poetry and painting as art forms that were conducted in the seventeenth and early eighteenth centuries.
>
> (Townsend 1997: 366)

Crucial to this debate was the manner in which 'Pictures capture the totality of a scene, while poetry can show temporal movement' (Townsend 1997: 366). This modelling assumes that pictures exceeded questions of temporarily. Poetry, however, happens as a temporal art form. Following the categorizations of Lessing's essay *Laocoon* (1766), painting and sculpture were positioned as 'spatial arts' as distinct from the 'time-based arts' of music and poetry. Yet, the notion of landscape painting presents an innate tension to these categories as 'natural scenes do not remain stable' (Townsend 1997: 368). The temporality of landscape is bound to ongoing processes of worlding.

In the *Critique of Judgment* (originally published 1790), Immanuel Kant (1724–1804) noted the ontological dilemma of landscape painting, arguing that it 'provides only the illusion of corporeal extension' (Kant 1987: 192). Gina Crandell, however, cites how the picturesque afforded an 'entirely new way of seeing' (Crandell 1993: 111) given that it aims to resolve Kant's noted dilemma through an aesthetic reversal. Rather than conceptualize representational painting as reducing the felt orientations of landscape, the picturesque imposes the conditions of painting to the 'appreciation' of landscape. Allen Carlson outlines the effects of this reversal and considers how the legacies of the picturesque 'requires us to view the environment as if it were a static representation which is essentially "two dimensional." It requires the reduction of the environment to a scene or view' (Carlson 1979: 271). The notion that landscape is assessed 'as if it were' a painting is crucial to my own argument on the distinction between scenographics and scenic politics. I adopt Carlson's phrasing to stress and isolate the role scenic politics play in the analysis of scenographics more broadly. If the scenic treats landscape *as-if-it-were* a painting and evokes a conceptual division (between subject and object), then scenographics result from interventional acts of orientation that explicitly affirm the situational potentiality and temporality of landscape.

The scenic concept is not apolitical insomuch that it speaks to a quality of pleasure. To describe a situation, defined vector, or view as scenic is to render it pleasant, charming, or attractive. Conceptions of 'nature' in art history are, likewise, positivity charged. Qualified by its distance from the human condition, nature is often considered in terms of being 'fresh', 'unspoiled' or 'divine'. Arguing that nature was an exemplary object of aesthetic experience, Kant observed how the 'abstraction' of landscape painting and the techniques of perspective, light, and colour afford a semblance of world that is isolated (removed, partitioned) from the worlds of onlookers. This ontological differentiation – of world from human – affirms the aesthetic politics of the picturesque that positions world as that which is looked upon and 'possessed' by humans. Malcolm Andrews suggests that the 'Picturesque habit of mind was – and indeed still is – deeply ingrained as a response to the casualties of environmental and social change. By the 1870s it had become absorbed into a rather more socially sensitive discourse, that of the conservation movement' (Andrews cited in Townsend

1997: 368). The notion that 'natural scenes' are good for you (see Hammond 1857) is bound up with the anti-industrial rhetoric of the conversation movement that views nature as divine and unspoiled, but also positive and enjoyable. This same reading positions landscape as discrete from humans. In this model, humans observe landscapes rather than recognize how the potentiality of a worlding assemblage changes and alters human experience: a potential that is predicated on humans *being with* landscape. The notion that landscape can be isolated from human and rendered a positive commodity is, Townsend argues, crucial to how the picturesque 'quantifies' the ongoing worlding of landscape.

Beyond the appropriation of landscape for conservationist aims, the scenic and conventions of landscape painting are firmly connected within the English language and Anglophone theatrical cultures. James Corner maps how landscape has been equated with theatre scenery, arguing that 'landscape objectifies the world – in the form of "scenery", "resource", or "ecosystem"' (Corner 1999: 11). The objectification that Corner outlines is also a process of quantification. The multi-sensory and intangible orientations of landscape are quantified into a singular object that can be exchanged and traded. The objectification and quantification of landscape 'fails to consider the profound consequences of the world's *constructedness* – its schematization as a cultural idea and, therefore, its subjugation' (Corner 1999: 3; emphasis in original). Corner's analysis stems from an argument put forward by Allen Carlson. In his article 'On the Possibility of Quantifying Scenic Beauty' (1977), Carlson outlines how a 'scenic cult' and a 'landscape cult' emerged following the advent of photography. In particular, Carlson argues that the methods of quantifying landscape through photography (although he stresses that this relates to a long history of landscape painting) and thereby assign it 'value' assumes that landscape can be understood *as-if-it-were* a two-dimensional static representation. Allen summarizes this impulse as the quantification of landscape. Intrinsic to this position is that, as Townsend outlines, 'the picturesque places the viewer outside the scene, which must be viewed in the proper way from the proper point of view' (Townsend 1997: 370). This literal positioning of the subject (the spectator) as discrete from the object (the landscape) is fundamental to the politics of the picturesque and, correspondingly, the scenic. Unlike the ontological indeterminacy of affective atmospheres, scenic politics enact a strict binary between subject and object that enable the viewer to possess, to partition, the experience of landscape through a system of value judgment.

The ontology of the scenic is counter to Stewart's position on scenes as 'things that happen' (Stewart 2007: 2) and the oneness Shearing (2014) cites as being formative to scenographic landscapes. Instead, the quantification of the picturesque and the scenic equates to the structural interpretations of the dramaturgical scene. The notion of a 'scene study' as a technique for rehearsing actors is an example of how the dramaturgical scene sequences action. Within a scene study an actor or actors will rehearse a particular part from a literary play. Typically, an author has written the play following the dramaturgical ordering of acts and scenes – dividing the places and time periods that occur as part of the action. In this situation, a scene is a means of organizing a sequence of action. One scene follows another scene follows another. The scene, in this instance, is wholly dramaturgical. It denotes the structure of action. A dramaturgical scene is the scene in *mise en scène*, where the scene is *observed* as a point interpretation and a codified transaction. A scenographic scene is the felt experience of *being with* an affective atmosphere and its othering potential. The dramaturgical scene and the scenographic scene operate in unison and without, in many instances, discernable division. They are, however, two distinct strategies that sustain an act of scene-making.

Stewart's scenes of 'impulses, sensations, expectations' (Stewart 2007: 2) denote the situational potentials of *being with* the scenographic scene. While charged with the learnt historicisms of painting appreciation (as 'high art' or even theological), I propose that the notion of the scenic aligns more with the interpretative systems of codified translation that render a dramaturgical scene a quantified object of study that sustains objective distance. Subsequently, the dramaturgical scene is representative of the ideological mechanisms that reduce world to a knowable human scale. Scenographic scenes, I argue, are the felt orientations and material relationships that afford and affirm the quantified worldings of the dramaturgical as felt encounters. Stage-scenes are ordered in terms of the dramaturgical, but felt through the orientating potentials of scenographics.

Scenographics

I am in Plymouth at the Theatre and Performance Research Association (TaPRA) conference in 2009. I am debating the remit of scenography with two colleagues – Emily Orley and Elizabeth Wright – in a coffee break. To test out the limits of our claims, I point to a lone chair within a seminar room and declare it 'scenographic'. The chair was similar to the ones we had been using throughout the day, but its placement (slightly angled, yet orientated towards us) and its situatedness (the sole object within a delimited area of the room) implied a distinct potential for dramatic action. It evoked the condition of theatrical objects where the act of placement on a stage speaks loudly and clearly; where the orientation of a stage object can articulate as much as the object itself. If the chair had been facing away from us or partnered with others like it, the encounter would have been different. Framed by an open doorway, our orientation towards the chair appeared composed, directed and purposeful. An orientation that implied the spatial logic of theatre; of voyeurs and stage, reflection and action. The response by my colleagues was straightforward: 'What do you mean by scenographic?' This book amounts to my answer.

I argue that scenographics are interventional acts of place orientation. These traits are formative to all manner of staged acts, whether the behaviours associated with gardening or interior design as well as the art practices of installation art and exhibition architecture. I propose that the attentiveness of the chair was relational to a perception that its orientations had othered, skewed or altered the normativities of the seminar room. The chair was also open to possibilities: an invitation for *potential* action. Yet, this attentive quality remained bound to the wider placements and orientations of the other chairs. The individual chair's position enacted an othering orientation that I labelled as scenographic. In this regard, I contend that the term 'scenographic' isolates and affords a particular perspective, or critical framework, that identifies the potentiality of stage architectures.

Jenn Joy applies a similar approach to the notion of a choreographic trait:

> Trespassing into the discourses and disciplines of visual-sculptural-audial-philosophic practice, *the choreographic works against linguistic signification and virtuosic representation; it is about contact that touches even across distances. The choreographic is a metonymic condition that moves between corporeal and cerebral conjecture to tell the stories of these many encounters between dance, sculpture, light, space, and perception through a series of stutters, steps, trembles, and spasms.*
>
> (Joy 2014: 1; emphasis in original)

Joy's approach argues how a choreographic trait exceeds the art contexts of choreography to afford a perspective on socio-political ruptures and events, claiming that the choreographic is 'a set of dispersive and generative strategies, calling our attention to these shocks and seizures and spasms within the contemporary' (Joy 2014: 27). As with my own position on the interventional circumstances of scenographics, Joy argues that a choreographic trait 'acts as a mode of provocation and address' (Joy 2014: 27). Correspondingly, a scenographic trait enacts a perceptual provocation that calls attention to the broader thresholds of worldly encounter: of how orders of world orientate action and regulate behaviour. Scenographics are predicated on the notion that they sustain a withness – a proximity as well as connectedness – that cultivates a potentiality for change and multiple practices within the same material environment. Scenographics isolate the potentiality latent within any staged atmosphere.

Scenographics afford a framework of specifying the 'stage-like' potentials of a situation that may otherwise be captured by notions of performativity and theatricality. Carlson summarizes how the adoption of these key terms by other disciplines has helped grow the artistic and scholarly identity of theatre and performance studies:

> [A]s performativity and theatricality have been developed in [other disciplinary] fields, both as metaphors and as analytical tools, theorists and practitioners of performance art have in turn become aware of these developments and found in them new sources of stimulation, inspiration, and insight for their own creative work and theoretical understanding of it.
>
> (Carlson 1996: 7)

While I agree with Carlson, I also call attention to the critique of performativity as posed by Tracy D. Davis and Thomas Postlewait: 'The public realm is the performative realm ... Perhaps, though, the idea explains too much and too conveniently. The temptation needs to be tempered, and the claims particularized' (Davis and Postlewait 2003: 29). My adoption of an institutional and operational understanding of theatre echoes Davis and Postlewait's argument for the claims of performativity to be particularized. The argument for scenographics is an argument for refining how these terms are employed. It operates as a call to re-evaluate the critical frameworks through which acts of staging are conceptualized in other disciplinary contexts. From gardening to installation art, these practices of staging are, I argue, bound to an enactment of scenographics that isolates interventional methods of place orientation. While scenography is peculiar, scenographics are commonplace.

My declaration of the seminar room chair as scenographic was not a statement on whether the chair was any more or less 'real' than those around it. I propose that scenographics do not seek to confirm an orientation as either true or false; rather, they account for how the relationships between objects, bodies and other objects enact a distinct form of place orientation. This is a trait shared with performatives. In October 1959, J. L. Austin delivered a lecture entitled 'Performatives' in Gothenburg. The title of this lecture captures a key tenet of Austin's theory of speech acts. Performatives are utterances that occur when a speech act – such as 'I do' at a wedding – amounts to doing, i.e. an action. Austin's argument for performatives were conceived in relation to the established conditions of constative utterances. These 'constatives' are statement values on whether a speech act confirms something as either true or false. Often described in the singular (as 'performative'), Austin details how the doing of performative utterances renders discrete forms – such as primary, explicit and pure – that constitute the shared linguistic condition of performatives.

I began by drawing your attention, by way of example, to a few simple utterances of the kind known as performatories or performatives. These have on the face of them the look – at least the grammatical make-up – of 'statements'; but nevertheless they are seen, when more closely inspected, to be, quite plainly, not utterances which could be 'true' or 'false'. Yet to be 'true' or 'false' is traditionally the characteristic mark of a statement.

(Austin 1962: 12)

Austin's decoupling of performatives from constative statements is significant. In doing so, Austin argues that the declaration of truth is not tied to performatives as a doing. One can say 'I promise to be truthful' (a performative) and, while this operates as the moment in which that promise was enacted, it does not confirm it to be a true statement. The act of promising, of saying 'I promise', is distinct from any ethical codes of conduct that qualify it as 'the truth'. James Loxley argues how Austin conceptualized this issue within a discussion on notions of seriousness and non-seriousness. Loxley outlines how performatives are not 'about a differentiation between reality and illusion' (Loxley 2007: 160). Instead, non-serious performatives – such as jokingly saying 'I declare war' – are qualified by criteria or a set of conventions that exceed the actual doing of the utterance. This distinction is also evident in scenographics. As with performatives, scenographics are utterances that happen as part of an assemblage that 'do' things with/to that assemblage. The arguments for scenographics consequently share many of the same epistemological indeterminacies as performatives. It also stresses – in its use of the plural – that scenographic traits do not pertain to essentialist positions on experiential encounter, as these orientations are shared and enacted through a number of methods, modalities and situational contexts that exceed strict definition. Crucially, scenographics account for intangible utterances that enact how certain crafted assemblages orientate, and how in turn are oriented by, human bodies.

My call to reconsider the expansive remit of staging concepts is most prominently evident in the use of the term 'performative' with art practices. Since the early 1990s, the idea of a 'performative artwork' has gained traction as a label for art that *does something*. Whether explicitly in terms of motion or implicitly through affect, a performative artwork is taken as a legacy of the New York avant-garde of the 1960s, with the term 'performative' potentially applying to the action art of Jackson Pollock (1912–1956) along with the happenings of Allan Kaprow (1927–2006). Dorothea von Hantelmann has, however, challenged the overuse of this term and suggested that the genrefication of performative is innately problematic – where performative artwork as a category 'remains stubbornly slippery, and for good reasons, because it is based on a complete twist of the word "performative"' (von Hantelmann 2010: 17). The misapplication that von Hantelmann outlines relates to Austin's mapping of performatives. Taking Austin's text as canonical, von Hantelmann suggests that performatives are often confused with a wider notion of performativity as 'performance-like'. The 'like' denotes that it is a proxy concept, whereas Austin's performatives are particular and relate to distinct qualities of speech. Diane Taylor agrees with von Hantelmann's position, proposing the term 'performatic' as a means of signalling how a 'lecture may be performatic (theatrical) without constituting a legal act' (Taylor 2016: 120). Taylor's approach renders 'theatrical' as politically distinct from 'performatic', the implication being that 'theatrical' suggests a potential politics of duality, whereas 'performatic' is a type of display act with no political associations in and of itself.

Von Hantelmann goes one step further than Taylor to declare that 'there is no performative artwork, because there is no non-performative artwork' (von Hantelmann 2010: 17). In positioning all artwork as performative, von Hantelmann argues that the 'doing' quality of speech acts applies to all forms of utterance. All art does something; all art sustains orientations. In this way, to describe an artwork as performative is to potentially misunderstand how all encounter is marked by acts of utterance. The notion of a performative artwork is, subsequently, redundant or nondescript. Von Hantelmann equally claims that the 'notion of performativity has nothing to do with the art form of performance' (von Hantelmann 2010: 18). To complicate this issue further, 'performance' in many continental European languages typically refers to the genre of performance art rather than disciplined behavioural traits. Von Hantelmann's conception of performance relates to my own usage of theatre as an extra-daily art event, which is distinct from the disciplined daily-enacted repetitions associated with performativity. Whether the narratological encounter of Tracey Emin's *My Bed* (1998) or the light-art of Anthony McCall and his *Line Describing a Cone* (1973), I argue that these artworks evoke methods of placing and orientation that are scenographic in conception and execution. If the argument for a performative artwork is rendered redundant, I propose that scenographics afford a useful counterpoint when articulating an artwork's affinity to staging. Theatricality, conversely, applies to acts of representation.

Theatricality has a distinct and prominent critical position within art theory, from Plato to the Romanticists of Jean-Jacques Rousseau (1712–78). Indeed, the use of performative as 'performance-like' – which in turn often denotes 'stage-like' – arguably navigates around an anti-theatrical bias that has formed the basis for certain approaches to art criticism. The art critic Michael Fried consolidated this position in his essay 'Art and Objecthood' (1967) by stating that 'Art degenerates as it approaches the condition of the theater' (1967: 164). Fried's position builds on the arguments of his counterpart, Clement Greenberg (1909–94). In 1948, Greenberg argued that modernist arts seek to 'achieve concreteness, "purity," by acting solely in terms of their separate and irreducible selves' (in Greenberg 1961: 139). Fried expands on this position to critique artworks that require the presence of an individual, a spectator, to 'complete' the work. Fried terms these practices 'theatrical'. Focused on minimalist painting and sculpture, Fried predicates his analysis on the notion that art is always wholly manifest at each moment in time. While arguing that this manifestation is continually in a state of reasserting its presence (where the 'presentness' of an artwork is remade in each moment), Fried contends that this is discrete from theatre in which the experience of durational time is central to the manifestation of the work.

> The literalist [minimalist] preoccupation with time – more precisely, with the *duration of the experience* – is, I suggest, paradigmatically theatrical, as though theater confronts the beholder, and thereby isolates him [*sic*], with the endlessness not just of objecthood but of *time*; or as through the sense, at bottom, theater addresses is a sense of temporality, of time both passing and to come, *simultaneously approaching and receding*, as if apprehended in an infinite perspective.
>
> (Fried 1967: 167; emphasis in original)

Fried concludes his essay by arguing that the very presentness of art is 'corrupted or perverted by theater' (Fried 1967: 168). The notion that art exceeds the durational experience of time and, in the words of Fried, sustains a quality of 'endlessness' reaffirms the popular conception of 'great' artwork as being timeless (in that it exceeds conceptions of time). The technical usage of theatre and theatricality within Fried's analysis situates theatre as that which is discrete from art. This builds upon a history of categorizing art practices as summarized by Lessing. Crucially, the use of the term 'spatial' by Lessing is focused purely on the conception of abstract dimension that exceeds any temporal duration. Likewise, Kant (1790) partitioned the 'visual arts' (including painting and the plastic arts, such as sculpture and architecture) as discrete from the 'art of speech' (poetry) and the 'play of sensations' (music and colour forms). Fried similarly conceives the abstract manifestation of art as being discrete from the situated experience of time. Whereas theatre is situated in time, for Fried art is timeless.

More generally, the notion of theatricality has been applied to a range of everyday practices that are enacted and/or staged. Elizabeth Burns (1972) has argued that theatricality 'in ordinary life consists in the resort [sic] to this special grammar of composed behaviour; it is when we suspect that behaviour is being composed according to this grammar of rhetorical and authenticating conventions that we regard as theatrical' (Burns 1972: 33). What Burns describes as authenticating conventions are the systems of codification disciplined by social contracts that situate an action as sincere or normative. Following the anti-theatrical rhetoric of critics such as Fried, the sincerity of a craft is assessed in relation to its distance from the theatrical. The impact of this positioning is evident in how the methods of scenography are positioned culturally. For instance, the orchestrated-ness of interior design (the placement of objects as well as surface textures) is understood as a crafting, yet this is removed from the negative politics assigned to theatricality. Likewise, within Naturalist traditions of theatre the term 'costume' has been consciously replaced with 'clothes' or 'garments'. This linguistic shift invites actors to wear costumes *as if they were their own*. The theatricality paired with costume is deemed counter to the psychophysical conventions of theatrical Naturalism.

While interior design and costume are representative of different interpretations of this critique, these anti-theatrical readings equally apply to all manner of material cultures where the conventions of scenery and stage management (as a 'managing' of events) are evident. Consequently, the politics of theatricality are tightly bound to the politics assigned to the methods of scenography.

Beyond the politics of theatricality, the study of theatre and performance in universities is arguably orientated towards the concerns of bodies and literature, performers and context: what bodies do and why bodies do it. While this reading is overly simplistic, the practical study of scenography is often reserved for a one-off module or a pathway within the degree (unless studied as part of a Performance Design degree). This situation partly stems from a misreading of scenography as set design or scenery. Of course, the place-orientating affects of lighting and sound, chairs and tables, are encountered in all theatre and performance curriculums – no study of theatre is without an enactment of scenography. Accordingly, the director of the first academic institution for theatre research, Max Herrmann, positioned the spatial qualities of theatre as vital. In his 1931 essay 'The Theatrical Experience of Space', Herrmann argued that '"performing arts are spatial arts", for they unfold and reveal their most essential qualities in real space' (cited in Fischer-Lichte and Wihstutz 2013: 1). Scenography occupies the critical juncture outlined by Herrmann, operating as 'the spatial' in theatre. The usage of the term 'scenography' in this instance has, however, been complicated by the prevalence of *mise en scène*, along with the established theatrical design lexicon. Schechner, as an earlier adopter of scenography in English, applies the notion of scenography more broadly, arguing that 'Theaters everywhere are scenographic models of sociometric process' (Schechner 1988: 157). Schechner positions the scenographic as a means of engaging social interactions through spatial intervention, but, significantly for this book, he also positions a scenographic trait as a condition of all theatre.

While scenographics may be a trait of all theatre, the implication is that scenography as a particular task exceeds the conventional Anglophone orthodoxies of theatrical production. Schechner points out that the institutional theatres enact conventional hierarchies that are ever-present, where even the 'building, like the events within it, is compartmentalized; the time for the audience to look at each other is regulated and is limited to before the show and to intermissions' (Schechner 1988: 154–5). As with Brook's opening paragraph in *The Empty Space* (1968), Schechner frames the institutional theatre as systematic and codified – rather than open and experimental. The argument for an expanded scenography has, in part, been fuelled by the perceived need to move away from the hierarchies of the institutionalized theatres and the study of scenography as separate or *for designers*. It also echoes a desire to articulate a scenography that has a greater resonance and profile within the academic study of theatre and performance, beyond a byword for design. This political repositioning of scenography beyond theatre, which also informs notions of Performance Design, is symptomatic of a wider tension between the *craft* of scenography and the *critical potential* of scenographics.

In her account of the transdisciplinary qualities of expanded scenography, Brejzek argues that '[s]cenographic strategies in the representation of the invisible and imagined, the virtual and the actual prove to operate within a contemporary interdisciplinary discourse that is informed by the praxis and theory of theatre, architecture, media and exhibition' (Brejzek 2011b: 5). Brejzek, while focused on the notion of an expanded scenography, presents a scenographic strategy as extending beyond the institutional theatre and its disciplinary orthodoxies. This argument is echoed by den Oudsten: 'Every scenographic piece of work, be it an exhibition or a play, an installation or a performance, will evoke a certain narrative space that is essentially unstable and that will cease to exist through time' (den Oudsten 2011: 17). The usage of 'scenographic' is noteworthy here. I argue that both Brejzek and den Oudsten's accounts can be read as applying the term as an ideological proxy to scenography. Likewise, my argument for scenographics complements a series of other critical-creative terminologies derived from stage cultures; namely, choreographic, filmic and photographic. In each instance, the quality attributed to the term exceeds any particular physical object to suggest an intangible structure or system of aesthetic discourse. The situation of an object, and its relationship to other objects or bodies, is where the notion of a filmic or choreographic reading derives its value. The same is evident for a scenographic reading. All situations that are operationally theatre will, as a matter of course, also be scenographic.

The framework of scenographics navigates the epistemological double negative that frames situations that are not not scenography. To return to my experience at the Sensing Spaces exhibition at the RA, my usage of the double negative for scenography's relationship to practices such as installation art denotes how scenographics operate beyond the institutional remits of theatre. In the same way as garden design or game design are not scenography, these practices are also not not scenography. Namely, these 'scenographic cultures' explicitly employ methods of scenography to orientate an experience of an affective atmosphere, whether in terms of lighting, soundscapes, costume or spatial configuration. Beyond theatre and performance studies, this trait is typically summarized in the notion of 'staging'. Curator Bridget Crone argues that the 'concept of staging provides a means for understanding curatorial activity whether an exhibition, time-based event, talk or screening as a moment of appearance that occurs through (and despite) the contesting movements of disintegration and potentiality' (Crone 2013: 210). Crone's focus on the moment, the act, of appearance signals my own position on scenography as place orientation. In this instance, Crone's application of staging evokes how a stage is rendered eventful: how it is composed, orientated and felt. The conditions of staging are the conditions of scenographics. While I hesitate to argue their equivalence given the history of scenography being rendered a terminological proxy, the richness of staging as both a practice and a concept is sustained through scenographics. To speak of staging is to speak of how scenographics enact an 'othering' of place.

Othering tactics

In *The Theatre of Tomorrow* (1923), Macgowan cites the producer Arthur Hopkins in his introduction to realism within theatre. Hopkins observes that the task of accurate reproduction, as evoked by material surrogacy, is:

> *only remarkable because it is not real*. So the upshot of the realistic effort is further to emphasize the

un-reality of the whole attempt, setting, play, and all. So I submit that realism defeats the very thing to which it aspires. It emphasizes the faithfulness of un-reality.

(cited in Macgowan 1923: 20; emphasis in original)

Hopkins' assessment exposes the intrinsic double negative of theatrical representation and what he argued to be the false ecology of theatrical realism. However, the 'faithfulness of un-reality' introduces a useful frame in which to examine scenographics – in particular, that the schism to which Hopkins alludes is predicated on the orders of knowledge that situate experiences as 'normative' or 'other'. The notion that the accurate reproduction's value is directly proportionate to the knowledge that it is 'not real' and ontologically other is crucial to understanding how scenographic orientations intervene into/with place. It is the capacity for place orientation – inclusive of empirical proxemics and felt subjectivities – to evoke and score these orders of knowledge that remains at the crux of scenographic experience. Yet, as with performatives, scenographics are not statements on the ontological criteria of a situation: real or false, authentic or inauthentic. Nevertheless, it is the 'un-reality' or interventional qualities of scenographics that rendered these orientations as discrete from normative worlding tactics. In that regard, scenographic traits are conceptually and practically tied to a capacity to enact othering orientations that score and draw attention to orders of worldly normativity.

Sara Ahmed articulates the processes of orientation as:

> different ways of registering the proximity of objects and others. Orientations shape not only how we inhabit space, but how we apprehend this world of shared inhabitance, as well as 'who' or 'what' we direct our energy and attention toward.
>
> (Ahmed 2006: 3)

Ahmed's approach to orientation conflates the sensory qualities of 'haptic' experience with learned orders of knowledge. Psychologist J. J. Gibson (1966) isolated the haptic qualities of sensory orientation when he challenged the division of the five Aristotelian senses (of sight, hearing, taste, smell and touch). Gibson's five perceptual systems of sensing include 'visual', 'auditory' and 'taste-smell'. Gibson's definition of sensory *systems* – as opposed to discrete and finite senses (a visual system is not only conditioned by stimulus from the eye) – is crucial to the holistic premise that defines haptic experience. Indeed, Gibson introduced the notion of 'basic-orienting' and 'haptic' systems. The basic-orienting system is the means by which bodies sense direction (up/down), motion or stillness, inside or outside. Gibson's haptic system includes all aspects of touch (pressure, warmth, cold, pain and kinaesthetics) that involve actual connection with a body. Gibson proposes that these perceptual systems often operate as complementary processes to active cognition, arguing that bodies sense before the mind has time to compute these stimuli as abstract thought. In terms of place orientation, Gibson's basic-orienting system relates to felt conditions of proximity. Ahmed, however, extends this system to the processes of apprehending others (and otherness). While both Gibson and Ahmed frame orientation as multi-sensory and psychological, Ahmed's focus on how orientation situates an individual in relation to questions of otherness extends its remit beyond the rudimentary proximity conditions of Gibson.

Ahmed summarizes the otherness of experiential encounter under the heading of 'queer phenomenology'. This loose heading adopts the precept that phenomenology, as a philosophical project, has been a study of the 'toward', focusing on the affordances that occur between bodies and objects, bodies and other bodies, or bodies and socio-political borders that render a situation as attentive. Queer phenomenology draws attention to how an othering of experience is felt and, consequently, enacted through means of orientation. While sexual orientation and heteronormativity provide an initial exemplar, Ahmed's analysis opens out to consider how phenomenological experience is conditioned by an ordering of difference. Likewise, the founder of proxemics, Edward T. Hall, stresses that any physical distances that define 'personal space' from 'public space' are relative to learned cultural traits, where 'people reared in different cultures live in different sensory worlds' (Hall 1968: 83). Hall recognizes that the 'patterning of perceptual worlds is a function not only of the specific culture but of the relationship, activity, and emotions present in a given situation' (Hall 1968: 83). The emotional and affective qualities of worlding are, accordingly, all part of a social patterning that charges certain places with a distinct feeling or otherness. Ahmed's argument is that orientations are qualified and reinforced through structural discourses of otherness, which builds upon Edward Said's position in *Orientalism* (1978) that humans 'have always divided the world up into regions having either real or imagined distinctions from each other' (Said 1978: 39). Said argues that there exists a 'universal practice of designating in one's mind a familiar space which is "ours" and an unfamiliar space beyond "ours" which is "theirs" is a way of making geographical distinctions that *can be* entirely arbitrary' (Said 1978: 54; emphasis in original). Understanding orientation in terms of material proximities *and* the felt orders of othering – whether in terms of strategies of orientation (spatial arrangement, intimacy, etc.), location (belonging, scale, etc.) or period (historical signifiers, tempo, etc.) – is crucial to the usage applied throughout this book.

I argue that the act of othering is hypertrophic in conception and reception. As with theatre and staging more generally, to engage in a conscious act of othering is to irritate the learned normativities of any given situation. The task of othering is integral to all manner of critical concepts for how phenomena are encountered in relation to ongoing subjectivities and ideological conditions. Most prominent of these is the notion of 'queering'. Ahmed's approach to queer phenomenology is predicated on analysing how orientations are crafted and enacted in response to learned orders of knowledge. Queering is an act of revealing or subverting how these orders of knowledge are manifest: from affirmative acts of gender play at a Gay Pride parade to the survival tactics of minority groups. In *European Others: Queering Ethnicity in Postnational Europe* (2011), Fatima El-Tayeb outlines how 'Europeans of colour' might adopt queering tactics that

> destabilize the ascribed essentialist identities not only by rejecting them, but also through a strategic and creative (mis)use, rearranging a variety of concepts and their interrelations, among them time, space, memory, as well as race, class, nation, gender, and sexuality.
> (El-Tayeb 2011: xxvi)

Thus, queering is approached as an affirmative tactic that is undertaken knowingly and with purpose that destabilizes orders of normativity – whether manifest as heteronormativity, homonormativity or structures of assigned authenticity.

The critical tactic of othering is notably distinct from the systematic processes that impose an assigned otherness which disciplines knowledge, situations or individuals in terms of the Other. Moreover, othering operates through the same affirmative tactics as queering and seeks to enact a conscious scoring of disciplined normativities that are codified through the repetition of a particular situation, object or speech act. In terms of this book, queering is approached as an othering tactic alongside notions of 'surrogacy'. With explicit reference to the histories of mimesis and representational discourse, the tactic of surrogacy is applied in order to re-evaluate orders of authenticity that privilege conceptions of originality over and above the affective orientations of surrogate objects as real assemblages.

In 1936, Walter Benjamin argued in his analysis of mass media and the reproduction of images that an art object's 'unique existence at the place where it happens to be' is the 'prerequisite to the concept of authenticity' (Benjamin 1968: 220). Citing how historically images were situated in particular places for particular time periods, Benjamin argues that the mass reproduction of images ruptured the synchronicity between image and place. This, in turn, challenged how images were understood epistemologically, as there could now be thousands of reproductions of the same image with no reference to the place of the original. Yet, Benjamin recognized that orders of authenticity operate as a disciplining apparatus that attributes value to some objects over others, arguing that 'the concept of authenticity always transcends mere genuineness' (Benjamin 1968: 244). Benjamin concludes that 'the function of the concept of authenticity remains determinate in the evaluation of art; with the secularization of art, authenticity displaces the cult value of the work' (Benjamin 1968: 244). The 'cult value' is when an object's presence is attributed greater social recognition that exceeds the materiality of the object in question (such as a religious artifact). Thus, Benjamin argues that authenticity operates as a secular enactment of cult values, which are equally predicated on questions of power, censorship and hierarchies of recognition.

One of Benjamin's key observations is that surrogate objects seemingly deplete the 'aura' of any original.

Yet, Benjamin is keen to stress that this aura is quantified in relation to the assigned orders of authenticity, which is discrete from any intrinsic quality of the object itself. Indeed, this notion of an object's aura is arguably an othering tactic that affords and sustains distinct orientations that enact a feeling of 'uniqueness' or 'specialness'. Since the assumed alignment with perspective painting as recounted by the Roman scholar Vitruvius (c.80–70 BCE–c.15 BCE), scenographics have been conceptualized in terms of surrogacy; of making somewhere or something else manifest in a timespace other than that of its 'original' place. Plato conceptualized the aura of an object in relation to its distance from the divine form. The divine form of an object, such as the schema of a chair, was for Plato its ideal conception and only known to the gods. The construction of a physical chair by humans was an abstraction from this ideal form. Accordingly, any imitations of chairs, such as an image of a chair, were twice removed form the ideal conception and thereby unworthy of serious analysis. Plato's order of imitations evokes a similar disciplining that is evident within notions of authenticity. Deleuze does, however, argue that the repeated object is rendered peculiar in its very status as a surrogate object. In *Difference and Repetition* (1968), Deleuze suggests that the repetition differs ontologically from the original in that the 'repeated cannot be represented: rather, it must always be signified, masked by what signifies it, itself masking what it signifies' (Deleuze 1994: 21). With explicit reference to the use of costume and masks in theatre, Deleuze argues that there 'is no bare repetition which may be abstracted or inferred from the disguise itself. The same thing is both disguising and disguised' (Deleuze 1994: 20). In this manner, the othering of surrogacy exposes underlying contrivances and constructions that discipline social, political and artistic practices. One innately scenographic example of this phenomenon occurs through the scenographics of a funfair Ghost Train.

As part of a weekend break to the UK coast with my partner and two friends, I visit a funfair in Hastings called Flamingo Park. After purchasing some tokens, my friend suggests that we ride the Ghost Train that has loudspeakers positioned on its exterior playing vocal sounds of groans and cackles that I immediately associate with the iconography of mythical monsters and Halloween. I hand over my token and clamber into the carts that comprise the train itself. I am sat at the front. As the train starts to move, I hold on to a metal bar as I adjust my body to the irregular sways of the cart. The entrance's double doors are flung open by the cart's front bumper. The sound of the cart's connection with the track below is augmented with the vocal sounds I had heard outside, which now seem louder and more immediate. We move between states of darkness into moments of strobe lighting that highlight and accent mannequins costumed as zombies or skeletons. Some of the mannequins have mechanisms that animate their limbs. Each time the train traverses a room, we enter a brief state of darkness before the jolt of the cart moves my body as it hits and opens the double doors for the next section. The mixture of light, costume, motion and sound are evidently crafted to afford a holistic experience that is potentially all-compassing, yet discrete from the 'world' outside. I cannot help but remind myself of previous experiences of immersive theatre that have sought to instigate a similar experience. Crucially, each crafted scene the train passes is a speculative manifestation of the familiar iconographies of monsters that I recalled upon hearing the soundscapes outside. In particular, these monsters are in and of themselves a fiction – a creation that symbolizes and enacts human fears of the Other. The monsters are literal manifestations of how humans conceptualize the 'undead' in terms of otherness. Yet, the materials and methods used to render these monsters 'real' are all identifiably scenographic. Indeed, I consider how the Ghost Train itself is only able to maintain the immersive experience or atmosphere that it seeks to sustain through means of scenographics. The recorded groans from directed speakers, costumed mannequins, sporadic lighting and motion of the train all add up to a feeling of worldly displacement and uncertainty. While the overall sequencing of the train is undoubtedly dramaturgical, the felt othering of this atmosphere is known through the Ghost Train's enacted scenographics. As the train exits back out into the 'real world', I consider how the situational otherness of the Ghost Train – as discrete from the iconographic otherness of the dramaturgical scenes – exposes a particular trait of scenographics: that scenographics are only known through their capacity for othering.

While the anthropologies of 'monsters as otherness' is a discrete line of enquiry, my experience of the Ghost Train exemplifies a wider argument on the othering traits of scenographics. The assemblages that comprise the various stage-scenes of my experience sought to impart a distinct and discrete atmospheric quality, which was peculiar to the lighting or soundscapes of the 'outside world'. My encounter with this atmosphere occurred through the accumulative affect of various scenographic orientations that sought to alter my attentive state. Yet, underlying all this was a conscious acknowledgement of the orders of knowledge that situated this experience as controlled and crafted. The affects of these orientations were also informed by the immediate recognition of the mannequins as mannequins, the groans as recorded and the lighting as sequenced. What is more, the subject in question is derived and enforced through a fictive worlding that, while familiar, is conceptualized ontologically as 'not real'. Nevertheless, my experience of the Ghost Train did occur. My body was really moved by the shudders of the cart and my senses were heightened by the shifting sound and lightscapes. The Ghost Train itself is an explicit exercise in othering how individuals encounter, in this instance a series of dramaturgical scenes of monsters, by intervening in how the rooms of the 'haunted mansion' are traversed. The objects and situations I encountered on the Ghost Train were all intentionally Other or, in the language of Ahmed (2006), 'queer'. Beyond any logocentric readings of narrative or message, the orientations that the scenographics sustained were encountered in terms of a situational othering – of bright lights, loud sounds, jerky motions, spatial uncertainty. My Ghost Train ride evidences how scenographics are predicated on the ability to intervene, to alter and impact how places are orientated that renders that experience as an extra-daily event, as Other. Therefore, this invites the conclusion that scenographics are only manifested as scenographics through their capacity for situational othering.

My overarching objective in positioning scenographic orientations as agents for othering is to consider how these traits irritate and score broader conceptions of worlding. While othering exceeds a strict focus on the politics of authenticity, I argue that notion of surrogacy – whether manifested through sound or light, as well as props and scenery – presents a lens through which to argue how othering is a fundamental tactic of scenographics. Notably, surrogacy introduces an additional ontological complication to queer objects as articulated by Ahmed (2006). Unlike queer othering that is predicated on skewing disciplined orders of behaviour, the othering of surrogacy stems from the recognition that an entity is knowingly and with purpose performing *in-place-of* another entity. The notion of surrogacy is directly related to the double negative of theatricality, yet it is also ontologically distinct in its capacity to sustain orientations that are unique to it. For example, Ghost Trains are predicated on the affective potential of surrogate objects. Whether the glow-in-the-dark painted bones of a mannequin skeleton or the use of red paint to paste red 'blood-soaked' handprints on the walls, these dramaturgically arranged messages invite and curate a specific iconographic association that is the order of the logocentric, of message and interpretation. The mannequin skeleton is a surrogate object *in-place-of* a 'real' skeleton. However, the surrogate objects used to manifest these messages are material assemblages of what, in ontological terms, are real objects: thermoplastics, cloth, metal bars, associated colours of paint. While symbolically loaded, the material assemblage of a mannequin skeleton is no less real than the materials from which it is constructed. In turn, these material assemblages afford real affects that orientate and score an individual's situational experience with place. The assemblage of the mannequin skeleton exists as a mannequin skeleton, a real surrogate object. The epistemological distinction exists in the overt theatricality of the assemblage; it is not not a skeleton. This epistemological double negative exposes an underlying ontological indeterminacy of surrogacy. The surrogate object affirmatively performs *in-place-of* another symbolically coded entity and, in doing so, sustains real orientations and affects. Even if a 'real' skeleton were to be used in place of the mannequin, the situational context of the Ghost Train renders the experience theatrical: the whole experience is predicated on the idea that it is not not a Ghost Train. When surrogacy is self-evident, this orientates any interactions or encounters in relation to the situational othering that the entity sustains. In that regard, this ontological indeterminacy recognizes the distinct and peculiar affordances that stem from the epistemological double negative of surrogacy.

Whether manifested through the tactics of queering or surrogacy, the othering trait of scenographics afford a means of arguing the underlying specificities that inform and shape a scenographic perspective. The notion of othering is also central to Soja's thirdspace. Outlined as part of an argument for 'thirding-as Othering', Soja suggests that a conceptual thirding, which complicates the demarcation between empirical and subjective experiences, 'is radically open to additional othernesses, to a continuing expansion of spatial knowledge' (Soja 1996: 61). Likewise, Anderson (2009) argues that atmospheres are impersonal and highly personal at the same time. Böhme (2006) too situates the ontological indeterminacy of an atmosphere as being equally conditioned by questions of psyche as well as the physical qualities of an environment. This position echoes Roland Barthes' (1977) argument on how a 'third meaning' obfuscates the philosophical exchange of subject and object. Foucault cites heterotopias, such as a theatre stage, as 'counter-sites' that either expose 'real space' as illusory or 'their role is to create a space that is other, another real space, as perfect, as meticulous, as well arranged as ours is messy, ill constructed, and jumbled' (Foucault 1986: 27). The counter-site of a stage enacts and demarcates its action as other, as beyond or as an irritant to place normativity. A stage, and by extension a scene, are implicational with an innate othering that enacts a distinct feeling of place and of placing. As with notions of atmosphere, orientation is ontologically indeterminate as it conflates empirical conceptions of distance and spatial dynamics with felt orders of knowledge. Consequently, scenographics are affirmative acts of othering that irritate the disciplined normativities of worlding through interventional orientations.

As a concluding note on orientation and othering, scenography as place orientation and scenographics as worldly othering resists an exclusively visual definition. When I speak of materiality as a distinctive concern of scenographics, I do so through the lens of orientation. In 1902, Appia outlined how the task of scenography is to navigate a 'particular atmosphere encompassing the actors, an atmosphere which can only be achieved in relation to the living and moving beings' (cited in Beacham 1994: 118). Materiality in this instance denotes not only a physical or visual object, but also a system of relations between objects, bodies and motion. Building on Ahmed's conflation of proximity with otherness, my approach of place orientation draws attention towards the means by which theatre *places* individuals and the modes by which these same individuals *place themselves* within a materiality (an affective atmosphere). Sculptor Kent C. Bloomer and architect Charles W. Moore articulate this in terms of how orientation requires the 'feeling of being bounded, possessed and centered' (Bloomer and Moore 1977: 54). I argue that the notion of orientation focuses on the bodily methods through which place, as a material situation of a spatial imaginary, is felt. As with Ahmed and Gibson's usages, place orientation is body-centric as it focuses on holistic systems of sensory encounter. Subsequently, the notion of place orientation as applied in this book isolates how affective atmospheres are conceived and traversed.

My argument for place orientation focuses on the interventional quality of scenographics as distinct from atmospheres that can be haphazard or beyond human agency. While atmospheres affect through assemblages of material affordances, scenographic place orientation sustains an othering quality: orchestrating peculiar assemblages that intervene according to certain timescales in relation to wider orders of worlding. Of course, place sustains the geopolitical spatial ideologies of ordering, but the othering context of scenographics focuses on how place is oriented through systems of crafted materiality inclusive of scent and temperature as well as terrain and objects. Scenography as place orientation is an act of composing these stimuli, or being intentionally aware of their affects, with a distinct focus on how a constellation of these methods becomes manifest as an affective atmosphere.

Skenographia has many legacies.

CHAPTER 2

Scenography and the Anglophone theatres

While I argue that scenographics are innate to all staged events, its parent concept is not a common term within the English language. 'Scenography' is representative of a theatrical practice and linguistic idiom that derives from a long history of continental European theatre. It is not a term, nor concept, that has been born of the Anglophone theatres. Of all the summaries within the English language, theatre and performance scholars Paul Allain and Jen Harvie capture the allure and uncertainty often synonymous with the terminology:

> Even though the practice has existed for hundreds of years in various forms, as a term 'scenography' is relatively new and still unfamiliar. It has superseded the phrase 'theatre design', for 'scenography' denotes the integrated work on all elements of a production, from costumes through soundscapes to masks, a breadth which the expressions 'stage design', 'scenic design' and 'theatre design' cannot encompass.
> (Allain and Harvie 2006: 203)

The sentiment that scenography is representative of a holistic approach to theatrical design is echoed by English-speaking theatre scholars (Howard 2002; Aronson 2005; Baugh 2005; McKinney and Butterworth 2009; Rewa 2009; Collins and Nisbet 2010). Arnold Aronson argues the term 'carries a connotation of an all-encompassing visual-spatial construct as well as the process of change and transformation that is an inherent part of the physical vocabulary of the stage' (Aronson 2005: 7). With regards to the Anglophone usage, scenographer and theatre director Pamela Howard is often cited as the key instigator for the contemporary usage. However, many have overstated her role within its overall adoption, as she herself protests, 'I have not invented scenography ... It is not a new religion or even a new idea. It's just that I have begun using and speaking the name, and others do it, too' (Howard 2002: 128). The term 'scenography' has now been appropriated into the Anglophone theatre discourse, albeit it almost wholly within academic or academically aligned circles. The usage is in these contexts is, however, far from consistent.

The origin of the Anglicized appropriation of the term is a topic that is rarely discussed in depth. Often assumed to be a direct English-language translation of its continental cousins, this position is counter to the competing definitions of within Europe. Along with German, English was one of two major European languages not to employ a linguistic variant of the original Greek to denote the place-orientating role of design practices in the theatre. Whereas the German *Bühnenbauer* ('stage builder') and the English 'stage designer' denote the practice of realizing a stage environment, each semantic coding of *skenographia* is representative of a distinct set of practices and/or readings of the scenographer's institutional role with each national context. Revealing, until the 1960s the term in English typically denoted a form of architectural perspective drawing with no direct association with theatre.

The first adoption of scenography

Scenography enters the English lexicon in the early 1600s. Architect Sebastiano Serlio (1475–c.1554) uses the term within his fourth book of architecture, translated into English by Robert Peake in 1611 using the French spelling: 'The Scenographie or Sciographie, that is, the insight, by shortening of the most part of the Buildings that are in Rome, Italie, &c. diligently measured, and set by them in writing' (Serlio 1611: A2). This usage follows a mistranslation of Vitruvius's *scaenographia* by the architect Daniele Barbaro (1514–70), a disciple of Andrea Palladio (1508–80). Barbaro assumed Vitruvius's *scaenographia* to be synonymous with *sciographia* ('to draw in perspective'), a mistake that architect Alberto Pérez-Gómez outlines as the source of the confusion: 'Barbaro believed that *sciographia* (the third Vitruvian idea), translated as "perspective," resulted from a mis-reading in the original text of the word *scenographia*, whose application was important only in the building of stage-sets' (Pérez-Gómez and Pelletier 1992: 28). Pérez-Gómez notes that later translations of Vitruvius's original text often repeat Barbaro's mistranslation:

> These modern translations fail to do justice to the original text, in which there is no allusion to a vanishing point or to linear perspective. Even if *scaenographia* means 'to draw buildings in perspective,' the Latin origin of perspective, *perspicere*, is a verb that means simply 'to see clearly or carefully, to see through.'
>
> (Pérez-Gómez and Pelletier 1992: 29)

Pérez-Gómez's observations are evident in Joseph Gwilt's English-language translations of Vitruvius's text originally published in 1826, where 'scenography' 'exhibits the front and a receding side properly shadowed, the lines being drawn to their proper vanishing points' (Gwilt 1874: 10). Morris Hicky Morgan (1914) replaced 'scenography' altogether with 'perspective'. Morgan and Gwilt's translations are still in use today. To complicate the translations of Vitruvius still further, Erwin Panofsky (1991: 101) argues that Vitruvius describes an act of 'scene-making' (*scenam fecit*) rather than an explicit focus on 'scene-painting'. Painting is often taken to be the 'making' that is implied within the use of the Latin *fecit* ('he made'), but, as Panofsky observes, there is no direct connection to the craft of painting within the original text. Vitruvius does, however, cite the painter Agatharchus as the first to apply the craft of scene-making to the plays of Aeschylus. This contradicts the lineage as outlined by Aristotle, who cites Sophocles as the first to employ *skenographia*. Whatever the exact lineage, it is evident that a strict focus on painting as the only potential method of place orientation in Greek theatre – or at least as implied within the term *skenographia* – is potentially disingenuous to the term and the practices that can take place under its name.

One legacy of Barbaro's definition is that scenography had a greater recognition in English, prior to the 1960s, as a method of perspective drawing than for its relationship with theatre. This first adoption into English is no doubt derived from the prevalence of the Grand Tour in the 1600s, enjoyed by English gentry. With stops across northern Italy, this rite of passage was in equal parts a schooling in the latest ideas emerging from the Italian Renaissance and an exercise in excess. Most notably, English architect Inigo Jones (1573–1652) partook in the tour and would go on to collaborate with Ben Jonson (1572–1637) and lay the foundations for British theatrical design. Jones's designs took inspiration from Palladio and Vincenzo Scamozzi's Teatro Olimpico (built 1580–85). In particular, Scamozzi completed the theatre following Palladio's death during construction and sought to realize the impression of streets receding to a horizon. This was influenced by Vitruvius's depiction of the Greek theatre as overlooking a city, a task that was impossible in the marshland of Venice. Scamozzi designed a raked platform that supported physical constructions scaled following the rules of the Vitruvian vanishing point. Through openings in the Roman influenced *scaenae frons*, the theatre appeared to look out onto the streets of historical city of Thebes – connecting the drama with the places to which it pertains. Scamozzi's perspectival designs present an explicitly physical rather than figurative approach to staging place orientation. Scenography, following the mistranslations of Barbaro, becomes representative of how the Vitruvian vanishing point affords the semblance of distance without a feeling of space/place. Accordingly, the adoption of the vanishing point as a crucial element of the perspective stages of the 1700s established the raked stage and scaled scenery as theatrical orthodoxies. Moreover, these conventions resulted from the staging of the Vitruvian vanishing point that became a signifier for theatre that persists to this day.

Early approaches to stage design within the Anglophone theatres sought to translate the drawing methods associated with the vanishing point to give the semblance of depth and distance. The staggered painted flats synonymous with the British pantomime, and the scenic methods familiar to a high-school play, are legacies of this venture. Before the twentieth-century drawings of these stage environments would have been described as scenography, but the practice sustained no direct association with the term. The legacy of the Grand Tour and Barbaro's mistranslation are evident in the 1913 *Webster's Dictionary* entries for 'scenography' (with a 'y') and its related terms:

- Scenograph (*n.*) A perspective representation or general view of an object.
- Scenographical (*a.*) Of or pertaining to scenography; drawn in perspective.
- Scenographic (*a.*) Alt. of Scenographical
- Scenography (*n.*) The art or act of representing a body on a perspective plane; also, a representation or description of a body, in all its dimensions, as it appears to the eye.

(Webster 1913)

As late as 1993, the *Oxford English Dictionary* (OED) defined the term as 'The representation of a building or other object in perspective; a perspective elevation' or 'Scene-painting' as related to the ancient Greek practice only. Until recently, this focus on perspective was only paired with a second definition that accounted for 'The design of theatrical scenery; scenic design'. However, in 2013 a third definition was added to the OED entry that extended to the 'design and use of scenery, costume, lighting, etc., to create an effective performance environment; theatrical design; stagecraft'. Notably, this definition shifts from a previous focus on 'scenic design' to a broader conception of 'stagecraft', which stresses the *uses* of objects as well as their construction/design. This latest definition is also inclusive of costume and lighting as scenographic methods. Scenography's remit has seemingly extended beyond a pseudonym for scene painting and the physical construct of scenery, towards the recognition that it is representative of a distinctive strategy for theatre-making.

Continental differences pre-1960

While the English usage is not straightforward, this is confused still further by the multiple usages and applications of the term across continental Europe. Aside from one notable exception of Czech, continental variants on *skenographia* before the 1960s were typically conceptualized as a technical task relating to stage construction and/or decoration. In practical terms, the labours of a scenographer characteristically related to the execution of Restoration-influenced approaches to 'stage design' – as refined by practitioners such as Philip de Loutherbourg (1740–1812) – that situated 'stage worlds' as discrete from 'real worlds'. This worlding differentiation was manifested through the conventions of fixed perspective scale and the scenic politics of the picturesque. For instance, prior to 1960, in Spanish *escenografía* represented the practice of constructing the stage environment and properties only. In French, *scénographie* was a descriptor for the visual environment alone, with a *scénographe* being responsible for the technical realization of the stage constructions and decorations. Moreover, *scénographe* and *escenógrafo* (Spanish) conventionally denote the professional role of the 'set designer', as distinct from any other design roles on a production. This distinction is echoed by the Italian *scenografia* and, as a legacy of Barbaro, is extended to the practice of forced perspective drawing. The Danish *scenografi* likewise implies this notion of perspective drawing as well as stage design. While all definitions are connected to the OED's translation of Aristotle's *skenographia* as 'scene-painting', they are distinct from a radical take on the Czech *scénografie* that, by the mid-twentieth century, denoted a holistic composition of theatrical design practices. All pre-1960s continental designations of the ancient Greek *skenographia* exclude costume design. Admittedly, sound design as a compositional element within the theatre is a late twentieth-century addition to the institutional and creative theatrical roles. It is not surprising that this is not included as part of the pre-1960 definitions. For the majority of continental languages, there is no other established term that denotes the practice of designing for the stage. *Skenographia* has many legacies.

My rationale for citing the pre-1960 continental definitions is threefold. First, I wish to trace the particular histories of the radical Czech-influenced English-language variant. Second, after this time period the same factors that influenced that second Anglophone adoption also impact upon many of the continental approaches and readings. Third, along with the German *Szenografie*, the Anglophone variant is actively situated as different or distinct given the wealth of pre-existing terms in circulation before the 1960s: stage design, scenic design, set design, or just design, all precede the usage of 'scenography' as applied to theatre. Logically, the second Anglophone adoption in the twentieth century suggests that this term is representative of an idea, or approach to staging, that exceeds the remit of its predecessors. Or, as scenographer Frank den Oudsten outlines, '[t]he label of scenography apparently has a certain attraction to it. Scenography is an independent trade and the term "scenographer" has no fixed reference' (den Oudsten 2011: 13). Howard builds upon this perspective, as she argues that the term 'scenographer' offers a means of liberation from the dramaturgical servitude of theatrical design: 'It is very important to use scenography as a more accurate way of describing the role of the visual artist in the theatre, no longer being a servant but rather a leader, a creator or an initiator and a collaborator' (Howard 2002: 73). As a legacy of the New Stagecraft typified by the practices of Craig and Appia, it is only in the second half of the twentieth century that the term gains significant momentum within a theatrical context – albeit within a particular subset of English-speaking designers and scholars.

While not exclusive to this national context, American scenographer Darwin Reid Payne observes that '[w]hile the word has to some a faintly pretentious ring to it (some seeing a too-foreign influence in its use), others are beginning to see the real differences that lie between *scenographer* and *scenic designer*' (Reid Payne 1993: xxi; emphasis in original). It is, therefore, interesting to note that the notion of scenography as a holistic approach to theatrical design gained significant traction within the United States in the late 1960s. Most notably, this second adoption of scenography as a holistic approach aligns with the introduction of the Czech scenographer Josef Svoboda to the Anglophone context.

The second adoption of scenography

In 1948, UNESCO began funding the International Theatre Institute (ITI) in Prague. Initially focused on peace and cooperation following the Second World War, the ITI would provide the forum from which OISTAT would emerge. Originally founded in 1968 (with *architectes* being added to the title in 1985), OISTAT employed the French variant *scénographie* in its official title and documentation, although many core members were based in Prague. Svoboda was one such member. Indeed, Svoboda held the position of General Secretary for OISTAT from 1970 until 1984. Importantly, the translated 'scenography' is informally introduced to Anglophone peers as a conceptually inclusive term that encompassed all aspects of staging. Reflective of the postwar spirit for cooperation, the term was seen as that which bound the various design groupings – whether lighting or sound, set or costume – together as part of the same organization. This was discrete from the Anglophone terms that separate tasks into specialist areas or crafts: whether set design, lighting design, costume design, etc. The profile of these international organizations initialized the reintroduction of 'scenography' into the Anglophone stage lexicon. Yet, the decision to base these discussions in Prague, and the political upheaval of the preceding years, significantly shaped how the second adoption emerged as a holistic and conceptually inclusive practice in the 1960s. Svoboda was a key figure throughout this period.

In 1958, Svoboda presented the stage production of *Laterna Magika* at the Brussels World's Fair. It is a revelation for Anglophone theatre practitioners and designers. Svoboda's integration of video, scenery, music and dialogue went far beyond the remit of a theatre/stage/scenic designer as conceived within English-speaking theatres. Baugh recalls Svoboda's influence on those who witnessed his work, observing that, 'To those who "discovered" the work of Svoboda during the late 1960s, it appeared to represent a degree of synergy and integration that went far beyond a seemingly straightforward bringing together of visual and aural ingredients' (Baugh 2013: 82). With knowledge of the experiments of Craig and Appia, along with Bertolt Brecht (1898–1956) and designer Neher, Svoboda's work represented the most recent accumulation of the Wagnerian *Gesamtkunstwerk* that, while employing the techniques of scenic art, operated beyond the remit of vision alone. Baugh outlines how Svoboda 'extended the "Neher/Brecht-like" quality of creating a "text" of performance using the materials and technologies of theatre as a palette of opportunities' (Baugh 2013: 90–91). Moreover, Svoboda was renowned for his steadfast usage of 'scenography' to describe and define his practice becoming 'synonymous with the establishment of the word' (Baugh 2013: 82) within Anglophone communities. To discuss the second adoption of scenography is to trace the influence of Svoboda, and his Czech contemporaries, on English-language theatres.

Laterna Magika tours to New York in 1964. Two years later the *Tulane Drama Review* published a series of short excerpts of material sourced on Svoboda. The term 'scenography' is clearly used within a subtitle and description of the Czech's practice (Svoboda, Morris and Munk 1966: 146). In 1967 the same journal published an article by Grotowski with an excerpt from his manifesto, *Towards a Poor Theatre* (1968). Grotowski used the term to denote 'modern staging – scenography using current sculptural or electronic ideas' (Grotowski, Wiewiorowski and Morris 1967: 60). The following, in a special issue on 'Architecture/Environment', the French architect Jacques Polieri (1928–2011) made reference to 'scenographic principles' and 'scenographic problems' (Polieri, Goff and Goff 1968: 181–2). Kelly Morris is the article editor for the Svoboda and Grotowski piece. Under the overall editorship of Richard Schechner (editor 1967–9, 1986–present) and Michael Kirby (editor 1970–86), the rebranded *TDR: The Drama Review* continued to employ 'scenography' throughout the 1970s as a compositional strategy of theatre-making. For instance, by 1972 theatre scholar Brooks McNamara (1937–2009) is liberally applying this idea in support of an interview with the performance artist Meredith Monk. Describing Monk as a 'scenographer', McNamara proclaims:

> Monk's scenography involves more than just radical use of theatre materials; it approaches theatre production without preconceptions about objects, or space, or light, and it suggests fundamental questions about the function of theater architecture, design, and technology in contemporary performance.
> (McNamara and Monk 1972: 90)

Awareness of scenography was growing within American academic circles. While not exclusive to *TDR* (other examples include B. N. 1967; Schechner 1968; Gress and O'Horgan 1970), it is notable that this journal embraces the term more than any other, as it published numerous articles using the term on subjects as diverse as traditional Indian theatre (Awasthi 1974) and the work of Vladimir Mayakovsky (Deák 1973).

Crucially, in the same period Czech theatrical practice more generally received an increased level of attention within Anglophone scholarship. The principal instigator of this was the theatre researcher Jarka Burian. Following a research visit to Czechoslovakia in 1968–9, Burian published the first of several articles on Svoboda (1970, 1971, 1973). This material would culminate with the publication of *The Scenography of Josef Svoboda* in 1974. The holistic remit of scenography is clearly outlined by Burian: 'the premise that a scenographer must be more than a designer and that a theatrical production is an organic, existential process, the specific configuration of which will inevitably vary each and every time, depending on the given elements' (Burian 1974: 19). The holistic reading of scenography and the scenographer as 'more than a designer' is undoubtedly a phrase that has shadowed the second adoption of 'scenography'. Correspondingly, a year before Burian's visit to Czechoslovakia, the PQ had its inaugural event in 1967. This government- and ITI-funded international exhibition of scenography would offer the Anglophone community sustained dialogue with the Czech approach (although English-speaking nations would not formally contribute until 1975). Organized as national exhibitions, the original format was to convene and share the work of scenographers within a particular nation. Prizes are then awarded for the most innovative or timely collection of works.

Today, PQ has expanded this remit to include 'performative installations' or full-scale performances on the state of scenography more broadly. While still retaining the national format in terms of organizing the event, since the mid-1990s there has been a distinct rise in national exhibitions presenting a manifesto or argument on scenography as opposed to a curation of current works. Notably, the idea of a national variation on the practice of scenography has remained a focus point of the curatorial remit for PQ. This approach to scenography as a nationalized practice is reflective of the linguistic distinctions that occur across continental Europe. Both historically and today, PQ continues to exemplify the idea that there are multiple scenographies, whether practically or linguistically defined, as opposed to a universally agreed scenograph-y.

The notion of multiple scenographies with national variants informs Kirby's editorial for a special issue of *TDR* entitled 'International Scenography' (1984). Kirby states that the term 'international' was employed in the issue's title to recognize 'the way in which scenography varies from country to country, reflecting national characteristics' (Kirby 1984: 2). The special issue features ambitiously titled articles such as 'American scenography' (Aronson 1984) and 'West German scenography' (Graue 1984). Indeed, Kirby begins the special issue with an introduction to the term in question:

> The visual is, of course, crucial in the theatre experience. Scenography, however – perhaps because of the emphasis on theatre-as-literature in our educational system – has generally been neglected. Few recognize the names or styles of even the leading designers. Critics mention scenography, if at all, only in passing. Many designers themselves expect and seem to want their work to be utilitarian, and 'safe' merely predictable backgrounds. In this issue of *The Drama Review*, we have attempted to deal with scenography that is both unusual and ambitious.
>
> (Kirby 1984: 2)

While equating scenography with the visual elements, Kirby appears to recognize the tension between the established orthodoxies of theatre design and the qualities of scenography. Svoboda is cited by Kirby as a prominent figure within the field, although he concludes by stating: 'It is our belief, on the other hand, that the most significant scenography is being produced by an American: Richard Foreman' (Kirby 1984: 2). Although not the first instance of an English-speaking practitioner being framed in this way, it is notable that Foreman's work is a synthesis of text, action, vision and sound. His scenographies are complex and extend beyond questions of vision and figurative depiction, although these methods are clearly evident, to consider a holistic experience of performance encounter. Foreman's performances contest the very notion of a setting or background – the methods of scenography are foregrounded and rendered integral, experiential. While not employed nor educated as a 'designer', Foreman is representative of a group of directors who have been assigned the label 'scenographer' alongside auteurs such as Robert Lepage and Robert Wilson (although Wilson studied architecture, he describes himself as a director). The holistic circumstances of the second adoption of 'scenography' have rendered it an inclusive practice that, as evident in application to Foreman, positioned its scope beyond the exclusive remit of a conventional 'designer'.

By the end of the twentieth century, scenography has become an established term within the Anglophone academic study of theatre and performance. Symptomatic of this is Howard's establishment of the European Scenography Centres in 1994 at institutions in Prague, Helsinki, Utrecht, Zurich, Barcelona and London as the MA European Scenography at Central Saint Martins. These centres go on to educate many of the practitioners and academic scholars within the field today. Baugh goes as far as declaring that scenography is now 'universally accepted' (Baugh 2013: 82). It is, however, notable that beyond the realm of universities and art schools the term retains a distinctly academic quality and is often viewed through this lens. In the early twenty-first century, 'scenography' remains for many English speakers an alien term and is rarely adopted within the professional Anglophone theatres. Indicative of Reid Payne's (1994) comment on the 'too-foreign influence', Howard summarizes the current state of affairs by suggesting that:

> A decade ago, the word and the practice of scenography were relatively unknown except in parts of Eastern Europe. Some thought it was a spelling mistake, others a grandiose word for set design and many thought it was a symptom of designers getting above themselves.
>
> (in Collins and Nisbet 2010: xxiii)

While Howard argues for its acceptance, it would be foolhardy to suggest that scenography is commonplace beyond the academic study of Performance Design. Theatre designer Michael Pavelka confirms this, stating: 'you're unlikely to argue the toss about [scenography and] all this unless you're in a scholarly situation' (Pavelka 2015: 4). What is interesting about Pavelka's statement is that arts and humanities academics may struggle to recognize the term's relationship to theatre and design more generally. Scenography, it would appear, remains distanced from industry practices due to its alignment with academic and experimental contexts, as well as a limited profile within the Anglophone academy due to a historical lack of interdisciplinary scholarship.

Scenography is not currently a concept that is readily employed outside of theatre and performance scholarship. There are, however, four areas of academic study where it does appear, albeit irregularly: architecture, classics, spatial design and museology. While fields such as architecture employ it derogatively (a topic discussed in Chapter 7), classics employ the term when translating or discussing Ancient Greek or Roman theatrical cultures. The application within museology and spatial design effectively equate to a discussion on the same exercise – what might be termed 'experience design' spanning the use of dioramas within museums and the design of commercial pavilions. The term is employed within these exhibition and museum contexts to describe the processes of staging and presenting a temporary environment. Den Oudsten provides the most direct account of the relationship between these disciplinary positions. Describing both the exhibition and theatre as 'narrative environments', he argues that 'both construct an island of the extraordinary, a situation where physical presence is essential' (den Oudsten 2011: 1), and even goes as far to situate the two activities within a common ancestry of the marketplace: 'The theatre and the exhibition share a common rudimentary form which had its origins in the marketplace of old, where the convincing merchant would display his articles with just that extra bit of flair' (den 2011: 2). While origin arguments are fraught, the idea that exhibitions sustain shared qualities with the techniques and strategies of theatre is a useful one – in particular, that the situation of an exhibition is arguably operationally theatre, as it enacts events through a crafting of place orientation, of theatring.

Den Oudsten provides a particular history on the German-language adoption of *Szenografie*. He argues that a project manager named Martin Roth (who went on to be Director of the Victoria and Albert Museum, 2011–16) introduced the notion at the Hanover World Fair in 2000. As part of a response to the event, Roth argued that:

> The term *szenografie* does not exist in Germany ... On the surface it can be assumed that scenography is a derivative of event cultures. When progress is fast-paced, theaters leave the theater, the classical trade fairs are trimmed and the tourist industry styles the holiday as an event, the creation of artificial worlds becomes necessary, a director is needed to stage the alleged reality.
>
> (Roth 2000: 84)

Notably, the practice of *Szenografie* is clearly situated, in this instance, within a context that is institutionally beyond theatre. Roth cites the establishment of a new department of scenography at the Staatliche Hochschule für Gestaltung in Karlsruhe by Heinrich Klotz, which explicitly spanned theatre and exhibition studies, as the impetus for the German understanding of *Szenografie*. Roth does acknowledge that the term had some association with the theatre in Germany prior to this time, albeit to a lesser extent than *Szenenbild* ('scene image') or *Bühnenbild* ('stage image'). Nevertheless, den Oudsten and Roth's account of scenography as aligned with the exhibition assumes that this practice is operationally theatre. Den Oudsten recognizes this explicitly, as he states: 'both stage and exhibition need to be considered as one unified thematic field' (den Oudsten 2011: 12). He goes on to argue that this thematic field 'is relevant not only within the walls of the theatre and the museum, but increasingly so in the urban and rural spaces of city and landscape' (den Oudsten 2011: 12). While this speaks to the notion of an expanded scenography, den Oudsten's reading also reinforces the operational definition of theatre beyond defined institutional orthodoxies.

In German, there exists the notion of *Inszenierung* that is typically translated as 'staging', but is literally a variant on *mise en scène*. The linguistic distinctions between *Szenografie* and *Inszenierung* echo that of 'scenography' and *mise en scène* in the Anglophone contexts. While principally connected to the act of staging, *Inszenierung* denotes notions of enactment and orchestration, with the term implying an act of construction – of making or presenting an event. In the German lexicon, *Inszenierung* spans the practices of directing (*Regie*) and scenery (*Kulisse*). *Bühnenbild* is, however, the more common expression when discussing the physical qualities of a designed stage and is akin to the term 'stage image' in English. *Inszenierung* affords a conceptual and professional overlap between the pictorial conventions of *Bühnenbild* and the directorial concerns of *Regie*.

The term *Szenografie* sustains a similar politics of liberation to that of 'scenography' in English. To paraphrase Burian, a *Szenografen* is accordingly 'more than a *Bühnenbildner*'. This position echoes the thoughts of Brecht and Neher with particular regard to the distinction between a *Bühnenbildner* and a *Bühnenbauer* ('stage builder'). As Baugh (2010: 191) recounts, the pair saw *Bühnenbild* as the crafting of perspective that distances a 'theatre world' from 'reality'. Neher, however, argued in 1951 that 'a "realistic stage picture" is a nonsense' (in Willett 1986: 75). *Bühnenbauer* was Brecht and Neher's preferred term, as it focused on the crafting of felt environments that occur with, and in acknowledgement of, a theatre's surrounding geographies. This tension between theatre as an event and theatre as an image – of stage place and stage image – is one I return to throughout this book. Nevertheless, *Inszenierung*, as with *mise en scène*, carries with it a politics of servitude and potentially enforced hierarchies of authorship that those who adopted scenography in the 1960s onwards had sought to critique and transgress.

Den Oudsten does suggest a point of departure between the German and English variants. In particular, the study of *Szenografie* and its practice are presented by different terminologies: 'In the German region the notion of scenography doesn't seem to suffice and the concept of *Szenologie* has been introduced to cover the theoretical discourse of scenography' (den Oudsten 2011: 12). *Szenologie* ('scenology') is conceived in the same mould as musicology, where the focus is on the '-ology' (study of) rather than on the '-graphy' (doing) of a craft. This approach is not to be confused with the French notion of *ethnoscénologie* ('ethnoscenology'), which Pavis describes as a discipline 'concerned with cultural performance and performance practice without imposing upon them the overly reductive model of Western theater' (Pavis 2003: 288). The notion of *ethnoscénologie* was proposed by Jean-Marie Pradier (1995) as an ethnocentric approach to the study of performance. Partier aligns this usage with the metaphorical iteration of *skenos* (as distinct from *skēnē*) that denotes a body as well as a tent or hut – the two conditions are seen as allegorical. The French *scénologie* is therefore principally concerned with a form of biopolitics where the 'artist's body … as well as the viewer's' (Pradier 2001: 63) is studied first and foremost.

While Pradier's *scénologie* is discrete from the usage as implied by den Oudsten (the 'study of scenes' not bodies), an anthropological framing is evident within Schwarz's reflection on how the fields of theatre and spatial design might coalesce. Echoing Brejzek's reading of scenography as transdisciplinary, Schwarz argues that 'the scenographic impulse, with its border-crossing ambitions, may even be seen as the dynamic centrepoint around which those fields of art taught' (Schwarz 2011: xviii). Influenced by Roth's positioning of *Szenografie* with the wider event cultures of the exhibition and tourism, Schwarz locates the notion of scenography as an 'in-between' practice – an idea that the PQ has embraced describing scenography as 'a discipline existing in-between the visual and the performing arts, which uses the best of both worlds' (Lotker 2009). From *Szenografie* to *scénographie*, *skenographia* to *scénografie*, the relationships between 'scenography' and its continental variants remain in a state of flux. While there may be no definitive translation, one thing is clear: throughout continental Europe, and with its second adoption into English, scenography is a practice that derives from the conditions of theatre. Unlike the first adoption via a mistranslation of perspective drawing, the second adoption of 'scenography' as a linguistic idiom and cultural practice is firmly 'of the theatre': a product of the conditions and methods of the theatrical.

Sound and costume as scenography

The argument that scenography is representative of a holistic approach is most directly evident in the inclusive incorporation of sound and costume. While lighting inherits two of the core characteristics of set design (light aligns with conventional visual and spatial critiques), there has been some resistance to sound and costume being readily accepted into the fold of scenography. Sound as a method of theatrical place orientation is indicative of a shift in the technological innovations of recorded sound and directed speaker systems. Svoboda described how the recorded sound of a door opening offered a means of staging in and of itself where scenography is 'raised to scenographic *direction*' (cited in Burian 1974: 19; emphasis in original). Sound, for Svoboda, was crucial to arguing how a scenographer considers the manifestation of theatrical rhythm within the affective atmosphere of scenography. Nevertheless, the inclusion of sound as a scenographic method has been met some resistance. Notably, in 2010 Ross Brown outlined how as a

> sub-discipline of theatre design or scenography, sound designers have been encouraged to adopt the orthodox stage design approach, which is to develop a concept that is consistent with and coherent within an overall staging concept, emanating from the words of the text and guided by a unifying directorial vision.
>
> (Brown 2010: 131)

Brown argues that the visual conception of scenography is predicated on a situational distance from the subject, where 'sense is derived on the basis of detachment from the scene' (Brown 2010: 132). Yet, theatre sound, Brown argues, is always experienced as part of a wider assemblage of experience:

> Sound, however, whatever events the sources of individual sounds might represent, is *in totum* an immersive environment. One cannot stand back from it and see the entire picture; one's aural attention does not have the equivalent of sightlines; the theatrical mode of listening does not gaze uniformly, but is, by nature, a state of continual omnidirectional distraction.
>
> (Brown 2010: 132)

Central to Brown's understanding of scenography is the notion of a 'stage image' that is detached from the holism of a situated experience.

Yet, as I argue throughout this book, the reading of scenography as innately visual and detached from its situated geographies is reflective of how the ideological aesthetics of 'the scenic' – as discrete from scenes – that reduces experience into quantifiable images. Scenography is never detached from its situational circumstances; rather, it intervenes as a worlding irritant. Interestingly, in 2015, Brown retracted his argument against sound as scenography, stating that his 'argument is now differently nuanced: that in theatre history (if not historiography), concepts of *picture* and *spectacle* have never been visual, but always sensorily multimodal' (in Curtin and Roesner 2015: 112; emphasis in original). Brown now cites how the notion of a sound-*scape* arises from the order of land-*scape*: a conventional aligned with the pictorial that is inclusive of a broader conception of experience beyond the strictly visual (see Shearing 2014). Adrian Curtin confirms the acceptance of sound within the holistic conception of scenography, observing that sound design 'belongs to the order of the scenographical (that which is crafted, intended, "written")' (Curtin 2010: 218). Curtin's positioning of sound design within the 'order of the scenographical' is to evoke the means by which theatre sound now operates as a distinct method of place orientation. While Curtin positions this crafting within the province of a sound designer, the implications are that sound is a part of a wider collaboration of designers that enacts a holistic scenography. Curtin's focus on scenography as a crafting equally speaks towards the conclusions of this book – that scenography is a crafting of place orientation that occurs in time.

Costume, as the most intimate of designed theatrical environments, is unmistakably aligned with the conception and reception of bodies in theatre. McKinney and Butterworth recognize the difficulties posed by the separation of costume from body, as 'it is sometimes hard to distinguish clearly between what is achieved through the performer's body and movement of the performer's costume' (McKinney and Butterworth 2009: 6). This innate relationship between a theatrical body and costume aligns with sociologist Joanne Entwistle's definition of dress as a situated bodily practice: '[w]ithout a body, dress lacks fullness and movement; it is incomplete' (Entwistle 2000: 10). Costume exists as a design practice that, out of all the methods of scenography, is intrinsically connected with how bodies appear. However, scenographer Delbert Unruh has observed that costume has, thus far, not undertaken the same material and aesthetic 'revolution' as the other methods of scenography:

> The development, dissemination and wide acceptance of the idea of scenography was a process that relegated costume design to a supporting role. In many ways, the development of the idea of scenography sought and achieved a unity of directing, scene design and lighting design. The issue of costume design was momentarily set aside in the effort to forge this unity.
>
> (Unruh 1991: 28)

For the most part, costume practice remains centred on the narratological strategies of what Lehmann would describe as dramatic theatre (see Hann 2017 for further discussion). If scenography is to be viewed as a holistic practice, then the question of costume is paramount. As evident in the dance practices of Loïe Fuller (1862–1928) or Martha Graham's *Lamentation* (1933), costume is a compositional element that responds to, and shapes, the conception and reception of action. Pavis cites a similar position when he observed that a 'body is "worn" and "carried" by a costume as much as the costume is worn and carried by the body' (Pavis 2003: 175). While choreography is centred on the composition of body movement, costume is an inescapable intermediary that conditions the choreographic process. Aoife Monks suggests that '[c]ostuming might be read as a verb rather than as a noun therefore: an act or event that is centered on the ways in which audiences look at an actor dressed up onstage' (Monks 2010: 3). Both the experience of dressing *within* costume, and interpreting its semantic overtones, offer a means of positioning costume as a mode of place orientation, where costumes affect performers as part of a reciprocal conditioning between body and fabric. In designing costume, we are designing action, for the process of costuming is a situated bodily event that is composed in relation to the wider scenographic scheme and requirements of theatre. Costume choreographs action, while choreography activates costume.

The inclusion of costume within the concept of scenography can be traced through the Kennedy's encyclopedia and companion entries published by Oxford University Press. Notably, in his latest 2010 account, Kennedy positions costume as a principal concern of scenography:

> Scenography (literally, painting of the skene) thus includes stage architecture, scenery, machines, costumes, and lighting, but does not include speech, non-verbal sounds, actors' actions, actors' personal properties, or the non-ludic areas of the playhouse such as lobbies and bars.
>
> (Kennedy 2010: 536)

For the 2003 entry, Kennedy does not list costume as part of the scenography family. Following the same structure as the entry in 2010, Kennedy notes that 'actors' appearance' as well as 'non-verbal acoustic signs' (2003) are excluded from conceptions of scenography. While the most recent edition still excludes 'non-verbal sounds' and thereby sound design, costume is now cited alongside the mainstays of scenographic practice. Costume, of course, also places action in the manner of the dramaturgical. Pavis evokes this position when he argues that 'Costume often constitutes a kind of traveling scenography, a set reduced to a human scale that moves with the actor' (Pavis 2003: 177). Pavis's 'travelling scenography' stresses how costume orientates a reading of place where, independent of linguistic reinforcement, the learned semantics of costume can locate action within a certain period or geographic place.

One of the possible counterarguments to a holistic understanding of scenography is that the second adoption inadvertently positioned set design as the principal design practice within theatre. While the disciples of Svoboda and the radical Czech *scénografie* promoted the unifying aspects of scenography, this holistic reading benefits the spatio-visual logic of set design – as opposed to a lighting, sound or costume design. When colleagues speak of scenography, individuals note the 'stage picture', 'image' or 'visual aspects' – rarely will this begin with a question of costume or sound. Indeed, within theatre programmes and academic literature, it is not unusual to see the term 'designer' employed when inferring to the individual responsible for the physical environment only. From Inigo Jones to Craig, Svoboda to

Howard, throughout the history of theatrical design the individual who had responsibility for the physical landscape has taken priority – albeit within a historical model of theatrical production that situates design as illustrative rather than critical. Partly, this is due to the technologies of light and sound having only emerged as a specific design choice in the late nineteenth century. Costume, while arguably preceding notions of stage design in terms of a historical lineage (see Barbieri 2017), has always been the forgotten partner. Nevertheless, it is important to recognize that the logic of scenography as an inclusive and holistic approach appears to present the physical constructions and spacing of the stage as its principal concern. While sound may offer complementary or integrated aspects within these staged environments, the manner in which scenography is typically discussed prioritizes a visual-based encounter of the stage. There is no avoiding it. In the argument to have the designed aspects recognized as an equal partner within the theatrical experience, the voice of the set designer – as conceptualized through strictly visual conceptions of stage image – has historically been the voice of scenography.

To follow this argument to its conclusion is to arrive at the notion that, whether inadvertently or otherwise, set designers have historically cemented their status as lead designers through the holistic qualities of scenography – superseding colleagues in light, sound and costume. While I do not feel that this was any one individual's intention, it is useful to recognize the influence of this reading and the tensions it brings to any readings of scenography today. Importantly, it is high time that scenography, both in terms of practice and theory, discussed itself as a fully holistic practice. Costume and sound are as important aspects of scenography as the physical spacing or stage structure. While the balance of these elements will shift from production to production, from scenario to scenario, the notion that scenography is a visual practice negates the complexities of a scenographic experience. While scenography exceeds notions of set design, it is equally important to recognize that it is not exclusively visual either.

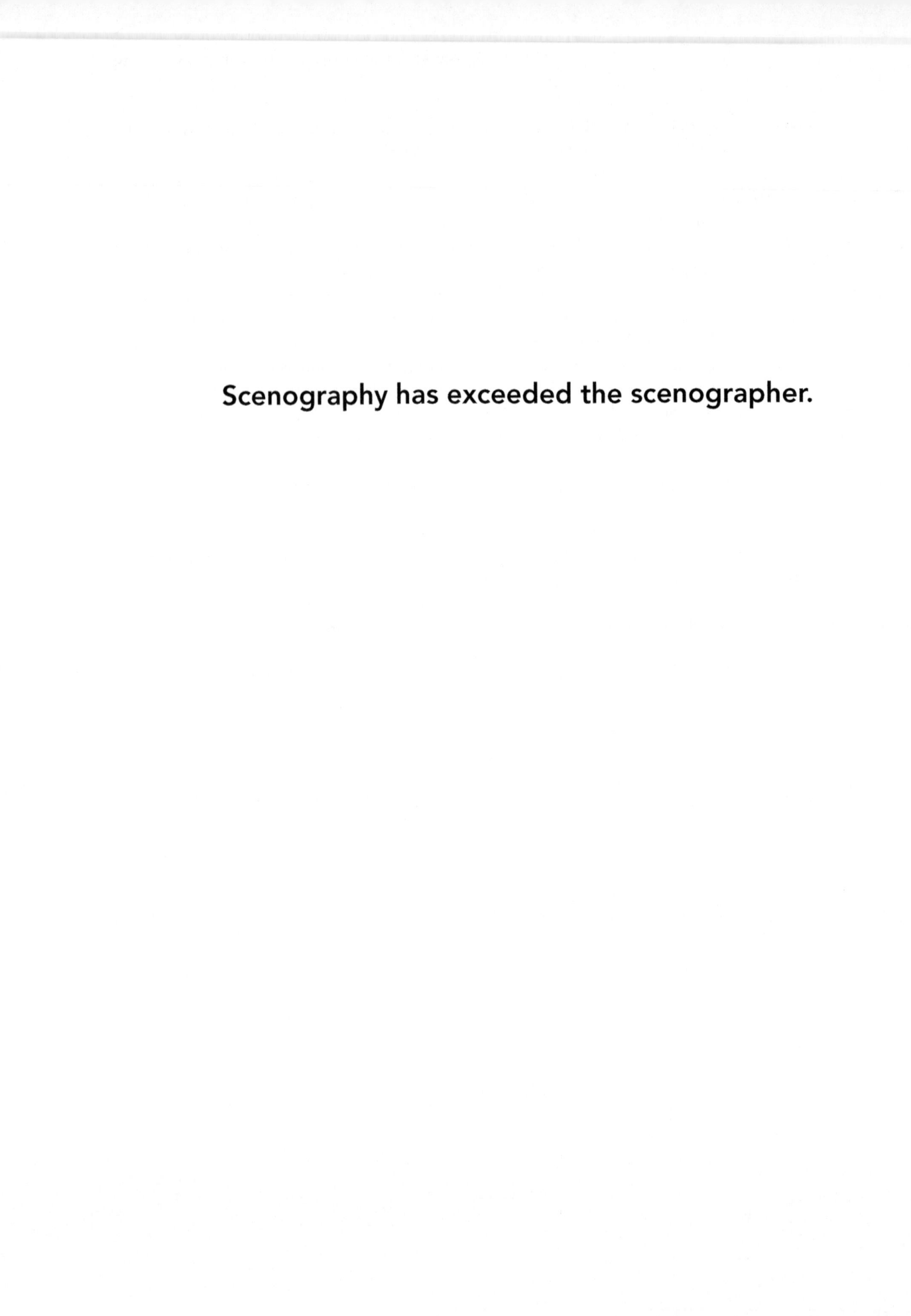

Scenography has exceeded the scenographer.

CHAPTER 3

Scenography beyond scenographers

First and foremost I wish to forestall any misunderstanding. My argument for a renewed distinction between scenographer and scenography is not a call for the role's terminal culmination; the creative and technological knowledge of scenographers (those who undertake theatrical design tasks) offers a vital and discrete contribution to theatre as a collaborative undertaking. Rather, my intention is to argue how scenography as place orientation is central to a number of complementary production roles and concepts. Whether focused on *mise en scène* or dramaturgy, director or choreographer, I argue that the conceptual and practical remit of a holistic scenography has always exceeded the finite duties of individual production roles. If we acknowledge that scenographics are inclusive of direction and movement, then any definition of scenography as being exclusive to one production role fails to fully account for how scenographics become manifest within theatre.

The second adoption of scenography responded to a perceived need for a practical and theoretical framework that afforded a voice for those undertaking or studying 'design' in the theatre. Howard's *What is Scenography?* (2002, 2009) is an argument for why those who undertake theatrical design tasks should be treated equally within the creative act of theatre-making. This was a worthy and very necessary argument that needed to be profiled. In this chapter, I review how the scenographer concept operates within Anglophone theatres to propose that the implied 'ownership' of scenography with a named scenographer renders the concept exclusive (rather than inclusive and vital). I argue that this conceptual, more so than practical, differentiation affords a renewed platform to fully realize scenography's status – alongside dramaturgy and choreography – as a stage strategy that is intrinsic to all theatre practice. Scenography is a task of all theatre-makers.

The second Anglophone adoption is linked to a radical Czech understanding as an inclusive and holistic approach to theatrical staging. The influence of Burian's work on Svoboda is evident in Aronson's definition. Whereas Burian notes that a scenographer is 'more than a designer', Aronson states:

> ['Scenography'] implies something more than creating scenery or costumes or lights. It carries a connotation of an all-encompassing visual-spatial construct as well as the process of change and transformation that is an inherent part of the physical vocabulary of the stage. In that sense, it bears some relation to the French term *mise en scène*.
>
> (Aronson 2005: 7)

Aronson recognizes the innate overlap between a holistic reading of scenography and the conceptual remit of *mise en scène*. Indeed, the holistic reading disputes the established territories of complementary terms. As already outlined, it is important to recognize that the second adoption bears a greater relationship to the radical Czech *scénografie* than to the pre-1960s French *scénographie*. Scenography is, following Svoboda's articulation, concerned with encounters of staging and the crafting of stage-scenes that exceeds a strict focus on 'stage pictures'. While scenography is inclusive of painted scenery and numerous methods for the figuration of place symbols, it is not, as with the pre-1960s French variant, a practice solely directed towards the production of a visual setting or background.

Mise en scène and scenography

I'm sat in the cheap seats for a revival of Robert Lepage and ExMachina's Needles and Opium *(2016) at the Barbican Centre, London. I look down towards the stage. A large sliced white cube rotates as the credits are projected on its surfaces. A section of the white wall of the cube folds out. It has a duvet and pillows attached. A lamp is placed on an open box that also hinges out from the flush white surface of the cube. I notice that the textures of the cube are changing, altering colour and gaining patterns. These projected textures also progressively define and transform the whiteness of the cube into the features of a familiar room. An assemblage of textures and objects builds towards the schema of a bedroom. The cube keeps turning. It becomes apparent that this white cube will provide a form of 'playframe' for the production, with its projected surfaces and mechanical traps reshaping and reconfigured throughout the show's duration. The awkward angle of the cube's rotation is confirmed as I hear the squeak of an actor's shoe as he steps out on to the raked surface. The signs of place and texture are vivid. I struggle to see beyond the* mise en scène*: the systems of interpretation. Yet the individual methods of scenography, the crafts of stage mechanics, of lighting design and costume are apparent. The technological crafts of digitally rendered imagery, projection mapping and vision mixing are equally discernible. The fade of a swirling hypnosis spiral transitions into a projected texture of a circular sewer cover scores how orientations of place are continuously merging and re-merging with the progressive rhythms of this scenographic assemblage. I consider the scenography of* Needles and Opium*, not in terms of interpretation, to which I would assign* mise en scène*, but how Lepage's company of Ex Machina have crafted the rhythms of staging that give the production a distinctive spatio-material quality. How the transition to the warm glow of the projected floorboard texture orientated my experience of the greys on the corresponding walls. The crafts of composition, tonal balance and material rhythm were all part of* Needles and Opium's *scenographic scheme. A speed of transition scores the eventful qualities of this stage place. I think to myself this is not an image, a photograph: this is an event. The scenography is what renders the* mise en scène *eventful – it is what transforms it from a referential sign system to a moment of encounter.*

Conventional readings of the French *scénographie* present an emphatic division between the conceptual concerns of a production's dramaturgy and theatrical design. Theatre scholar Patrice Pavis applies this distinction, as he states, 'Scenography is the visible and material part of mise en scène. It is only one component among others' (Pavis 2013: 63). Pavis's definition of scenography implies that it is a material, rather than conceptual, operation and is concerned only with the display of a visual setting. Notably, Pavis confronts the confusion between these two terms and aims to clearly position scenography as a challenge to the conceptual remit of *mise en scène*:

> There is an underground struggle between scenography and mise en scène: since the appearance, or at least awareness, of mise en scène, scenography has been on the defensive, as if it had definitively lost the powers it acquired during the Renaissance.
> (Pavis 2013: 63)

It is notable that very few theatre scholars have presented the tension between scenography and *mise en scène* as forcefully as Pavis. However, the absence of this debate can be read as implied when one is employed over the other. In a survey of keywords in theatre and performance, *Contemporary Theatre Review* hosted a special issue in 2013 with concise statements on the established disciplinary lexicon. Theatre scholar Brian Singleton provides an article on *mise en scène*, which does not employ the term 'scenography'. Singleton's account outlines some of the same tensions noted by Pavis as it focuses on the authorial qualities of the *mettre en scène*:

> She or he who, in the past, had simply put things on the stage (*mettre en scène*), would become, through choice of form, content, and perspective, the principal author of creativity. All the other practitioners in the theatre (such as the actor, designer and stage manager) would become subservient to the totalizing vision of the 'author'.
> (Singleton 2013: 48)

While Singleton goes on to problematize this authorial model, theatre scholar David Bradby related the rise of *mettre en scène* to an increase in state funding for French theatres in the 1980s. This simultaneously furthered the power of the *mettre en scène* (as the individual whom the funds were assigned to) while also facilitating a greater focus on the visual aspects of performance. The *décorateur* (set designer), Bradby argued, was therefore a principal beneficiary of this new funding landscape. Indeed, the increased status of visual design led to a shift in language:

> The use of the words *décor* and *décorateur* for designer and set design were abandoned in favour of the terms *scénographe* and *scénographie*, and this change in vocabulary signaled a shift of emphasis in the production process, as the visual element acquired greater importance in the construction of meaning.
>
> (Bradby 1991: 257)

While the French *scénographie* retains a distinct focus on visual execution and the technical knowledge required to realize sophisticated stage technologies and environments, Bradby's observations imply an influence or correspondence with the holistic Czech understanding. What is more, it also offers yet another example of a concrete distinction between set design and scenography – even in the contemporary French the two are not synonymous, but are representative of distinct tasks or remits. Bradby does not, however, extend the notion of scenography to non-visual conditions of staging or consider scenography as a distinct theatre-making strategy.

In terms of the Anglophone context, both terms have been adopted from the continent in the absence of an established equivalent. Yet I argue that 'scenography' is derived from radical Czech theatrical conventions, whereas *mise en scène* is a product of the French theatres that first emerged within the context of the theatrical practice of Molière (1622–73) and the perceived need to connect the place of performance with the focus of the action. Pradier, however, points out that the full term is a recent convention, arguing that in 'seventeenth-century France one spoke merely of "la mise" (setting) for the placing of actors and the mechanics of their entrances' (Pradier 2001: 64). Moreover, Pradier positions the critic Jules Janin (1804–74) as the first to apply this exercise to a particular individual as an exercise in interpretation, namely the *metteur en scène* (a director). While the exact focus of *mise en scène* is contested, the collision of this French term and a Czech-influenced scenography within the English language provides some productive distinctions. The first of these distinctions is located within the shared conceptual lineage of *mise en scène* with the German task of the dramaturg, in that both are concerned with the narratological interpretation of a production.

McKinney and Butterworth provide a blunt position on how the dramaturgical concerns of *mise en scène* are aligned with the Anglophone usage: '"Mise-en-scène" refers to the process of realising a theatrical text on stage and the particular aesthetic and conceptual frames that have been adopted as part of that process ... The mise-en-scène does not refer to the performance itself' (McKinney and Butterworth 2009: 4). Theatre scholar Alexander Dundjerovic also identifies this conventional reading of *mise en scène* and aligns the conceptual task of 'placing' the action with the labours of the director or the playwright:

> Traditionally *mise-en-scène* is preconceived and reflects the movement that is found in the dramatic text. It develops hierarchically, following psychological cause–effect analysis, and justification of action, using the previous section as a building block upon which to create the next level. Conventionally, it remains within the parameters of the director's or playwright's conceptualisation.
>
> (Dundjerovic 2003: 70)

Dundjerovic builds upon this hierarchical reading of *mise en scène* to suggest the notion of a 'transformative *mise-en-scène*'. Unlike the conventional understanding as denoted by McKinney and Butterworth, Dundjerovic offers this differentiation with regards the work of Robert Lepage. Citing Lepage's characteristic application of projected imagery and stage machinery as a fluid and vital part of his production's narrative progression, Dundjerovic argues that Lepage's work evidences how theatre materiality occurs as part of a singular theatre-making strategy that is *of* and *with* performers rather than separated as a background or setting. Dundjerovic defines this as a transformative *mise en scène* that is continually developing, using 'all the elements of theatricality as its own resources, being organically connected with the performers, their experience and their individual expression' (Dundjerovic 2003: 70). Dundjerovic does employ the term 'scenography', particularly when discussing how Lepage's work corresponds with innovations in Czech theatre and Svoboda's approach to staging. While used sparingly, Dundjerovic's application stresses a focus on a physical materiality or object with *mise en scène* providing the conceptual glue – although the crossover between these concepts is not confronted directly.

Dundjerovic is one of many to have proposed variants on the concept of *mise en scène*. It is notable that in each instance of this linguistic expansion there is a full acknowledgement that the term alone does not account for the experiential qualities of contemporary performance. In 1992, Pavis offered three categories of *mise en scène* that related to particular phases of theatrical experimentation in the twentieth century – autotextual, ideotextual and intertextual. Autotextual *mise en scène* operates on a purely visual logic that has no social context. Pavis aligns this with what he describes as the 'symbolism' of Appia and Craig. Ideotextual *mise en scène* denotes how metatexts on the social or psychological conditions are communicated through staging, as typified by the theatrical landscapes of the Berliner Ensemble and the designs of Neher. Intertextual *mise en scène* infers metatexts of previous productions, most notably found within adaptions of classical dramatic texts in the 1970s. Pavis's modelling has, however, changed over the years as a reflection on the questions posed by contemporary practices. Nevertheless, Pavis remains consistent in the position that *mise en scène* operates as an 'organising principle': an 'object of knowledge, a network of associations or relationships uniting the different stage materials into signifying systems, created both by production (the actors, the director, the stage in general) and reception (the spectators)' (1992: 25). In his most recent approach, Pavis questions the influence of Schechner's performance on contemporary practice. Pavis asks whether, in an age when literary text is no longer central to theatre, we need to 'find another word, and thus another theory, for a mise en scène that does not represent an already-written text but which works with silence and non-verbal signs (be they visual or musical)' (Pavis 2013: 289). It's notable that scenography is not proposed as a possible avenue of investigation.

Lehmann, on the other hand, does not orientate his reading of *mise en scène* to distinct historical phases of theatrical experimentation nor to the prefiguration of literary text. Lehmann proposed in 1989 that that the practical implications may be better understood in terms of 'metaphorical *mise en scène*', 'scenographic *mise en scène*' and 'theatre as situation' or '"event-like" *mise en scène*'. The first of these relates to the conventional French reading as a visual manifestation of the playwright's dramaturgy. Interestingly, the second recognizes how the visual qualities of the theatrical event may exceed the communication of pre-existing literary decisions:

Scenographic theatre does not communicate or represent something else but appeals in its concrete essence to the sensual ability of the spectator to connect and structure meaning as a possible effect and not as a predetermined origin of the aesthetic realisation, as an effect which remains necessarily, not accidentally, ambiguous.

(cited in Balme 1997: 26)

Notably, Lehmann positions 'scenographic theatre' as a particular mode or genre of theatrical expression: echoing ideas of 'designer's theatre' or 'director's theatre' in German. The third approach offered by Lehmann also proposes a distinct form or genre: theatre as situation. In this instance, Schechner's notion of 'performance text' is rendered dominant where, as theatre scholar Christopher Balme outlines, the 'social and aesthetic experience is then the primary object of analysis, not an aesthetic product presented to the spectator' (Balme 1997: 26). Lehmann points to the work of Allan Kaprow and the notion of a 'happening' as an exemplar of this third variant. Whereas Pavis's categories are all orientated towards a semiotic interpretation of place orientation, Lehmann resists this approach and instead stresses 'the systemic ambiguity of theatre signs' where the 'necessity of making the materiality of theatrical signifiers [is] the primary problem of analysis' (Balme 1997: 26). Lehmann's focus on materiality seemingly stresses the significance of scenography, as an affective atmosphere and place orientation, within the act of theatre reception.

Lavender observes, as with Pavis and Lehmann before him, how the conventional understanding of *mise en scène* struggles to articulate the eventful encounter of contemporary performance. Lavender's approach is to discuss three linguistic variants on the term: *mise en scène*, *mise en événement* and *mise en sensibilité*. Lavender suggests that *mise en scène* has fallen out of fashion within Anglophone scholarship, but states its significance to the 'arrangement of space, presence and appearance that produces an effective figuration for the spectator' (Lavender 2016: 78–9). The focus on figuration, of description, is positioned centrally for Lavender. *Mise en événement*, Lavender proposes, moves to recognize the eventfulness of certain participatory performance practices. Akin to Lehmann's 'theatre as situation', this variant focuses on performances where the event of participation operates as the organizing principle. Whereas Lavender assigns *mise en scène* to the 'mediators of action', *mise en événement* is concerned with the structures of participation within an event – the design of action. *Mise en sensibilité* moves one step further and aims to account for how, within immersive works, an individual becomes situated in a web of personal decisions and choices: a series of implied and explicit questions that are simultaneously political and ethical, felt and witnessed.

> It implicates the *matter* of theatre – what it is about, deals with, dramatises – with its *mediation*. When we are within mediation, as participants or immersants, we are differently response-able. It is tempting to suggest that with response-ability comes power, but that would oversimplify things. The power at stake here is a mixture of agency, authentic feeling, witness from within and – not least – the power to withdraw, not to participate. It is not always easy to make our own choices, but that too should remain a possibility.
> (Lavender 2016: 100)

Lavender's argument oscillates between ideas of *scène*, *événement* and *sensibilité* when describing the multitude of organizing principles that inform a staged performance. One is not a replacement of the other. While the variants he introduces appear innate to the conditions of immersive and participatory theatre, Lavender offers a useful thesis on the limits of *mise en scène* and the need to account for the eventfulness of theatrical experience.

One thing is clear: *mise en scène* struggles to articulate the eventful encounter of contemporary practice. One, quite straightforward way, I personally approach *mise en scène* is to frame it as a form of 'design dramaturgy'. While questions of dramaturgy and scenography are dealt with more explicitly later in this chapter, I use this phrase to isolate how spectators understand the narrative messages of a production. This is principally an exercise in interpretation and translation. It focuses on the practical task of spectatorship as the point at which a *mise en scène* is rendered – how an outsider reads its figurative associations and socio-political connotations. Moreover, I align this interpretative process with the aesthetic politics of the 'scenic' that treats landscape *as-if-it-were* a painting or quantifiable image. In this regard, *mise en scène* has a greater focus on the allegorical sign systems of theatre than scenography. While the methods of scenography will in many instances provide the means for this communication, in positioning *mise en scène* as a form of design dramaturgy my aim is to recognize its relationship to ideas of reception studies and the semantic overtones of the stage. Whereas *mise en scène* is a system of interpretation and translation, scenography is a crafting of place orientation.

While this is a debate that I return to throughout this book, as a closing note on the shared tasks of *mise en scène* and scenography it may be that professional territories disguise much of the critical debate: insomuch that certain communities of practice have an implied ownership over certain terms. As with *Inszenierung* in German, *mise en scène* – to put it bluntly – is a terminology that has a strong historical connection to literary conventions of theatre and the rise of the director. The idea of literary text, rather than text as a post-structural weaving, is historically fundamental to this terminology. Den Oudsten presents this tension within a parallel argument from museology. Focusing on the task of *muséographie* (curation) and *scénographie* (referring to exhibition design), den Oudsten presents a Cartesian split between thinking and doing, the conception and its execution.

> A crucial pointer appears to be the francophone development from *muséographie* and *scénographie*, which essentially relates the world of things to the world of thoughts, and establishes, also in the theatre, a fundamental equivalence of the expressive power of the dramatist's text and the curator's collection of objects.
> (den Oudsten 2011: 12–13)

Den Oudsten's cited division between dramatic intention and practical implementation is echoed within certain contemporary Francophone and Anglophone models of theatrical production. As outlined by Bradby and Singleton, these tensions derive from the question of authorship and disciplinary terrain, as much as linguistic differentiation. In the French theatres, conceptual approaches to staging are the domain of the *metteur en scène* (literately 'scene-setter'), whereas the practical execution of theatrical design lies with the *scénographe*. This distinction maps on to the contemporary usage of director and stage designer: the purpose of these roles is clearly situated within a hierarchical model. The English variant on 'scenographer', however, presents an innately more problematic discussion with regard to questions of authorship.

Whose scenography?

Within an Anglophone theatre production team there will typically be a series of named individuals for each method of scenography (costume, light, set, sound, video). Only on a rare occasion will a theatre practitioner choose to adopt the label of a scenographer. The reasons for this are multiple: from the role of unions in protecting the status of certain practices to the contractual stipulations proposed by an employer, as well as the preferences of the individual practitioners. Pavelka offers a summary on the perception of the term 'scenographer' within the Anglophone commercial theatres and applies a degree of cynicism in doing so:

> In the main, as a designer, I avoid using the term ['scenographer'] on a daily basis as it tends to create a twinge of panic in directors (because they might perhaps think you're stomping through their intellectual space), in a design team (because it smacks of pulling rank and could sound pretentious/ competitive) or to technicians (because they probably don't care what you call what you do … and they're probably right!).
>
> (Pavelka 2015: 4)

Pavelka's reading evokes a number of political tensions that have followed Burian's positioning of a scenographer as 'more than a designer'. Interestingly, fifteen years after Burian's publication the theatre director Peter Hall (1930–2017) echoes the sentiment of this phrasing, as he argued that a 'designer does more than design. He or she is the helpmate and critic of the director' (in Goodwin 1989: 14). While still couched within a hierarchal model, Hall's position implies a line of collaborative dialogue within the Anglophone theatre between designer and director that possibly extends beyond the technical remit of figuring place (as in the French *décorateur*). The implication of a 'critic', more so than a 'helpmate', is that in certain production models a designer may be invited to argue how the stage materials are encountered: how the performers interact and complement the ethos of a production's overall design.

It could be assumed, following Hall's reading, that a designer is synonymous with that of a scenographer given this level of collaborative dialogue. However, Macgowan and Jones, while talking about the relationship between scenic painting and the New Stagecraft, cite that 'as a designer of picture-settings, the artist can only suggest action, but not dictate it, through shapes and atmospheres [they] create' (Macgowan and Jones 1923: 126). Hall confirms this hierarchy, as he noted that there remains a focus on the literary or narrative readings of theatre within the Anglophone model, where a designer 'must support, not embellish' (in Goodwin 1989: 14). This approach to 'British stage design' was evident in the first British contribution to the PQ in 1975. Curator John Bury outlined how, 'Today, as in Shakespeare's time, the theatre of Britain is a writer's theatre and the concern of British designers is a proper response to the text and the author's meaning' (Bury 1975). While this position may read as historic for some contemporary designers, the ethos of design as 'proper response' to narrative or literary text remains an undercurrent to how design practices are assessed in certain quarters of the British media and, unfortunately, by some theatre colleagues. Recently, the playwright David Hare evoked a similar historicism to argue British theatre as distinct from continental practice:

> Now we're heading in Britain towards an over-aestheticized European theatre. We've got all those people called 'theatre makers' – God help us, what a word! – coming in and doing director's theatre

where you camp up classic plays and you cut them and you prune them around.

(in Alberge 2017)

While Svoboda also stated the importance of not over-designing, the English helpmate of the designer as defined by Hall echoes the implications of Hare's directorial 'over-aestheticisation'. In both instances, the implication is that a 'British' designer is concerned with the technical execution of the *mise en scène* as it relates to physical objects. The overall authorship of the production's composition or rhythm remains the director's remit, with Hare suggesting that this should be limited to the creative positions as evident in a playtext.

While Hare rejects the 'theatre-maker' ethos, Svoboda encouraged a blurring of the conventional tasks assignment to a scenographer or director:

A good director is one who understands design, and a good scenographer can only be one who is also a director, at least in terms of his [*sic*] knowing the principles of blocking, movement, rhythms, and the expressive forces of the actor.

(in Burian 1974: 19)

The concerns of the director and the remit of the scenographer are shared when considering the overall material encounter. Notably, the tensions outlined within this reading expose how the concerns of scenography may extend beyond the remit of a named scenographer. Consequently, an underlying motive for the term's resistance within the Anglophone context may be the fundamentally collaborative context of scenography.

While focusing on the concept of *mise en scène*, Singleton recognizes the blurred distinctions between the individual roles within contemporary theatre-making: 'Standing for nothing but itself, *mise en scène* has achieved a materiality over and above the work of the individual practitioner whose role has been blurred and blended into a creative process' (Singleton 2013: 49). Brejzek (2011a: 8) confirms this position by suggesting that scenography is rarely ever singularly authored, as it can relate to the movement of the actor, the execution of the lighting and the spatial composition of soundscapes. Scenography is operationally a collaboration between the designed elements within theatre, as well as a collaboration between the individuals who formulate these elements. While an individual may choose to adopt the term 'scenographer', the technical and artistic realization of scenography will always exceed the remit of one individual outside of a one-person production. Subsequently, this fusion of scenography into the intrinsic time-based and collaborative qualities of theatrical production poses some interesting questions when positioned against the other established production roles and perspectives of the Anglophone theatres.

McKinney and Butterworth summarize this confusion by suggesting that:

Scenography and its production sit uneasily within the existing functions of writer, director, choreographer, designer and performer becomes each, or any combination, of these roles is capable of producing scenography in ways that will not accept restriction implicitly imposed by such singular identities.

(2009: 5)

The composer Richard Wagner (1812–83) in his manifesto on *The Artwork of the Future* (1849) poses a similar question when he asks 'Who, then, will be the Artist of the Future? The poet? The performer? The musician? The plastician? — Let us say it in one word: the Folk' (Wagner 1993: 85). Wagner's 'Folk' arguably speaks to the collaborative practices associated with devised theatre – where is it the 'people' or group that make theatre rather than the individual – as much as the integrated philosophical premise of the *Gesamtkunstwerk*. It also denotes how the collaborative labours of theatre resist finite definitions of practice in favour of an artwork's needs. Scenography's shared contexts are arguably a consequence of this artistic diktat. Therefore, fundamental to the radical Czech understanding of scenography is the proposition that the practice may not be carried out by an individual who self-identifies as a scenographer. As evident within the Peter Brook's (1968: 11) famous definition, all theatre is spaced or staged in one way or another – even if enacted through the delineation of a bare stage by movement alone. Scenography is not a practice that is intrinsically linked to the labours of a scenographer or, following the logic of this argument, that a scenographer is definitively someone who recognizably 'designs'.

Within one of the first publications to discuss scenography in the Anglophone context, performance artist Meredith Monk outlines her resistance to the idea that the stage environment had been 'designed' for a production entitled *Vessel* (1971). As a devised project with a flat hierarchy of collaboration, for one sequence the performers constructed a 'mountain' of clothes. Monk outlines that 'No one *designed* that mountain. We did it ourselves. In my group are weavers, and calligraphers, and people who dye fabrics – that is our group's sensibility' (in McNamara and Monk 1972: 98; emphasis in original). While Monk's depiction is circumstantial, the question of who formulates or authors scenography is one that Lotker and Gough confront directly. The pair argue that scenography can be found in the work of 'a scenographer, a collective of artists, an architect or nature itself. It can be found by an actor, a dancer or a spectator' (Lotker and Gough 2013: 3). Overlooking the authorial implications of 'nature', Lotker and Gough offer an understanding of scenography that is not tied to the individuals who design performance. As with the term 'performance', 'design' is both a noun and a verb or, as performance scholar Elin Diamond defines it, 'a doing and a thing done' (Diamond 1996: 5). Interestingly, Aronson argues against the usage of design due to its connotations of material description in the Anglophone theatres: 'I still find [scenography] far more useful, more encompassing, and more inclusive than the word *design*, which, particularly in the United States, refers to a very specific and limited aspect of the spatiovisual experience of performance' (Aronson 2005: 7; emphasis in original). Beyond the typical usage in the United States as implied by Aronson, Hannah and Harsløf (2008) apply Diamond's definition to the notion of Performance Design – approaching design as an active process which is ongoing and reactive. The implications of this assertion are that the reception of design practices may not be completed by the author of an object or image. The process of designing (and scenography, following Lotker and Gough's remarks) may instead become complete only within the experience of material encounter. While this latter observation is discussed in the next chapter, it is indicative of the broad conceptual remit that the ideas of scenography now inhabit. What is evident in this depiction is that scenography is not the exclusive product of a named scenographer.

The collaborative conditions of scenography are not to suggest that it is only conceived outside of a hierarchical structure of authorship. Focused on correlations between exhibition and theatrical design, den Oudsten identifies how issues of authorship arise when individuals who had, in previous models of production, taken a 'realization' or 'technical' role, now inhabit the realm of the (co-)author.

> It promotes the view of a new type of scenographer, which in the German region is now commonly referred to as the '*Autoren-Gestalter*' (author-designer). Within the traditional framework of the exhibition trade the scenographer as author-designer principally takes a position in the middle of the axis that connects, or separates, curating and design.
> (den Oudsten 2011: 14)

The work and collaborative practices of the scenographer and director Robert Wilson exemplify de Oudsten's reading of the German *Autoren-Gestalter* or the French *auteur*. In taking a lead in the majority of creative roles, from writer through to designer, Wilson is indicative of how an individual with a design background (architecture) can supplant those with a literary or acting background to formulate a different, yet innately similar, hierarchical structure of theatrical production. While the designed aspects may now have a greater prominence within the narrative encounter of the drama, as in *A Letter for Queen Victoria* (1974), the question of authorship within Wilson's productions are, at least in terms of the listed programme, self-proclaimed. What is more difficult to discern is how the distinct 'theatre-making strategies' – such as scenography, dramaturgy and choreography – interact within this milieu of new authorial and production models. As with Baugh's (2013: 224) comment on the lack of a centralizing practice of the theatre, it is also clear that the boundaries between what is scenography and 'not-scenography' are becoming increasingly difficult to discern.

Beyond dramaturgy and choreography

The advent of conceptual, if not always professional, overlap between the discrete theatre-making strategies offers a method of tracing the distinctive and shared traits of scenography. The expanded criterion of dramaturgy in recent years has made it increasingly difficult to discern the labour of the dramaturg from that of the scenographer when practical, professional and conceptual concerns overlap. Theatre practitioner Eugenio Barba began to question the remit of the dramaturg when he suggested that, '[i]n a theatrical performance, *actions* (concerning the dramaturgy, that is) are not only what the actors do and say, but also what sounds, noises, lights, changes in space are used' (Barba 1985: 75; emphasis in original). This inclusive remit informs the notion of an 'expanded dramaturgy' as outlined by performance scholar Peter Eckersall. For Eckersall, dramaturgy is 'a confluence of literary, spatial, kinaesthetic and technical practices, worked and woven in the matrix of aesthetic and ideological forces' (Eckersall 2006: 283). This expanded definition derives its underlying focus from the literary discipline of the dramaturg, a conventional production role within German repertory theatres.

The conventional task of the dramaturg is to consider the socio-political contexts of a text-based production and, where appropriate, recommend alterations to the structure or dialogue of a play. An expanded dramaturgy takes the critical and analytical perspective as honed within the institutionalized theatre and seeks to apply it beyond literary concerns and, more broadly, to the structure of events. As performance scholar Cathy Turner and dramaturg Synne Behrndt suggest, 'The "dramaturgy" of a play or performance could also be described as its "composition", "structure" or "fabric"' (Turner and Behrndt 2008: 3). Correspondingly, Howard describes scenography as 'the seamless synthesis of space, text, research, art, actors, directors and spectators that contributes to an original creation' (Howard 2002: 130). As with Eckersall's focus on 'spatial' and 'technical' practices, Turner and Behrndt's definition could also signify the 'synthesis' of scenography as outlined by Howard. Indeed, Turner applies the notion of dramaturgy to the time-based qualities of architecture, arguing that it 'can be used to suggest an understanding of architecture that includes the time-based, narrative and lived elements within it, the folding processes implicit, latent, resistant or simply possibilities within its structures' (Turner 2010: 152). Consequently, the concerns of dramaturgy are shared, at least in part, with the concerns of scenography. Each distinct practice relates to the processes of folding the constituent parts of an event together to enact a fleeting assemblage, whether materially or metaphysically.

This conceptual and practical convergence between notions of scenography and dramaturgy has, unsurprisingly, led to a degree of confusion. 'Visual dramaturgy' has been suggested by scholars such as Howard (2009) as an example of this convergence. Visual dramaturgy is often mistakenly articulated as a synonym for scenography. In part, this confusion derives from Lehmann's definition and subheading within *Postdramatic Theatre* (2006: 93) entitled 'Scenography, visual dramaturgy' that equates visual dramaturgy with scenography. Lehmann's outline, however, states that 'Visual dramaturgy here does not mean an exclusively visually organized dramaturgy but rather one that is not subordinated to the text and can therefore freely develop its own logic' (Lehmann 2006: 93). The term was originally coined by Norwegian theatre scholar Knut Ove Arntzen and outlines how a dramaturg approaches the visual elements of performance from a textual perspective. Visual dramaturgy, or as Ove Arntzen prefers it 'a visual kind of dramaturgy', denotes a particular organizational strategy for staging that relates to the German notion of designer's theatre (such as the work of Hotel Pro Forma or Robert Wilson). Lehmann (cited in Balme 1997) goes one step further to imply a genre of 'scenographic theatre'. If, however, it is acknowledged that scenography is concerned with place orientation, then the genre of scenographic theatre is rendered problematic, as all theatre is scenographic – in the same way that all theatre is choreographic or dramaturgical. While it could be argued that this reading follows notions of physical or visual theatre (that sustain a dominant staging characteristic), in terms of the argument put forward in this book the genre of scenographic theatre is critically unproductive. When approached as a condition of dramaturgy in general, visual dramaturgy is one element of a production's design dramaturgy inclusive of sound. In this regard, visual dramaturgy is of the order of *mise en scène*: a mode of interpreting and translating visual approaches to staging. Scenography as a creative-critical practice exceeds a visual remit.

Linguistically, a more productive convergence can be located when the two terms, 'scenography' and 'dramaturgy', are used in relationship to another. The notion of a 'scenographic dramaturgy' is floated by Howard, who cites Neher's close working relationship with Brecht as an example of how 'a scenographic dramaturgy emerges that supports the text from its inception' (Howard 2009: 46). Theatre scholar Natalie Rewa implies that the conceptual concerns of dramaturgy offer a form of liberation from scenography's historical servitude (to the figuration of place), as she argues: 'the creative work of the designers is dramaturgical, rather than primarily decorative or representational, and articulates vocabularies for the synesthetic dialogue with the spectators' (Rewa 2009: xi). Baugh takes this linguistic and conceptual convergence a step further, as he argues that 'scenography has become the principal dramaturgy of performance-making' (Baugh 2013: 240). Baugh suggests that, with the increase in intermedial and immersive practices over the last decade, the scenographic elements (from light to architecture) of theatre have gained greater narrative and time-based prominence than ever before. A number of individuals have spoken about the 'designer as dramaturg' in recent years, whether in theatre (Curtis 2016) or urban design (Carter 2015). In arguing that scenography is a principal form of dramaturgy, Baugh hints at a distinction where each stage strategy of theatre-making relates to a set of intrinsically theatrical methodologies: ways of approaching the shifting and unstable construct of a stage.

The methods of scenography (model boxes, directed sound, spotlights, etc.) and the methods of dramaturgy (structural sequencing, textual composition, period research, etc.) are rendered distinct by their historical lineage as products of theatre orthodoxies. To position scenography *as* dramaturgy, as Baugh phrases it, is a statement on how the methods of scenography can reveal or instigate the analytical qualities of dramaturgy. Turner similarly stresses the importance of beginning from the conditions of theatre, arguing that 'theatre dramaturgy needs to be understood as distinct from everyday life, in order to understand how it takes its place within, or indeed contests the development of that everyday dramaturgy' (Turner 2015: 3). If scenographics are to be understood as distinct agents within the wider geographies of the everyday, then focusing in on the peculiarities of scenography within theatre affords a methodology for isolating and unpicking the orientating qualities of this practice and the perspective it affords beyond theatre. While notions of *mise en scène* or design dramaturgy account for the conceptual interpretation of a staged environment, Baugh's phraseology implies that the encounter of stage materiality is in and of itself a distinct point of interpretation. This reading operates in a similar way to Lavender's *mise en événement*, albeit with a greater focus on the affective qualities of stage material. There are, however, other strategic approaches to the continental European stage that emerged from a uniquely practical context – choreography.

The adoption of choreography into Anglophone theatres offers a number of intriguing parallels to that of scenography. While now established as part of the popular English vernacular, the application of the term 'choreography' to denote an active process of composing dance practice only emerges in the popular realm in the 1930s. Before this time, the term existed within English in relationship to the practice of recording dance only. A 'choreographer' was a form of scribe, rather than a named dance practitioner. One suggestion as to how the term became adopted as a compositional practice is through the introduction of George Balanchine (1904–83) to the fledgling musical comedy on Broadway. Having danced in Paris with the Ballets Russes and a keen disciple of Sergei Diaghilev (1872–1929), the originally Russian Balanchine embraced experimentation and the development of new dance forms. Central to this was the compositional role of the choreographer, as defined within continental theatres. When invited to work as part of a production of *On Your Toes*, Balanchine's biographer Bernard Taper recounts an important exchange with an American producer:

> Before *On Your Toes*, the playbill credit line for the dancers in musicals had always read, 'dances by – –.' Balanchine asked the producer, Wiman, whether his billing might read, 'Choreography by George Balanchine.' This was an unfamiliar word in the United States in 1936. Wiman said he feared the public would not know what it meant. Balanchine replied that maybe it would intrigue the public to see a new word, and Wiman agreed to make the experiment.
>
> (Taper 1996: 180)

Balanchine and Wiman's experiment paid off. 'Choreography' is now a common English-language term, in part, due to the profile of dance practices in popular culture. Nevertheless, definitions of this theatre-making strategy are, as with dramaturgy and scenography, being increasingly applied as part of an expanded field of movement studies.

While trained in ballet, the choreographer William Forsythe's practice is indicative of the artistic and institutional contexts that the expanded field of choreography now operates within. To encapsulate his interdisciplinary collaborations within the fields of architecture and graphic design, Forsythe developed the notion of 'performance installation'. The term is intended to denote Forsythe's practice that is centred on the development of choreographed environments, where the dance is enacted between participant and material, body and environment. Choreography is, for Forsythe, 'about organising bodies in space, or you're organising bodies with other bodies, or a body with other bodies in an environment that is organised' (in Spier 2011: 139). While clearly focused on 'bodies' as a defining material of choreographic practice, Forsythe's definition facilitates the application of choreography to an expanded field. Joy extends this focus on bodies to consider how to 'speak of choreography, or to speak choreographically, is also to speak of history and of writing and of dancing as entangled forms' (Joy 2014: 17). Joy's argument is that the corporality of choreographic traits are formative to all manner of other modes of doing and thinking.

To stress these indeterminate qualities, Joy compares the choreographic to Barthes' critique of 'filmic' as a conceptual thirding, 'disturbing as a guest who persists in staying at the party without uttering a word, even when we have no need of him' (Barthes 1977: 48). As with scenographics and the dramaturgical, awareness of the filmic is derived from the episteme of film that renders it discrete from painting or theatre. Filmic is the quality that transcends film to acquire a third meaning that is neither wholly film nor something distinctly other. Yet, this proxy concept is bound to the discrete methods of film: of montage and editing. The epistemology of the filmic is, therefore, relational to a knowledge of film and film-making. Following this model, Joy argues that choreographic traits are manifest within all modes of participation – from the choreography of architecture to the choreographics of crowds – that focus in on conceptions of movement and bodily placement. It also, as with Turner and Behrndt's use of 'fabric', invites comparisons to scenography and the porous exchanges that occur between choreographics, dramaturgies and scenographics.

From an Anglophone perspective, it is telling that the theatre-making strategies of dramaturgy and choreography were imported concepts that do not directly align with the orthodoxies of English-language theatres. It is also interesting to note that the currency of 'choreography' (now an everyday term) as a theatre-making strategy came to prominence as a legacy of theatre and dance modernisms. The development of European theatre practice in this era influenced Anglophone theatres, in the first instance, through the introduction of individuals into English-speaking theatres. As typified by Balanchine, these European innovations demanded a renewed lexicon that linked theory with practice, idea with execution. It is notable that Craig and Appia did not employ the term 'scenography', although there is some evidence that the established stage lexicon was insufficient. In a study on Appia's usage of the term *choréographie*, scenographer Scott Palmer (2015: 44) translates Appia's usages of '*la conception scénique*' as 'scenography'. Appia applies this term in a passage on the interconnectedness of the disparate stage elements, rather than a narrative figuration of place, for which he applies the term *mise en scène*. Equally, Kantor (1961: 212) stressed that the merging and transformation of scene techniques, along with the interconnectedness of stage practices, would necessitate a shift from terms such as 'scenery' and 'stage design'. Indeed, this is evident in how, since 2003, the performative installation has gained recognition at PQ as a principal mode for exhibiting scenography, positioning the event of scenography as the primary 'object' of study. Notably, this shift in practice has been mirrored by a shift in language.

Expanded scene design?

The post-disciplinary status of Performance Design has been argued in response to many of the same practices and linguistic challenges that define notions of an expanded scenography. The idea of an expanded scenography draws obvious parallels with Eckersall's expanded dramaturgies. The application of this same modelling to scenography, in order to better account for the current plurality of contemporary practice, sustains a logical sense of progression. I would, however, argue that this logic is based on the histories of continental European theatre, as typified by a conventional reading of the French *scénographie* as defined by Pavis, rather than the second adoption into English. I offer this observation for two reasons. First, if the first adoption into English is taken as a mistranslation, then scenography as a holistic approach arguably does not have a 'classical' form within the Anglophone theatres. Second, in the absence of a classical form, the modelling of an expanded field is made intrinsically problematic given the holistic premise of the second adoption.

The idea of an expanded field is based on art critic Rosalind Krauss's analysis of contemporary sculptural practice in the 1970s. Borrowed from Gene Youngblood's *Expanded Cinema* (1970), Krauss argues that the classical definitions of sculpture were being contested, where 'the word *sculpture* became harder to pronounce' (Krauss 1979: 33; emphasis in original). While noting the tensions facilitated by the earthworks of Mary Miss or Robert Morris's mirrored installations, Krauss argues that sculpture had been defined by a historicism: 'I would submit that we know very well what sculpture is. And one of the things we know is that it is a historically bounded category and not a universal one' (Krauss 1979: 33). Rather than assessing an object's legitimacy as sculpture in relation to what came before, Krauss proposed that, by situating sculpture within a matrix (see Figure 3), composed of other aligned art forms, this offers a means of mapping the practice of sculpture beyond a linear historicism. In particular, Krauss's mapping positioned sculpture outside of, but in relationship to, a binary between architecture and not-architecture, landscape and not-landscape. The implication being that sculpture might be understood as an undertaking that took place as a counterpoint between a number of defined historicisms.

Krauss's modelling situates the historicized sculpture at the periphery, along with architecture and landscape. The insinuation is that within the field between these established historicisms exists the site of artistic practice: 'Thus the field provides both for an expanded but finite set of related positions or a given artist to occupy and explore, and for an organization of work that is not dictated by the conditions of a particular medium' (Krauss 1979: 42–3). All sculpture can be plotted on to Krauss's matrix, as it focuses on how the medium is deployed rather than a defined grammar to which it is rendered (whether made of marble or earth, as well as placed on a pedestal or part of the landscape). The notion of a base is, however, paramount to how Krauss approaches sculpture as sculpture. Krauss

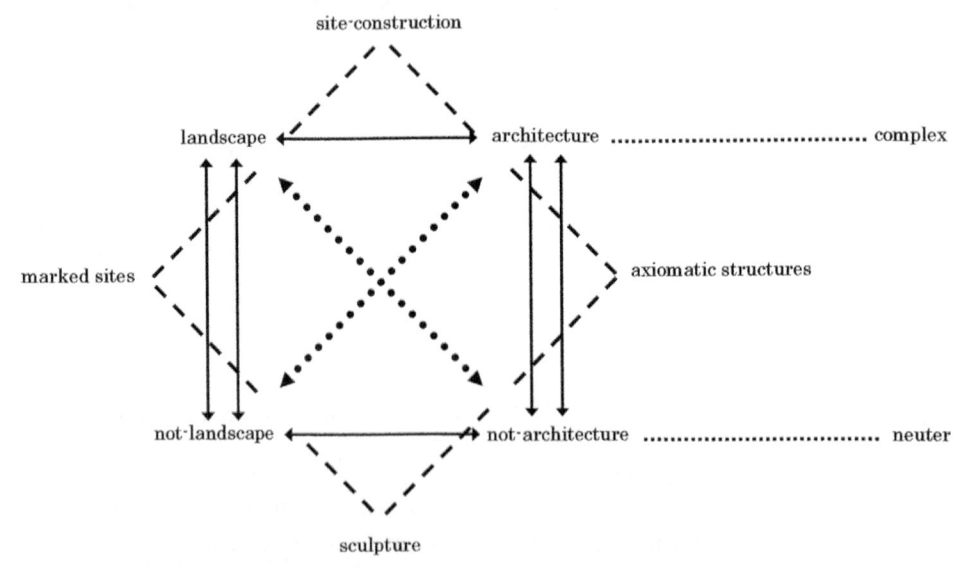

Figure 3 Krauss's modelling of an expanded field
Source: Krauss (1979: 38)

critiques the classical understanding where 'sculptures are normally figurative and vertical, their pedestals an important part of the structure since they mediate between actual site and representational sign' (Krauss 1979: 33). While modernist sculpture had become 'siteless' and focused toward abstract forms, Krauss argues that the base had merely absorbed the pedestal. The classical logic extended into this new phase of sculptural practice, where the pedestal had been amalgamated with the base and form had replaced figuration. Moreover, the process-based practices of postmodern sculpture further reinforced the base as an intrinsic quality of sculpture. As evident in Morris's mirrors and Miss's hole in the ground, the medium of sculpture was not predefined, yet all retained a sense of grounding, of base.

The central attraction to positioning an established practice within an expanded field is, as Krauss outlines, that 'one has thereby gained the "permission" to think these other forms' (Krauss 1979: 38). Whereas previously only those trained within a certain craft had an implied authority over that art form, the expanded field opens out questions of authority and ownership in an altogether different way. In that regard, it is not surprising that this reading has been applied to other practices, such as dramaturgy. Indeed, the expanded logic as applied to dramaturgy refers to two distinct operations. The first expansion of dramaturgy, as typified by Barba, was from a literary strategy of theatre-making to a more holistic account for how all the elements of theatre are structured, inclusive of light and sound, as well as text and environment. The second expansion of dramaturgy occurred when this holistic reading was then applied to non-theatrical events. The first phase of dramaturgy's expansion echoes the second adoption of scenography. While 'dramaturgy' was by no means a common term within the Anglophone theatres before Eckersall's proposal, the second expansion of dramaturgy that he promoted amounted to the application of dramaturgical thinking to other disciplines. As far as I am aware, there has not been a prominent argument put forward that expanded dramaturgy, or dramaturgy, might operate as an academic discipline in its own right.

In English, the notion of an expanded scenography, becomes confused when presented against the premise of scenography as a holistic practice. Krauss alludes to a related issue when arguing for a logic of sculpture: 'As is true of any other convention, sculpture has its own internal logic, its own set of rules, which, though they can be applied to a variety of situations, are not themselves open to very much change' (Krauss 1979: 33). Krauss reduces this logic down to the notion of a base. As outlined throughout this book, scenography is a crafting of place orientation rather than the objects of theatre: a theatre-making strategy on a par with dramaturgy and choreography. Following Krauss's methodology, to capture the technical grammar or historicisms that an expanded ethos implies the English-language variant should be read as 'expanded scene design' or 'expanded stage design', as these terms denote a technical and institutional framing that is present in the continental variants. The second adoption of 'scenography' does not have a specific medium or material. The only parallel with the fixed syntax of a pedestal is that of a stage, where notions of scenography and stage are arguably synonymous. The deterministic assumption that stages precede scenography is, however, contested in relationship to the scenographies of distributed mixed-reality assemblages and telepresent performances. Nevertheless, the associations evident within a continental reading of an expanded scenography are rendered problematic within the Anglophone context, given its complementary status against an established bank of technical terminologies – from set and lighting design to scene and sound design.

While the expanded position implies that scenography can supersede the institutional theatres, it could also be taken to denote how the holistic second adoption of 'scenography' is already expanded beyond the orthodoxies of theatrical design. Arguments for an expanded scenography become relational to an understanding of scenography, although this same argument can be applied to expanded dramaturgies and choreography as well. It is, however, useful to present the argument that the second adoption of scenography is already expanded beyond any classical context. While this speaks directly to the continental politics and associated tensions aligned with the term, the distinctions between the first and second Anglophone adoptions confirm a history of expansion. Subsequently, the argument for 'expanded scenography' acts to confirm 'scenography' as scene painting and frames the second adoption as a progression beyond this technical reading.

I apply the term 'scenography' to denote the place-orientating imperatives as conceptually aligned with the second adoption. The first adoption's technical focus on scene-painting is symptomatic of how scenographics are rendered superficial, illustrative or conceptualized as 'mere' background. This is why I do not use the term 'expanded scenography', as it gives credence to this reductive position and affirms the politics of the scenic as being formatively scenographic. I nevertheless acknowledge that this critique of 'expanded scenography' is almost unique to the Anglophone and Germanic contexts given the linguistic familiarity of its complementary terminologies. In most other languages aside from the radical Czech, variants on *skenographia* conventionally denote the role of set design within the theatre and are not readily understood as a holistic practice. Even in Czech, the principal position is from a spatial-material counterpoint to the more literary or bodily focused director or choreographer. It is important to note that this is a primary reason why scenography gained currency within the Anglophone context. It also echoes my commitment to arguing scenography as being distinct from set design and beyond an academic pseudonym. Equally, I remain wary of how the expanded ethos sustains a decentring, away from theatre as a formative practice. Instead, the critical affordances and interdisciplinary potentials of this terminology are captured within the term 'scenographic'. This renewed alignment, I assert, positions scenography as 'of the theatre', and as a strategy of theatre-making. To understand scenography is to understand how theatre works. While also acknowledging practices that operate in other disciplinary contexts, a distinction between scenographics and scenography presents the capacity for a more nuanced discussion on the critical qualities of both.

In arguing for a critical understanding of scenography as theatre-making, it is my contention that this can reaffirm the richness of contemporary theatre practice as existing beyond the archetypes propagated by antitheatrical rhetoric and the politics of the scenic. It also avoids the production of new terms and instead focuses on a renewal of the lexicon, for 'scenographic' is a familiar term. What is more, I am not proposing scenography as an independent academic discipline. This is an argument that features as an undercurrent in much of the critical material on an expanded scenography. Aronson confirms this position arguing that it is 'perhaps time that "scenographic studies" emerges as a fully developed discipline to stand beside performance studies' (Aronson 2018: 4). I honestly feel that there are already too many boundaries and fixed centres of practice. I have no desire for the regulatory and intellectual disciplining that comes with the establishment of a new set of disciplinary walls. Instead, I am interested in proposing strategies for navigating the porous exchanges that take place between fixed centres and communities of practice. Moreover, I would contend that the scope of Performance Design sustains and supports the recognition and mobility that colleagues desire from disciplinary status. In this regard, I approach Performance Design as a post-disciplinary home of scenography that equally draws upon the practices of architecture to spatial design, interactive media to social geography. Scenography amounts to a particular strategy of theatre-making. Consequently, I propose that scenographics afford a framework for identifying and debating how the methods of scenography operate beyond the institutionalized theatres.

Overall, my intention is to differentiate scenography's distinctiveness from other possible strategies of Performance Design, such as topography or psychogeography. I argue that scenography is rendered distinct by the methods and modes of encounter that it has acquired from the necessities of theatrical enactment. While this includes the use of two-dimensional forced perspective and surrogate objects or costumes, I would contend that this is also inclusive of the methods employed to delineate and demarcate defined places for action (stage-scenes) as well as the crafting of place orientation (staging). Light is central to this practice. The use of a tightly focused lantern within a darkened environment can immediately shift the felt affective qualities of that atmosphere through a distinctly scenographic technique. Sound and movement are equally important for the transformation and reformation of place orientation. These techniques are, in part, derived from the conventions of scenery along with the learned material and spatial grammars that come with acts of staging. Nevertheless, the radical Czech-influenced second Anglophone adoption of 'scenography' is centred on a holistic strategy that focuses on the encounter and conception of theatre materialities. Scenography, rather than an account of theatre objects, is understood as an intangible crafting of theatrical place orientation. Most explicitly, the implications of this reading are that scenography *happens*; that it occurs in theatre, *as* theatre. Accordingly, to speak of scenography is to speak of the time of scenography.

Scenography is not set; scenography happens.

CHAPTER 4
Scenography happens

In English, the term 'set' is used to denote that which is 'fixed', 'concrete' or 'rendered solid'. While also conveying the ordering of objects as well as shorthand for a contextual 'setting', I argue that the linguistic positioning of scenography as a synonym for 'set design' is indicative of a wider dramaturgical bias against scenographics: that they are subsidiary and in-service, technical and illustrative. Contrary to this reading, I argue that scenography is an act of place orientation that simultaneously complements and exceeds the linguistic implications of set design or conventions of scenery.

With obvious parallels to time-oriented conceptions of dramaturgy and choreography, scenography, following the radical Czech usage, is conceived as a means of isolating how the material and spatial elements of theatre *happen*; how they are encountered and how they orientate feelings of place. Maaike Bleeker summarized some of these issues in her thesis on theatrical visuality, arguing that 'Visuality happens. Visuality is not a given property of things, situations, or objects' (Bleeker 2008: 2). Critically, Bleeker's reading of visuality extends beyond the context of vision and the hegemony of the visual within Western aesthetics. In situating visuality as an event, Bleeker focuses on how the interpretation and experience of images are composed at a particular moment, where experience is equally concerned with subjective analysis as well as holistic processes of sensory reception.

My own approach applies Deleuzian thinking on 'assemblages' along with a new materialist articulation of 'affective atmospheres'. Deleuze argues that encounters are constituted from a range of elements that are then composed or aligned to imply something greater than their individual virtues.

Assemblages exist, but they indeed have component parts that serve as criteria and allow the various assemblages to be qualified. Just as in painting, assemblages are a bunch of lines. But there are all kinds of lines. Some lines are segments, or segmented; some lines get caught in a rut, or disappear into 'black holes'; some are destructive, sketching death; and some lines are vital and creative. These creative and vital lines open up an assemblage, rather than close it down.

(Deleuze 2006: 178)

Building on the conclusions of Deleuze, Ben Anderson argues that it is the 'very ambiguity of affective atmospheres – between presence and absence, between subject and object/subject and between the definite and indefinite – that enable us to reflect on affective experience as occurring beyond, around, and alongside the formation of subjectivity' (Anderson 2009: 77). The indeterminate qualities of an affective atmosphere as a coalescing of seemingly distinct components (of light, sound, scent, texture, etc.) are fundamental to understanding what scenography does and how scenography happens. Crucially, Deleuze's notion of assemblage relates to an encounter that occurs in time: it is an event of potential that may be distinct for each individual and different upon each encounter. Set is to be stagnant, unchangeable. Scenography is anything but set.

To illustrate and evidence my claims, this chapter includes a case study on the scenographic principles of the Ipswich-based physical theatre company Gecko's production of *MISSING UNPLUGGED*. My attendance at this performance is used as a case study in order to argue how scenography happens through the material and immaterial encounters of theatrical design. This is particularly significant as the original 'set' for *MISSING* (2012) was destroyed in a fire, only for Gecko to re-stage the event in the absence of their technological and physical materials a week later. I argue that the conditions of this re-staging isolate how scenography happens through ideas of staging and blocking, as well as the performance of materials. The particular conditions of this case study outline how a system of scenography operates between and betwixt the individual methods that sustain a stage atmosphere. While others have posited this position before (Böhme 2013; Lotker and Gough 2013; von Arx 2015), in framing the eventful qualities of scenography as paramount, this focuses on the holistic operation of scenography as outlined by Svoboda. What is more, in arguing that scenography happens this locates the Anglophone usage in relation to the established stage lexicon – from scene painting to theatre design, *mise en scène* to design dramaturgy. It also reveals the critical distinction between a method of scenography and scenography itself shifting from the orthodoxies of scenery and the scenic to a holistic understanding of stage-scenes as affective atmospheres.

The time of scenography

In Greek, the term *graphos* has multiple meanings that have been translated as 'scribing', 'writing' or 'etching'. Each translation denotes a distinct act: of making an impression upon something with something. Numerous definitions have focused on positioning the methods of scenography in equivalence to the logocentrism of literary structures, such as 'scenic writing' (Aronson 2005: 7; Collins and Nisbet 2010: 140). The theatre director Roger Planchon (1931–2009) stressed in 1964 that, following Brecht, a director was required to take 'responsibility' for all aspects of scene-making. Planchon stresses that

> Brecht is to have declared that a performance combines both dramatic writing and scenic writing; but the scenic writing – he was the first to say this and it seems to me to be very important – has an equal responsibility with the dramatic writing.
>
> (cited in Bradby and Williams 1988: 55)

Central to Planchon's adoption of Brecht's scenic writing is that this denotes a process of interpretation, by an audience, and translation, by a director. Kennedy offers a useful summary of this position, stating that the 'suffix *graph* helps to remind us of the ways in which scenography is a form of writing, a formulated code or language of the visual. In this light, scenography is also a text, and requires a separate reading' (Kennedy 2001: 12). The move to argue the equivalency of non-literary elements as text or writing has become an established trope in theatre and performance studies.

From Schechner's 'performance text' to Pavis's ideo-textual *mise en scène*, the post-structural position on text as an interweaving of signs and concepts informs a number of academic positions on how performance is *read*. However, Lefebvre argues that to conceptualize an affective atmosphere in terms of a message is to evade the nexus of potentiality innate within a spatial act:

> Any attempt to use such codes as a means of deciphering social space must surely reduce that space itself to the status of a *message*, and the inhabiting of it to the status of a *reading*. This is to evade both history and practice.
>
> (Lefebvre 1991a: 7; emphasis in original)

To argue scenography in terms of the logocentrism of writing privileges the reception of a message above and beyond a scenographic assemblage's potentiality for action through an enactment of place orientation. As a material-spatial assemblage, scenography resists a strict logocentrism of message and interpretation.

Influenced by Lefebvre, I argue that the translation of 'graphy' as 'writing' is problematic for two reasons. First, it equates the logocentrism of writing with the relational and, following Böhme (2013), the ontologically diffuse experience of worldly encounter. Second, the application of this translation does not always sufficiently stress the active qualities denoted within the original Greek: graphy is a doing, a verb. The suffix of 'writing' arguably flattens and quantifies a material event into a formal system of codification, whereas the term *graphos* in Greek is not aligned with the logic of reading. *Graphos* is focused on the act of mark-making and does not imply, in and of itself, a formal means of interpretation or language. 'Drawing' offers a useful and, for many scenographers, familiar interpretation of *graphos* that upon first reading counteracts the logocentrism of writing. Drawing does, nevertheless, still imply the production of a distinct product in that manner of a quantifiable object (a defined interpretative meaning) that echoes writing's logocentric imperative. Baugh notes the allure of writing as a preferred means of accounting for an imposed logic of scenography:

> Perhaps because scenography yields no useful verb, many contemporary artists prefer the linguistic familiarity of literature and refer to this inclusive manipulation of forms and materials in performance-making as 'writing' performance … Attempts at linguistic definition are generally reduced to an all-embracing, and not very useful, blandness as they aspire to express the breadth and inclusivity of the concept. We can only define scenography through a description of what it does and how it works.
>
> (Baugh 2013: 240)

Den Oudsten relates this argument more directly to the notion of *graphos*, where the suffix 'suggests time, implying that the syntax of fleeting signs carries the semantics of the message' (den Oudsten 2011: 17–18). Surprisingly, the time of scenography is rarely discussed, with the majority of scholarship focusing on the visual or the figurative. This approach is, however, implied by the architect Serge von Arx (2015) in his declaration that 'scenography does not exist'. In adopting this phrasing, von Arx is asserting that scenography as an idea or practice is not moot, but that scenography exceeds the conventions of quantifiable scenery. To study scenography is to study the act of scenography. Scenography takes place betwixt and beyond objects to account for how a sense of place happens within a theatre event. Consequently by shifting the focus from questions of writing I am also arguing that scenography is not *read*, for, as McKinney states, we 'experience a scenography rather than read it' (McKinney 2015: 80). My argument for a renewed focus on how scenography happens stresses that it *occurs*, in time, as an assemblage of place orientation.

The old English term 'wright' is arguably better suited to scenography. To wright means to fashion something into being from pre-existing materials, with the most germane example being a playwright (a fashioning of words). There are also shipwrights and wheelwrights. Accordingly, I approach the graphy of scenography as a *crafting* with a focus on wright-ing rather than writing. The act of place orientation is always encountered as a holism and cannot be reduced to an image or picture. Craig was conscious of this differentiation. Citing an exchange with the dancer and one-time partner Isadora Duncan (1877–1927), Craig offers a useful summary of the misunderstandings that have featured throughout scenography's history. Craig notes that Duncan had continually refereed to his work only as 'the perfect setting', with Craig exclaiming that 'even after 20 years … she thought I was thinking of scenery!' (in Innes 1993: 2). Instead, Craig's focus was a holistic approach to movement in theatre – an approach that would embrace light and architecture as having the potential for action. My own focus on scenography as a crafting of place orientation isolates how the event of scenography takes place from a multi-sensory and experiential position. Beyond the discrete conventions of scenery or the surrogacy of props, scenography orientates and scores how a feeling of place is constituted. To *do* scenography is to do staging; to do the situational act of theatre.

In emphasizing the necessity of a holistic conceptualization, my argument that scenography happens stresses the interventional quality of this practice at a particular moment in time. Herbert Blau argued that theatre's ontological situation is resistant to an uninterrupted continuity between life and art. Blau argued that theatre 'is not nor ever will be – though we may *imitate* it – the way in which life makes life' (Blau 1982: 288). While Blau acknowledged that human perspectives have been conditioned by theatrical conventions and vice versa, the temporal event of theatre disrupts the continuity of lifetime. Theatre is art time – it is extra daily. In this regard, Blau's argument echoes the critical positioning of durational performance artist Tehching Hsieh: 'I don't really blur art and life. The gap between each *One Year Performance* is life time. But the pieces themselves are art time, not lived time' (in Heathfield and Jones 2012: 463). Hsieh's artworks, from an observer's point of view, may appear to do the thing that Hsieh himself argues against. The punching of a card-clock while in a cage every hour for *One Year Performance* (1980–81) seemingly renders Hsieh's life time as art time. Yet, Hsieh's own temporal demarcation argues otherwise. Evidently, Blau's observations on theatre as beyond life time are equally applicable to the durational performance works of Hsieh. Art events and life events are temporally demarcated through a conscious othering that irritates normative structures of temporal experience – what de Certeau describes as 'everyday practice', as distinct from Barba's notion of the extra-daily. Scenography always happens as art time. Scenographic traits are that which complicate this demarcation by occurring in both art time and life time. This same modelling applies to choreography and choreographic, film and filmic, dramaturgy and dramaturgical.

Critical to the second adoption is that scenography accounts for how the art time of theatre is encountered as an affective materiality. McCormack stresses that affective atmospheres, or 'spacetimes', generate feelings and orientations that open up ways of thinking from within the happening of an assemblage:

> The experimental quality of affective spacetimes is not so much that they provide opportunities to prove or demonstrate a prefigured idea, but that they have the potential to generate a feeling of something happening that disturbs, agitates, or animates ideas already circulating in ways that might open up possibilities for thinking otherwise.
> (McCormack 2013: 9–10)

McCormack articulates the particular affects of an atmosphere through the Deleuzian idea of the 'refrain'. Echoing the Platonic idea of *chora* as the receptacle for all becoming, the refrain for McCormack is 'radically open: that is to say, while they may be repetitive, refrains are always potentially generative of difference, producing lines of thinking, feeling, and perceiving that may allow one to wander beyond the familiar' (McCormack 2013: 8). Moreover, McCormack argues that 'the refrain is radically impersonal, or at least more than human. It does not necessarily originate through the expression of some inner psychological impulse' (McCormack 2013: 8). Scenography is, accordingly, an assemblage of affective materials and technologies that craft a refrain into being as an affective atmosphere. Scenographies as matrices for refrains also sustain particular rhythms through the affective potentiality of an enacted assemblage, with ebbs and flows. Likewise, art critic Brian O'Doherty argues that 'Space now is not just where things happen; things make space happen' (O'Doherty 1986: 39). The potentiality of a scenography exists in its ability to 'make space happen'. Scenography occurs as an affective atmospheric assemblage that is configured and reconfigured over the duration of a situational art time.

The notion that scenography happens is nothing new. Craig argues that movement was crucial to the technological and aesthetic revolutions of the New Stagecraft. In particular, the conventional methods for demarcating strict boundaries between dramaturgical scenes – whether a curtain or a blackout – could be transgressed following the transformative qualities of light and kinetic staging: 'We pass from one scene to another without a break of any kind, and when the change has come we are not conscious of any disharmony between the new scene and that which is past' (in Innes 1993: 141). This flow between discrete dramaturgical scenes is explicitly evident within the scenographies of Robert Wilson and the Danish performance company of Hotel Pro Forma. The idea that scenography occurs as an affective atmosphere, and sustains an innate potentiality for change and re-modulation, echoes Böhme's observation that scenography

> is no longer confined to the design and furnishing of the stage space but, on the one hand, causes the action on the stage to appear in a particular light and, on the other, creates an acoustic space which tunes the whole performance.
> (Böhme 2013: 4)

Böhme continues to isolate how stages 'generated by light and sound are no longer something perceived at a distance, but something within which one is enclosed' (Böhme 2013: 5). Lefebvre confirms this position as he cites the assemblage of a stage atmosphere as an example of how social space is composed of multiple agents, where theatre 'in addition to a text or pretext embraces gesture, masks, costume, a stage, a *mise-en-scène* – in short, a space' (1991a: 62). Scenography is an exercise in scoring how extra-daily 'social spaces' are rendered knowable as an affective atmosphere that occurs in time.

One of the core points of differentiation between the Anglophone adoption of *mise en scène* and 'scenography' is a focus on the affective qualities of a staged atmosphere as distinct from acts of interpretation and translation. Lavender situates this usefully within his argument on the limits of *mise en scène*. In particular, Lavender reminds us that the French *mise en* literally means 'placed on' or 'put on'. All variants of the phrase, from *mise en abyme* ('put into the abyss') to *mise en place* ('put into place'), are situated as a 'past participle [that] indicates human agency – something was *arranged* – along with a *process* of construction' (Lavender 2016: 78). In situating *mise en scène* as a past participle, a more cogent understanding begins to emerge with regards to its relationship to scenography. Moreover, Hannah and Harsløf argue that notions of Performance Design acknowledge that 'places and things precede action – as action – is critical to performance design as an aesthetic practice and an event-based phenomenon' (Hannah and Harsløf 2008: 19). This argument informs the central provocation of this chapter. Unlike the conventional French variant, 'scenography' is not a past participle nor a pseudonym for 'set' or 'background'. As Böhme reminds us, '[a]tmospheres, to be sure, are not things' (Böhme 2013: 3). Scenography happens as an affective atmosphere that shapes and responds to action, as action.

Scenography beyond set

The experience of a stage atmosphere and my own conceptualization of place orientation are intrinsically bound to one another through scenography – where the potentiality of a stage atmosphere is derived from the orientating traits of scenographics. The arguments for the New Stagecraft were arguably predicated on the notion that a stage atmosphere was ephemeral and could sustain non-figurative encounters. Macgowan suggests that the 'new stagecraft sets itself to visualize the atmosphere of a play. Its artists aim to make … an emotional envelope appropriate to the dramatic mood' (Macgowan 1923: 20). In 1903, Appia echoed this position, arguing that 'we shall no longer attempt to give the illusion a *forest* but instead the illusion of a *man* [sic] in the atmosphere of a forest' (in Beecham 1994: 118; emphasis in original). Lighting designer Lucy Carter observes a similar trait regarding how light sustains atmospheres that 'make the audience feel, emotionally, that they're in the right place – to make them understand where the actors are just by the sensation of lighting' (Carter 2016). Carter's portrayal of how lighting affects spectators, and by implication performers, signals the event of scenography. The idea of feeling the 'right place' and the 'sensation of lighting' operates beyond the logocentric tendencies of *mise en scène* to focus on staging as an act of affective orientation. The resonance with place thus described is scored through the orientating qualities of light sensation. In this instance, Carter's reading exceeds the strict physical connotation of the term 'set'. The framing of scenography as place orientation seeks to encompass the immaterial affects, as well as the very material conditions, of contemporary staging. To position scenography as set is to misunderstand how the holistic remit must encompass these time-based forms of place orientation, which exceed strictly visual readings of the picturesque or the boundaried physicality of a set object.

The German set designer Katrin Brack offers a useful complication to the argument that set is inert or a fixed solid. Brack's work often employs ephemeral materials such as foam or haze as the principal material component for a set design. Critical commentaries on Brack's work have sought to distance her approach from notions of scenery or set. As Stefanie Carp puts it, Brack's stages are 'not sets and least of all stage sets' (Carp 2010: 20). Yet, Brack defines these environments as 'nothing other than a theater set' (Brack 2010: 175). Crucial to Brack's position is that, while her designs employ what might be deemed unusual materials, the working processes from which these designs emerge are that of a typical set designer. Brack works within an established theatrical hierarchy collaborating with directors and writers, as well as other members of the design team, to devise staging that reflects a production's dramaturgical requirements. Brack does not aim to exceed the conventions of set design. In this regard, Brack's foam architectures, while constantly in motion and seemingly resistant to the definition of a 'set object', are a result of a set designer's process. It is this process that, for Brack, renders them set. While Brack's position transgresses the codification of set as a strict reproduction of another place (another world image), the material qualities and affective atmospheres explicit within her foam architectures evoke a different connotation of set that embraces the arguments of

Svoboda and Performance Design: that a set is a collection, a gathering of materialities for display.

'Set' is a term with multiple connotations. The English usage, while taken to describe the physical construct of a theatrical environment, means to be fixed, static, rendered solid. Equally, the term denotes a collection, which can imply a pre-scripted form of sequencing as evident within the 'playing set' for a music gig. In this instance, 'set' is used to denote a dramaturgical collection of performances or scenes rather than accounting for discrete points of action. 'Set' can also be used to denote an alternation between states: to change a setting on a computer or to set the heating to off. The implications of this are evident within Kennedy's definition of 'scenography' as the 'accumulation of spatial and visual elements that creates a stage setting' (Kennedy 2010: 536). Scenography as an accumulation of elements gives recognition to the holistic reading, with the implication that a setting is a collection of items and things. Moreover, Kennedy stresses how scenography scores the changing between fixed states or scenes. Nevertheless, I argue that Kennedy's reading of scenography as a setting does not go far enough in terms of fully recognizing the eventful qualities of Svoboda's approach: as Burian outlines, 'Scenography is not a background or even a container' (Burian 1970: 125–6). My resistance to the idea of scenography as setting is centred on the notion that, to be set, or to 'set the stage', renders the act of scenography as a past participle: an activity that occurs before the event. Yet, Svoboda argued that scenography only exists within the act – the time – of theatre. While Svoboda stressed that physical movement is not a precondition of scenography, it is evident that the term 'set' does not appropriately account for the 'psycho-plasticity' that Svoboda describes as a defining characteristic of scenography. Linguistically, in English 'set' and 'setting' reflect the division of labour as evident in the pre-1960s French understanding, rendering the practice of scenography as a figurative, rather than transformative, exercise. My own approach to scenography echoes the recognition that Lavender extends to *mise en événement* or Lehmann's 'eventlike *mise en scène*' and the experiential focus of contemporary performance practice, albeit motivated by notions of an eventful materiality aside from the sequencing of participation itself (which would fall within the remit of dramaturgy). Whereas *mise en scène* is centred on the interpretation of stage place, 'scenography' relates to an affective *conditioning* of stage atmospheres.

In positioning the encounter and practice of scenography as time-based, this recognizes the simultaneity that occurs through the combination of multiple design practices. As McKinney and Butterworth argue: 'Scenography is not simply concerned with creating and presenting images to an audience; it is concerned with audience reception and engagement. It is a sensory as well as an intellectual experience, emotional as well as rational' (2009: 4). Appia equally stressed that the harmony of a distinct scenography is related to the complicated interactions that occur between the methods of scenography, writing in 1899 that the 'more types of media required for the realization of any work of art, the more elusive is this harmony' (in Beacham 1993: 29). While he did not employ the term 'scenography' as the agency for this harmony, Appia argued that a 'mutual influence still continues because a shared scenic principle binds them together under identical conventions' (in Beacham 1993: 35). The 'shared scenic principle' to which Appia refers is an account of scenography in all but name. While the constituent practices of scenography (light, sound, stage geography, object, costume) are distinct in terms of material and technological production, their relations to one another condition how they affect a fleeting stage assemblage – these discrete methods are part of a 'system' of scenography.

Lotker and Gough propose how the intangible qualities of scenography make us 'rethink scenography as a system' (2013: 3). Scenography as a system is a useful way of accounting for how the distinct methods of scenography are orientated within a theatrical ecology. Schwarz situates this form of holistic thinking as a legacy of the Wagnerian *Gesamtkunstwerk* that inspired Craig and Appia, where it 'does not represent an object, however complex, but a process whose complexity varies according to its degree of transdisciplinary' (Schwarz 2011: xiii). Scenography is concerned not only with the material constructions of theatre, but how these constructions *relate* to one another; *relate* to the performers; *relate* to the spectators. With regard to the expanded context, den Oudsten describes scenography in terms of a 'post-spectacular exhibition', as it 'deals with the relations between things rather than with the things themselves' (den Oudsten 2011: 4). Whereas once the exhibition was focused on the display of things, the post-spectacular exhibition is concerned with how things are related and how they connect. Indeed, den Oudsten identifies this as a condition of scenography and argues that it is this quality that makes it attractive to the expanded field:

> One of these tendencies is that those who dwell in the interdisciplinary wasteland recognise themselves in the notion of 'relative' or 'open' art, which refers to the relationships between things and the structures of the connecting chains rather than to the things themselves.
>
> (den Oudsten 2011: 21)

As with ideas of performance, the disciplinary migratory contexts of scenographics are facilitated by their relative qualities – the way in which it draws things together, connects them, communicates them to a community. The objects of scenography are no longer the primary medium within a holistic practice. The methods of scenography are the operational contexts in which these relationships are formed and sustained. Scenographics connect the disparate practices of light and sound, as well as linking the experiences of objects that are felt as distinctive atmospheric orientations. Scenography is an art of scenographic relations.

Scenography as a relational practice is not directly related to curator Nicolas Bourriaud's (2002) notion of relational aesthetics. Instead, it offers one method of mapping the intangible qualities of scenography. Bourriaud's definition of 'relational art' focuses on how artistic encounters evoke, sustain and enable social relationships (both with an artwork and with other 'viewers'). While scenography may evoke the qualities of relational art, insomuch that it may sustain a community of viewers, the notion of scenography as a system of relations is not an explicit extension of Bourriaud's writings. In describing scenography in terms of relations, the intention is to articulate how distinct stagecrafts correspond and complement one another through an act of place orientation. Costume is conditioned by light; light is informed by sound; sound is responsive to a physical environment. The methods of theatrical design are assembled through a system of scenography into an affective atmosphere.

It also, following Böhme's observations, denotes the experiential qualities of scenography as eliciting subjective emotional affects as well as empirical effects. Scenography offers a means of summarizing how theatrical design methods condition our overall orientation within a theatre event.

Gecko's *MISSING* set

In order to evidence my position that scenography happens, I return to an event that occurred on Friday 13 March 2015. I was planning to attend the physical theatre company Gecko's performance of *MISSING* the following week at Battersea Arts Centre (BAC), London. On this day, however, the BAC caught fire. The Grand Hall's ceiling collapsed. Gecko's set and stage materials were being stored in this area as part of a run at the venue. The materials for *MISSING*, which had been developed and constructed over the course of five years, were destroyed. An outcry of support from the artistic community followed, particularly centred on the significance of the BAC as a site for artistic development. Gecko is a mid-sized company; they had neither the resources nor the funds to recover the production, which was scheduled for a tour around the UK and abroad. A Kickstarter campaign was established to support Gecko in their commitment to rebuild *MISSING*, quickly amassing over £10,000. The original materials and other place-orientating methods were, however, lost in the fire.

What is significant about this event is that Gecko refused to allow this disaster to end their relationship with the aptly named *MISSING*. One week after the fire, the company re-staged the performance without any of the material elements that had defined the production's place-orientating methods. I attended this event. The original staging of *MISSING* employed a range of technologies, including stage travelators, a suspended monitor, as well as a precise choreography of light, stage trucks and physical action. Dance reviewer Sanjoy Roy described the original staging of *MISSING*: 'Nothing is stable. The performers track each other with wooden frames, like movable viewfinders, while travelators make every scene seem slippery' (Roy 2012). Theatre reviewer Jake Orr equally emphasizes the transitional qualities of the production's scenography, noting that the experience was akin to 'constantly floating between scenes in a dream state that never seems to end; a challenging but important element to the work' (Orr 2013). Interestingly, the artistic director and company performer Amit Lahav is accredited as a designer on the production alongside Rhys Jarman (set design), Chris Swain (lighting) and Enzo Appetecchia (sound). Lahav's direct engagement and involvement in the scenographic conditions of the production is evident in Roy's depiction of *MISSING*'s intertwined dramaturgy. The synthesis of numerous theatrical components leads Roy to conclude that, '[b]ut then, there is no main element: the work's distinctiveness comes from its mix of actors and dancers, sounds and images, subjects and scenarios, even of languages' (Roy 2012). With overtones of the Wagnerian *Gesamtkunstwerk*, Gecko's approach positions the scenographic encounters of *MISSING* as an integral feature of the performance's dramaturgy. The absence of the 'designed' physical structures, lighting sequences, monitors and travelators makes the challenge of a re-staging innately more noteworthy.

I am sat on the front row for the re-staged version, entitled MISSING UNPLUGGED, *at the Queen Elizabeth Hall on 20 March 2015. Performed for one night only, I look out on to the open stage at the Queen Elizabeth. The company had only been able to work in the space that day, meaning there was no time to bring in flats to alter the stage layout. The quick turnaround for a 7.30 p.m. performance meant that there was no time to focus any lanterns or program any lighting sequences. I watch from a front row seat as Lahav takes to the stage and outlines the context of this one-off event. Notably, Lahav asks those in the auditorium to raise their hand if they had seen the original production: in a packed auditorium, around half the hands go up. My own hand is raised. Lahav announces that the event will be staged without the lighting or stage trucks that had been such a prominent aspect of the original version's dramatic action. It becomes clear to me that the orange-tinted wooden floor of the hall, framed by a counterweighted fly system either side, would serve as the terrain for* MISSING UNPLUGGED. *The working lights remained on throughout the majority of the performance. There was no attempt to disguise the theatre architecture. The only lighting cue was towards the end, when Lahav, in his role as the father, reveals a bike light in his cupped hands in place of a glowing orb that had been in the original. To emphasize this moment, the working lights are turned off momentarily. During the performance, I note that one of my former students, the stage manager Tanya Stephenson, remained clearly visible in the wings, moving on stage to assist in the holding of wooden frames as surrogates of the monitors and truck reveals. I was drawn by the clarity of what was evidently the one original design aspect that had survived: the sound. Indeed, Appetecchia's soundscapes evoked the original's shadowy lighting design and murky aesthetic in a manner that underlined the technological complexity of the production. In particular, I felt Appetecchia's design amplified the production's ambient or narrative sounds, such as rewinding tapes corresponding to the 'rewinding' of the performers' actions and the foley artistry of closing doors. The sound design of the original production scored the re-staging of* MISSING UNPLUGGED. *I am struck by how the materialities of* MISSING *had been crafted without the physical objects in situ. I conclude that, while the set was gone, a scenography remained.*

Artistic director of the BAC, David Jubb, suggests that Gecko 'performed without most of their kit and their magical tricks and I think they invented a new form. I've never seen an unplugged version of a theatre show before' (in Tripney 2015). Practically, *MISSING UNPLUGGED* was closer to the principles of Grotowski's 'poor theatre' than the influences of Robert Wilson that the company cites. However, the context of this production asks the spectators to 'see' that which is no longer there. Bleeker argues that the term 'spectator' does not account for how visuality 'takes place' from a holistic perspective. Bleeker instead prefers the term 'seer', as a 'seer is someone who sees things that are not there: future things, absent things. Seeing always involves projections, fantasies, desires and fears, and might be closer to hallucinating than we think' (Bleeker 2008: 18). The seers of *MISSING UNPLUGGED* were overtly conscious that the minimal aesthetics were not intended. This exposes itself in a number of self-referral moments. For instance, when the backwards shuffling of the performers scored by the sound design raises approving laughter from the auditorium, everyone is now aware that this action is a surrogate for the absent travelators – whether you had experienced the original production or not. The spacing of the production is, for the most part, adhered to. Performers enter and exit through predetermined slots on the stage floor, while the appearance of a café reveal located within a stage truck is signified through the assembly of a large wooden frame. The spatial politics and material realities of the original production are re-performed through a combination of performers' movements and gestures, all scored by the original sound design. As regards the question of scenography, what was striking about the staging of this production was that the material and spatial conditions of the original endured. Aesthetically changed and materially removed, yet an affinity between the material and technological aspects of the production was maintained. Even without a change in the lighting state, the sequencing of the surrogate frames and the descriptive qualities of the sound design exposed how the production's scenographic scheme was not unique to the physical structures that had been destroyed in the fire. While the set was gone, a scenography remained.

Gecko's re-staging of *MISSING* offers a case study on how the relationships between material and immaterial elements constitute a production's scenography. While *MISSING UNPLUGGED* is a distinct version of the production, it exposes how scenography exists as a series of interconnected relationships that occur between the various performance elements. For instance, with particular regard to the sound design of *MISSING UNPLUGGED*, the quickly constructed surrogates for the technological objects of the monitors and the travelators were activated by descriptive foley sounds. Whether the recording of a found noise or high-tempo musical interlude, the sound design orientated and contextualized the theatre events – a task that is shared with the dramaturgical remit of *mise en scène*. Notably, Svoboda employs *mise en scène* when describing his theatrical approach, but stresses that scenography extends beyond geopolitics: 'The goal of a designer, according to this premise, can no longer be a description or copy of actuality, but a creation of its multidimensional model' (in Burian 1974: 31). Or, as McKinney (2015: 80) suggests, *mise en scène* denotes the interpretation of place whereas scenography, following Svoboda, is concerned with experiential orientations of placeness: of how an assemblage of materials and textures affect a state of orientation. As evident within the implied relationship between the surrogate objects of *MISSING UNPLUGGED* and the descriptive (original) sound design, the two operate alongside and in relation to one another. They are complementary readings of an interwoven process of place orientation more broadly construed.

In offering a distinction between *mise en scène* and scenography, the aim is not to facilitate a hierarchy or to propose a division between the signs (semiotics) of performance and its encounter (phenomenology). Instead, the intention is to better reflect the agency of 'things' and the affective potential of staging. McKinney unpicks this further, as she notes that the act of theatre is an assemblage of constituent parts, observing that 'these are all encountered, cumulatively, as members of a larger assemblage which includes the spaces and structures that contain and support them (the scenography, the site) and includes, too, the audience' (McKinney 2015: 91). This understanding is exemplified in the original staging of *MISSING*. Throughout the production, monitors and internally lit frames were employed to isolate a character's head or body. When held in position, the performers' movements would become sporadic: jumping between études that scored the dramaturgical through-line of the production of being 'out of sync', of being disconnected. With clear aesthetic references to the now ubiquitous fragmented streamed video or the functionality of 'skipping' (video) time, these 'frames' were choreographed as lenses that reveal a character's internal position as well as isolating moments of disconnection and distance.

Within this combination of action and material, the design of the production exceeded the remit of setting or background to include the uses and experiential potential of objects. The performers' movements scored by a bespoke sound and lighting formed part of the scenography. The blocking, positioning and tempo of the performers' movements simultaneously emphasized and constituted an assemblage of designed encounters that bound the constituent elements of *MISSING* together as an affective atmosphere. Scenography, as with readings of choreography or dramaturgy, is not exclusive to one particular stage feature (whether bodies or the physical environment). In 1921, Appia describes a similar process in his articulation of how the elements of a production form a productive harmony, where the designed aspects are 'managed within the range of technical feasibility and all made to converge at a single moment, the time of performance!' (in Beacham 1993: 24). As with his contemporaries Craig and the director Vsevolod

Meyerhold (1874–1940), Appia stressed that the act of theatre only exists within an eventual moment. The individual components (text, music, light, set, etc.) are only 'complete' when framed as an experiential whole.

To argue for the wholeness of scenography is, however, problematic. The value of scenography is not in its completeness or a boundaried conception of stagecraft, but of how the inanimate and material aspects of theatre also perform as part of an assemblage. Hannah has argued this point on multiple occasions, pointing out that 'it is high time we do speak of how design elements not only actively extend the performing body, but also perform without and in spite of the human body' (Hannah and Mehzoud 2011: 103). Accordingly, this focus on the affective performance of materials signals the innate eventfulness of material encounter. With regard to the scenography of MISSING UNPLUGGED, in the original production a small 'machine' used a crank handle to suggest a direct control of the travelators by a performer. In the re-staged version, a surrogate for this machine had been quickly rendered from a table, a wooden stick and gaffer tape. In the event, as the 'handle' is turned, the gaffer tape promptly breaks and elicits a knowing nod from the performer, echoed by knowledgeable laughter within the auditorium. The material condition of this new machine had spoken; it had performed its transient status as a 'stand-in' for a carefully designed stage object. The crank revealed the properties of its constituent parts. This distinct codified object was overtly exposed as an assemblage of other objects, each with distinct characteristics. The hardness of the stick and the elasticity of the gaffer tape were revealed within the collapse of the 'whole'.

Interestingly, this example echoes Bennett's reading on the emergent properties of an assemblage, where 'The effects generated by an assemblage are, rather, emergent properties, emergent in that their ability to make something happen (a newly inflected materialism, a blackout, a hurricane, a war on terror) is distinct from the sum of the vital force of each materiality considered alone' (Bennett 2009 24). The 'crank machine' was an assemblage of a range of constituent parts that expanded to the sound design of the travelator, as well as the movement of the performers. Significantly, the 'vital force' of the crank machine exceeds the materiality of any one element. While the emergent properties are intrinsic to each act of theatrical assemblage, the idea that the assemblage of scenography makes something happen equally dissociates it from the logocentrisms of *mise en scène*. Notably, in many scenographic encounters the individual elements remain, for the most part, discernible and retain their 'thisness' within the wider rhythms of an assemblage. Costume remains discernible from sound, which in turn is discernible from light. Bennett confirms this when she argues that each member element denotes 'an energetic pulse slightly "off" from that of the assemblage, an assemblage is never a stolid block but an open-ended collective' (Bennett 2009: 24). While scenography is not ad hoc, the assemblage of the disparate elements does not deny a thisness of scenography. Rather, scenography is understood as an entity that exists as a relational web of associated elements that exceeds the material conditions of its individual components. Scenography is not the objects of theatre, but how assemblages of materiality are sequenced and encountered *as* staging.

In approaching place orientation as an affective assemblage, I do not preclude the spoken word from my understanding of scenography. While bound with the dramaturgical concerns of *mise en scène*, theatrical place orientation has often been sustained through a combination of blocking and language - in particular, the performative utterance of placing action. Burns suggests that, before Shakespeare, place in English-language theatre was 'seldom clearly defined and that it is often difficult to tell where an encounter is taking place' (Burns 1972: 74). Burns argues that Shakespeare promoted the use of language as a means of orienting the feeling or thematic implications of a place, as much as signposting a distinct geographic location. With regard to MISSING UNPLUGGED, before the performance began the plot of the stage was described. We, as the spectators, were guided around the 'back wall' of the stage now marked by white LX tape and how the original lighting had sustained a dark aesthetic – which was quite different from the orange-tinted wooden floor of the Queen Elizabeth Hall. This description of a stage geography, inclusive of its spatial proxemics and textures, would qualify how place was encountered during the event. While the symbolic meaning-making of spoken language is a discrete ontological framework, the qualifying affects of this linguistic placing were undeniably a feature of how the scenography's assemblage was encountered, acting as a qualifying agent alongside the sound design or the use of props. The performative act of language evoked and disciplined a spatial imaginary that situated *MISSING*'s staging through spoken text. Scenography as an assemblage is, therefore, inclusive of the place-orientating factors of language and voice.

The affective occurrence of scenography operates in a similar mode to that of choreography. Dance scholar Arabella Stanger furthers this position, noting that:

> [Choreography] gives a heightened sense of space being made by moving bodies because, during the process of choreography and the performance of the dance that arises from it (which may happen after or at the same time as the choreographic process), space is plotted, shaped, and felt into existence by the organization of a set of bodily actions.
>
> (Stanger 2014: 72)

Stanger's reading draws from Lefebvre's position that our understanding of 'space' is constituted from a bodily encounter of movement. Notably, Appia in 1921 also applies a similar conceptualization of 'space making', as he argues that the 'actor is a compass for space, a pendulum for time ... In this sense [the performer's] body creates space' (in Beacham 1994: 289). McKinney confirms this in her discussion of cognitive perception and the idea of 'affordances'. In particular, McKinney observes that 'the "offer" of affordances is made apparent through the way the perceiving body detects changes in the environment' (McKinney 2015: 81). While Stanger and Appia stress the significance of the performer's body, McKinney extends this to consider how a spectator's bodily perception is equally engaged by the affordances of scenography (as an assemblage):

> The aesthetic experience of scenography involves not only the embodied response of the viewer but the action that occurs between the body of the spectator and the objects and environments it encounters, stimulated by the particular material qualities of the scenography.
>
> (McKinney 2015: 82)

What is significant in these definitions and approaches is how scenographic environments are 'felt' or 'organized' by a conditioning that is not, in and of itself, rendered fully in any one constituent element. While the schemes for scenography and choreography are planned and developed beforehand, the enactment of these practices is crucial to how stage events are manifested *in time*.

As illustrated by Gecko's re-staging, the linguistic associations of set as 'rendered solid' are notably distinct from the temporality and eventfulness of scenography thus described. While not writing in English, Appia offers an equivalent method for denoting the physical structure of a stage environment that exceeds the linguistic associations of set. Appia suggests in 1899 that the term 'terrain' may better account for this reactive qualities of a scenography's physical properties, arguing that 'by terrain I do not mean merely the part of the stage walked upon by the actor, but rather everything composing the setting that relates to the physical form of the performer and [his or her] actions' (in Beacham 1993: 49). The terrain of *MISSING*, its material conditions and place-orientating agents, remained within the re-staged version. As outlined by Appia, scenography as a shaping of terrain is inclusive of an overall atmosphere or felt environment. The experiential qualities of this terrain thereby feed another understanding of assemblage located *within* the affective atmosphere of scenography. In positioning scenography as an event, this confirms its complementary status alongside the established English-language stage lexicon. Whereas 'set design' relates to the objects of theatre, 'scenography' denotes how theatrical materialities are encountered and conceived *in time*: how the assemblage of theatrical design affects performer/spectator behaviours and how these behaviours in turn effect the assemblage of scenography. When viewed as an affective conditioning of stage material, scenography as assemblage exceeds the strict convention of scenery and evokes the affective qualities of materiality. Scenography stresses how assemblages of theatrical design practices sustain the immaterial and affective qualities of place orientation.

There are no stages without scenographics.

CHAPTER 5

Scenographic worlding

'Bunny Christie doesn't design stage sets. She creates worlds' (Jays 2017). Journalist David Jays' assessment of designer Christie's collaborations on productions such as *The Curious Incident of the Dog in the Night-Time* (2013) evokes a familiar – if critically unexamined – trope within contemporary scenographic practice: that scenography evokes a sense of 'worlding'. Heidegger introduces the notion of worlding in *Being and Time* (1927) and further refines this as part of this thesis on *The Thing* (1971): 'The world presences by worlding. That means: the world's worlding cannot be explained by anything else nor can it be fathomed through anything else' (Heidegger 1971b: 177). While stressing that the irreducibility of worlding is central to its conception and reception, Heidegger notes that this irreducibility stems from the ongoing task of worlding – in that it has no end. Stewart expands upon Heidegger's approach to define worlding as 'an intimate, compositional process of dwelling in spaces that bears, gestures, gestates, worlds' (Stewart 2011: 445). Worlding as a means of conceptualizing how orders of world are negotiated in daily life, leads Stewart to ask:

> What might we do with the proliferation of little worlds of all kinds that form up around conditions, practices, manias, pacings, scenes of absorption, styles of living, forms of attachment (or detachment), identities, and imaginaries, or some publicly circulating strategy for self-transformation?
> (Stewart 2011: 446)

The notion of a scene is adopted by Stewart to isolate how the 'sense of something happening becomes tactile' (Stewart 2011: 445). In this regard, the notion that Christie's scenographic practice 'creates worlds' is, I argue, a statement on the potential of scenographics to score felt situations of worlding that, in turn, reveals how thresholds of world are constituted and navigated. This is related yet distinct from the capacity to conceive or enact speculative worlds.

In *Heterocosmica: Fiction and Possible Worlds* (1998), Lubomír Doležel argues that the 'universe of possible worlds is constantly expanding and diversifying thanks to the incessant world-constructing activity of human minds and hands' (Doležel 1998: ix). With a focus on the 'world-building' evident within the literary narratives of *Robinson Crusoe* (1719) or the work of Franz Kafka (1883–1924), Doležel proposes that any 'actual world is surrounded by an infinity of other possible worlds' (Doležel 1998: 13). I propose that 'scenographic worlding' focuses on how the place orientations of scenographics can be deployed to affirm the material potential of speculative worlds. Scenographics are not, however, ontologically speculative. While Doležel notes that fictional (human-conceived) worlds are always radically indeterminate due to the impossibility of humans conceiving a universe in its entirety, scenographics are encountered in the same manner as a land border. This follows the position that scenographics are interventional acts of orientation that complicate, reveal or score processes of worlding. As with performatives, scenographics do not qualify an event as any more or less real than other worlding strategies such as cartography or psychogeography. Scenographics only 'create' worlds insomuch that they score how worlds are conceptualized as affective atmospheres and, in their very 'witness', condition human experience.

The notion that scenographic orientations are predicated on withness, of *being with*, is crucial to the overall argument of this chapter. The witness of scenographics stresses that to be orientated by a crafted atmosphere is to recognize how human and non-human agents are rendered complicit to, and active within, the assemblage of environments or atmospheres. Yet, notions of 'stage' and 'scene' have often been conceptualized under different terms that demarcate and position these attentive situations as distant or removed. Theatre historian David Wiles argues that the high walls and canopies of the Roman theatres insulated the 'festive or tragic world of the play from the natural world and from everyday life' (Wiles 2003: 40). Over time, this insulation cultivated the potential for 'stage worlds' to be emancipated from normative aesthetic and temporal conventions, while also situating these worlds as Other and ontologically removed from the 'realities' of life. However, stages also operate as attentive sites, as with the staging of political debate, that afford focus and render actions as conspicuous or attentive. Subsequently, stages arguably operate as perceptual borders that take place at the threshold between orders of world.

Unlike the essentialist readings of Heidegger, who positions 'the world' as the receptacle for all becoming, Stewart (2007, 2011, 2014) implies that multiple worlds are encountered as part of daily life. From the 'Natural World' to 'Disney World', the 'Anglophone World' or the 'Third World', the notion of a 'world' operates as conceptual threshold that orientates a feeling of scale and belonging. Worlds are also highly personal, as with the 'dreamworld' or a 'worldview', and can demarcate a state of being or perspective. World concepts orientate how ontologies of experience are disciplined that can privilege the assigned labours of the 'real world' above the speculations of 'fictive worlds'. Operating at the threshold of the politically real and the contrived, stages have come to conceptualize human-centric enactments of worldly phenomena that denote how experience is partitioned *in terms of world*. Consequently, the concepts of stage and scene (stage-scenes) isolate how worlding occurs as an ongoing negotiation of thresholds, whether framed as fictional or real, that scores and orientates situational experience.

I approach the attentiveness of a stage-scene as a consequence of a scenographic othering that irritates the disciplined normativity of human worldings. Böhme evokes Adorno's definition of art to argue how atmospheres operate as potential scenes, where 'atmospheres are something like the aesthetic quality of a scene or a view, the "something more" that Adorno refers to in somewhat oracular terms in order to distinguish a work of art from a mere "piece of work"' (Böhme 2013: 2). Böhme suggests that the ontological indeterminacy of atmosphere does not exclude it from the totalizing qualities of a scene as attentive.

> The reason is primarily that atmospheres are totalities: atmospheres imbue everything, they tinge the whole of the world or a view, they bathe everything in a certain light, unify a diversity of impressions in a single emotive state. And yet one cannot actually speak of 'the whole', still less of the whole of the world; speech is analytical and must confine itself to particulars.
>
> (Böhme 2013: 2)

The notion that an atmosphere can 'tinge the whole of the world or a view' is, I argue, a quality that equally relates to stage-scenes as worlding irritants. This same interventional quality is evident within the enactment of a stage. Wiles (2003) argues that stages are conceptualized in relation to ritual practices that position the physical place of a stage as beyond world, as a 'plateau'. Accordingly, in this chapter I review how situational encounters with stages isolate how worlds are crafted in relation to material assemblages *and* felt ideologies. Likewise, I argue that the mutual interchange and co-relationships between scenes and stages are paramount to any discussion on scenography. Stage-scenes operate as worlding hypertrophies that manifest from the thresholds that demarcate the porous boundaries of perceptual worlds, inheriting certain qualities and transgressing others. While a stage-scene will always host a nexus of worlds within any perceived or disciplined boundary, I propose that stage-scenes isolate a particular feeling of worlding that renders this process attentive or at least discernible. I conclude this chapter by outlining the theoretical and practical implications of a stage-scene as a hybrid concept along with the affective qualities of a 'scenographic scene' and quantification enacted by a 'dramaturgical scene'. To reconsider the symbiotic relationship between notions of stage and scenography, I begin by isolating the situational circumstances of 'stage geography'.

Stage geographies

If, following David Harvey (1993), 'geography' conflates the felt qualities of landscape with ideological systems of power, stage geographies enact a re-ordering (or othering) of place that scores how geographies are constructed and assigned meaning (power). The notion that stage geographies sustain a potential for power – from situational attentiveness to the enactment of social hierarchies – is evident in Schechner's argument that the principal convention to have endured from the ancient Greek theatre is that 'a "special place" is marked off within the theatre for the performance' (Schechner 1968: 48). Equally, art critic Thomas McEvilley argues that from the ritual practices of the Palaeolithic period distinct theological geographies – places charged with theology that renders them a point of contact between a distant 'heaven' and an immediate 'earth' – have sustained a 'specially segregated space [as a] kind of non-space, ultra-space, or ideal space where the surrounding matrix of space-time is symbolically annulled' (McEvilley 1986: 8). The 'ultra-space', for McEvilley, is the 'construction of a supposedly unchanging space' as a 'space where the effects of change are deliberately disguised and hidden' (McEvilley 1986: 9). The notion of an ultra-space aligns with Foucault's 'heterotopias' as counter-sites that are 'outside of all places, even though it may be possible to indicate their location in reality' (Foucault 1986: 24). As evident within the Ancient Greek and Roman cultures, theatre has typically been cited as one of these ultra-spaces where citizens engaged with theological ideas and practices (as exemplified by the festival of Dionysus and its conclusion at the *theatron* in Athens). Curator Bridget Crone argues that stages in contemporary art practices are a 'highly visible site of encounter' (Crone 2013: 208). Equally, fellow curator Jean-Paul Martinon cites how a stage in curatorial practice is distinct from theatre, where 'a stage is usually a raised floor or platform' (Martinon 2013: 11). For Martinon the curatorial stage 'expands beyond all recognition, taking in buildings, sites, geographical areas and event, in some cases, countries' (Martinon 2013: 11). While inadvertently confirming an archetype of theatre before cinema (theatre stages are a raised platform), Martinon contends that stages mark the 'co-appearance of subjects, objects, architectures, communities and worlds and with it, the formation of a polis' (Martinon 2013: 11). In this instance, Martinon is equating the event of public appearance with the stage in order to signal a collapse of these concepts in the manner of the Theatrum Mundi.

Gay McAuley argues that theatre 'consists of human beings *in a defined space* watched by other human beings' (McAuley 1999: 245; emphasis in original). The Theatrum Mundi concept and the general conception of world as stage sustain a potentially utopian notion of 'defined space'. This reading invites the counter-intuitive supposition that stages are either a symptom of worlding orientations or that the idea of 'the world' (as defined by humans) is a symptom of stage. Whether applied to immediate physical markers or the imagined community of a nation, the idea of 'stage' is evidently related to how worlding, or the demarcation of sequential worldly thresholds, are understood both conceptually and experientially. The ability for a stage to apply to a finite square in a room as well as the scale of 'the world' denotes a paradox central to its attraction. A stage is totalizing, all-encompassing.

The stage concept represents a human desire to position world as singular, as a unit, which can then be studied and understood. In reducing the complexities and multiplicities of the 'world' concept to stage, this is to reduce worlding to a human scale. No one individual can ever know a country (the people, the places, the materials, the earth, etc.). As Benedict Anderson (1991) has argued, countries are imagined communities reinforced by the secondspaces of maps and linguistic disciplining. The concept of 'place', much like a stage, is subject to the same totalizing traits of human worlding. Tuan argues that, at 'one extreme a favorite armchair is a place, at the other extreme the whole earth' (Tuan 1977: 149). Whether literally on a finite perspective stage or metaphysically through world as stage, the stage concept provides a means of reducing the complexities of worlding to a point of attentive action. This conceit, that to know the world is to reduce it to a point of action, has long been the concern of theatre. Therefore, what connects Schechner's 'special place' with McEvilley's 'ultra-space' is the charged potentiality for action that comes with the attentive power of stage geographies. This 'power geography' sustains a distinct affective assemblage that irritates normative experiences of worlding that would otherwise recede into everyday landscapes. Stage geographies irritate the ongoing practice of worlding as charged places that sustain a distinct potentiality – a potential for drama.

I am touring Vatican City with a group of friends and colleagues in early January. As we begin our walk out of the precinct and into Rome, we approach a large wooden hut positioned on the white stone of the Vatican mall. The texture and material of the hut is evidently out of sync with the overall architectural scheme. This hut intervenes and disrupts the normative rhythms of this place. As we get closer, it becomes apparent that the hut opens out at what is evidently the front. Inside the open wooden structure is a collection of 'life-size' mannequins and stable objects. There is a red rope barrier between the structure and a number of tourists taking pictures with camera phones. The dramaturgical 'scene' presented within this hut is that of a Christian nativity. The mannequins are positioned towards a figurine of a baby in a cradle. While I recognize the learned cultural signifiers of this practice from my own childhood, the dark-brown wooden structure against the white stone of the Vatican presents a distinct orientation for how I interact with this installation. This structure is evidently Other, a worlding irritant. It is an event and merits attention. Consequently, the placement of this structure and its material features has rendered this area as 'special', demarcating it from the wider landscape of the geographies beyond. The distinct arrangement of this assemblage has orientated my attention towards an area that would otherwise be part of the general flow of the architectural precinct. Importantly, I note that this intervention has been crafted without a formal stage. The structure of the hut and its interventional qualities has rendered the area of this structure a 'stage'. The nativity scene is a scenographic assemblage. I realize that the methods of scenography have formed and shaped this stage-scene into being. Once the structures of the hut and the mannequins are removed, this place will no longer be discernible as a discrete stage. The scenographic qualities of this event have rendered this stage as knowable. Without scenographics there would be no stage, no scene.

The example of the Vatican City nativity scene isolates how stages are crafted through scenographics. The orientating methods of scenographics are what irritate the wider situated geographies in which a stage intervenes. Yet, the nativity scene is not a 'new' world. It remains bound to the situated geographies and wider worldings from which it emerged. The nativity scene does, however, draw attention to the perceptual thresholds that score ongoing negotiations of worlding. The stage-scene is encountered as a situational rupture that, in turn, highlights the normative architectural flows of the Vatican mall: it is attentive only in relationship to the perception that its placement and materiality is temporary and eventful, as well as speculative and representational.

To return to Jays' (2017) statement that Christie 'creates worlds', the notion of scenographic worlding is seemingly tied to an investigation of how stage geographies become manifest as perceptual worlds. Beyond the learned semantic concepts of 'sky' and 'earth', 'nature' and 'universe', Nancy argues that worlds are felt constructions that evoke the Greek concept of *techne*, of bringing forth.

> *World* is the name of a gathering or being-together that arises from an *art – tekne –* and the sense of which is identical with the very exercise of this at (as when one speaks of the 'world' of an artist, but also of 'the world of the elite [*grand monde*]'). It is thus that a world is always a 'creation': a *tekne* with neither principle nor end nor material other than itself.
>
> (Nancy 1997: 41)

Gaston Bachelard (1994) equally points out that worlding occurs in relation to questions of scale and attentiveness. As a critique of Heidegger, Bachelard argues that such formulas as 'being-in-the-world and world-being are too majestic for me and I do not succeed in experiencing them. In fact, I feel more at home in miniature worlds, which, for me, are dominated worlds' (Bachelard 1994: 161). Bachelard observes how worldings can go unseen, as with the microscopic, or are so vast to render them unavoidable. Worlding recognizes the enduring concession of worldly thresholds that become manifest, albeit fleetingly, in relation to other worlds already transgressed and the worlds that lie ahead. Moreover, a definitive world (as universe) that encompasses all life and material can only be understood by humans through abstraction. While Graham Harman (2016) has contested this position, arguing that it is human-centric and privileges worldly subjectivities, I argue that the stage concept is a symptom of how humans (as discrete from non-human agents) conceptualize worldly encounter. The attentive situation of a stage seeks to confirm world as only being observable in pieces, in slices.

In *Dramaturgy and Architecture* (2015), Turner argues that to 'consider dramaturgy as architectural is also to consider it as a project upon the world, as world-building, socially as well as aesthetically' (2015: 5). Turner's position on the architectural potential of dramaturgy elaborates on Lehmann's suggestion that the postdramatic is representative of 'a new kind of architecture – an architecture of theatre' (Lehmann 1997: 56). Crucially, Turner collapses the orientating qualities of scenographics into the wider architectural structure of dramaturgy. This position seeks to isolate how the dramaturgical world-building – of sequencing and interpretation – affords experiences that sustain discrete feelings of worlding. This same intention is evident in notions of immersive theatre. Josephine Machon articulates how immersive theatres isolate the potential to craft worlding orientations where 'the feeling of being submerged in another medium – as with immersion in water – is established from the outside. The world operates both within and outside the timeframe, rules and relationship of the "everyday" world' (Machon 2012: 93). While 'the world' is conceived in terms of the dramaturgy's architectural wholeness, Machon implies the potential for scenographics (as the theatre environment itself) to sustain the 'in-its-own-worldness' as an 'artistic intention as well as a strangely elusive charm' (2012: 93) is intrinsic to immersive experience.

Appia equally argued that performers needed to exist within the temporal and material circumstances of a stage-scene if theatre was to achieve a harmonious *Gesamtkunstwerk*. The predominant agent in this unification was, for Appia, the living qualities of performers rather than the 'space' itself. Appia's notion of a 'living art' was predicated on the idea that scenography was rendered attentive by the lived encounter sustained by the interactions of the human *with* the non-human. The overall aim of the living art was to collapse the representational borders between viewing and, in doing so, Appia anticipated the dramaturgical and scenographic perspectives that have shaped the emergence of immersive art practices in the late twentieth and early twenty-first centuries. Yet, it is the capacity of scenography to render place eventful that situates this practice particular and peculiar. If stages geographies are places of potential action *and* enacted power, then scenographics are arguably the agents that render places as attentive and extra-daily.

The charged potentiality of stage geography is not, I propose, a negation of a stage's placeness. In the same manner that a bus stop is a place, a supermarket is a place, or a festival is a place, a stage is a place because it is situated. Stage-scenes are always enacted as part of wider ecology of material circumstances, albeit potentially only fleetingly. While the institutional theatre building is politically understood as a place (it is listed on the secondspace of a map), the stage concept has been framed as resisting a claim to placeness. The notion of a 'stage space' denotes this tension. The phrasing positions stages as being open to many and multiple places. Artistically, it also implies a focus on the volume of an environment that is divorced from the socio-political politics of its immediate geographies. This reading is evident in Oskar Schlemmer's (1926) usage of *Raumempfindung* ('felt volume') when describing his experiments into theatrical composition at the Bauhaus. A stage space evokes a reading akin to McEvilley's ultra-spaces, as a place that exceeds material geographies of the real. Stages have, subsequently, been described as spaces that transgress their situated place. Nevertheless, a renewed critical vocabulary of scenography as place orientation invites a critique on the centrality of stages as the medium through which theatre transgresses a prescribed politics of place. Schechner (1988) implies this approach when describing a 'theater place' as a condition of humanity, where a

> theater is a place whose only or main use is to stage or enact performances. It is my belief that this kind of space, a theater place, did not arrive late in human cultures (say with the Greeks of the fifth

century BCE) but was there from the beginning – is itself one of the characteristics of our species.

(Schechner 1988: 148–9)

Schechner continues to argue that the

> transformation of space into place means to construct a theater; this transformation is accomplished by 'writing on the space,' as the cave art of the Palaeolithic period demonstrates so well. This writing need not be visual, it can be oral as with the Aborigines.
> (Schechner 1988: 148–9)

The suggestion here is that stages are 'written' into being. Stages do not precede action; stages are rendered attentive through intervention.

While origin claims are often unproductive, I contend that Schechner's reading of how stage places are 'written' or crafted implies how the orientating traits of worlding thresholds are scored through scenographics. My understanding of a 'stage place', influenced by Massey, does not dictate that its geographic location, its situation, is ideologically fixed or reductive. A place can be transitional, open or unfamiliar. Schechner's depiction of how a stage is rendered eventual – through a 'writing of space' – echoes my argument on scenography as the crafting of place orientation. Scenography amounts to the methods through which a stage is wrought and rendered spatially and materially attentive – in other words, staging. In discussing a stage in terms of place, I argue that this exposes the underlying relationship between scenography and its material circumstances that encompasses the mechanics of a West End show to the encounter of a site specific performance installation. Stages enact and score a spatial ideology that defines and segments place through demarcation. Accordingly, scenography is an interventional crafting that irritates normative spatial ideologies and render stages as affective and knowable. There are no artistic stages without scenography.

Scenographic worlding is a strategy for negotiating the perceptual thresholds and ideological frameworks that orientate, govern, and regulate the potential for attentive action. Heidegger argues that a 'boundary is not that at which something stops but, as the Greeks recognized, the boundary is that from which *something begins its presenting*' (in Soja 1996: 142). The worlding irritant of a stage stresses that 'something is happening', something is becoming. Similarly, McCormack's application of the refrain to the study of moving bodies articulates how an affective atmosphere presents a feeling of worlding, of being *within or besides something*:

> Refrains have a territorializing function: that is, they draw out and draw together blocks of space-time from the chaos of the world, generating a certain expressive consistency through the repetition of practices, techniques, and habits. These territories are not necessarily demarcated or delineated, however: they can be affective complexes, 'hazy, atmospheric,' but sensed nevertheless, as intensities of feeling in and through the movement of bodies.
> (McCormack 2013: 7)

The 'intensities of feeling' that McCormack describes as a symptom of a refrain is equally a quality of a stage or scene, in that they craft a feeling of attentiveness that is discrete, yet potentially porous at the sometime. However, the geographic porousness of stage-scenes is often overwritten by ideologies that position the stage as a *tabula rasa*, a 'blank slate'. Yet, these same ideologies had been foundational to the New Stagecraft that sought to overcome the verisimilitude of theatrical realism. The stage as a void operated a mechanism for exceeding the representational and embracing the atmospheric potentials of a holistic scenography. Nevertheless, the critical positioning of stage as discrete from world has, I argue, nullified the formative role of scenography to theatre-making and restricted its interdisciplinary uptake. Scenographics are the potentialities for change and multiple possibilities that remain latent within any crafted atmosphere. Stage ideologies are the manner in which these potentials are regulated and apportioned as fictive, illusory, and beyond world.

Stage ideologies

From Craig and Appia, to Schlemmer and Svoboda, modernist artists viewed the stage as a means of transcending the geographic and material circumstances of a lived encounter. In 1991, Svoboda captures the allure of the stage as a timeless void:

> When I sit alone in a theatre and gaze into the dark space of its empty stage, I'm frequently seized by

fear that this time I won't manage to penetrate it, and I always hope that this fear will never desert me. Without an unending search for the key to the secret of creativity, there is no creation. It's necessary always to begin again. And that is beautiful.

(cited in Burian 2002: 123)

In the twentieth century, the idea of a stage as a dark void that exists beyond the timespace logic of its own architectural geography is notably different to how the notion of stage has been understood throughout history. The notion of a stage as a neutral or empty place emerges with the usage of 'plateau' in medieval Cornish theatres. Glynne Wickham states that *platea* in Latin 'means simply "the place", no more, no less' (1974: 36). The plateau in Cornish theatre was a site where stories where enacted, typically configured in the round with scaffold structures from which speeches were delivered. Richard Southern (1957) argues that performers and spectators would have inhabited a plateau together, with performers moving down from the scaffolds to interact with other performers or to re-orientate the spectator's focus. Wickham equates the concept of the plateau with the contemporary usage of 'acting-area', which is functional above all else. Butterworth (2005) suggests that the stage of the English Playhouse imported this convention of the stage as plateau, yet with the usage of a raised platform also sought to partition the stage from the place of the spectators. 'Plateau' is also used to describe a levelled ground at a high attitude, with the term *plat* meaning 'level' in Old French. Deleuze and Guattari apply the plateau concept as a means of navigating the nomadic impulses of contemporary philosophy. Whether in terms of a levelling clear of distractions that sustains nomadic thought, or the raising (literally with the English Playhouse) of stage beyond placeness, there is an idea of a plateau as that which is beyond the situation of its immediate geography – free of the socio-political ideologies typically attributed to place. In the case of the plateau as a 'high level', a plateau is geographically and metaphysically beyond the messiness of human life. This positioning of a stage as beyond echoes the theological framing of ultra-spaces as a meeting point between a higher plane of existence and a reality of earth – of beyond world.

The ideology of an empty stage sustains a contemporary variation on ultra-spaces that have been symbolically annulled. Stripped of a distinct theological dogma, the empty stage concept presents a platform that elevates the situation of theatre beyond the messiness of lived geographies. High modernism appropriated these ideals as emptiness and neutrality, arguing that the most suitable environment from which a work of art might emerge is the *tabula rasa* ('blank slate'). Lefebvre accounts for how modernist architects 'offered – as an *ideology in action* – an empty space, a space that is primordial, a container ready to receive fragmentary contents, a *neutral* medium into which disjointed things, people and habitats might be introduced' (in Wiles 2003: 265; emphasis in original). Likewise, O'Doherty argues that the white cube of the art gallery is seen as a

> ghetto space, a survival compound, a proto-museum with a direct line to the timeless, a set of conditions, an attitude, a place deprived of location, a reflex to the bald curtain wall, a magic chamber, a concentration of mind, maybe a mistake.
>
> (O'Doherty 1986: 80)

Consequently, the neutrality of an empty stage is predicated on a learned historicism that is counter to the often miscited work of Brook and his manifesto on *The Empty Space* (1968). Hannah has argued this persuasively, noting that

> Brook's demand was not for a modernist *tabula rasa* in which architecture and its history are obliterated ... Instead, his *Empty Space* challenged us to regard any space (with its intrinsic character) not only as a site for performance, but also as a performer in waiting.
>
> (Hannah 2008: 42)

Brook's preferred theatre at the Bouffes du Nord (1974) in Paris, with its 'found' architectural status and scarred walls, is representative of Hannah's position. Brook's stage place at the Bouffes du Nord is evidently filled with memory and detail. The scarred walls of this old Parisian music hall echo Brook's philosophy that a theatre is a site of storytelling, of memory. Indeed, Brook's first line of his manifesto offers an alternative that is less ideological, where a 'bare stage' is prepared for shaping and open to renewed possibilities. An 'empty stage' is impossible. Beyond the disciplined conventions of symbolic annulment, stage-scenes can never be empty. Stage-scenes are always situated.

Stage ideologies remain ever-present within contemporary theatre-making. The postdramatic black box studio aims for a return to Grotowski's (1968) call for the theatre as a sacred or ultra-space. After Appia and Craig, along with Artaud and Brook, the whole studio was approached as a potential stage. As evident in *The Constant Prince* (1965), Grotowski's darkened walls and floor signal an attempt to further this claim by neutralizing the lived experience of theatre as a situated place. The white cube of the art gallery draws influence from the whitewashing of the Protestant churches as outlined by Michael O'Connell (cited in Greenblatt 1980). However, the black box studio remains distinct in that, while the white walls of the Church aimed to reflect back only a 'pure self', the intention of the black box is to reflect nothing, to allow the ritual of drama to emerge from a performed nothingness, from the modernist notion of the stage as void. Unlike the whitewashed church as a civic beacon that draws attention, the black box attempts to recede from its immediate socio-political geographies. The black box situates itself as an anywhere place, in the manner of a plateau: it is not geographically bound, but transcends the physical immediacy of the building, town or country in which it is located. This is, however, a utopian aim. The black box never recedes. It remains. Located in the time and space in which it occupies. A black box is not neutral in the same way that the white cube of the gallery is not neutral. All are loaded with a spatial imaginary that has been practiced and assigned. These are places of art, of action, of drama. The timeless void is a utopian preoccupation of the modernist project, whether rendered as a blank canvas or an 'empty space'. All are impossible. While the experimentations and practices that strived towards these aims were highly productive, the black box and its associated environments rely on a convention of spectatorship and making that – particularly when compared against previous environments and methods – denies the material circumstances of a stage place. No stage-scene is neutral.

While originally positioned as a rejection of theatrical orthodoxies, the liberating context of the black box studio has settled into a stable sign of theatre. Now arguably as loaded a theatrical environment as the proscenium against which it rebelled, Wiles laments the loss of the black box's original attraction:

> I search through my own memories in an effort to recall the sense of liberation that those spaces once generated in me and my generation. Today the illusion of flexibility has gone. The insistent rectilinearity of walls and of units positioned according to the dictates of the safety officer, the fixed position of the control box and the glowing green exit signs impose their iron discipline.
>
> (Wiles 2003: 255)

Whereas once the black box had heralded a new age of theatrical experimentation for practitioners and spectators alike, it now sits within the context of contemporary theatre-making – situated within its wider socio-political geographies as the Roman *scaenae frons* was before it. Questions of theology are replaced with the economics of responsibility and litigation that direct neo-liberal politics. Moreover, the situation of a black-walled cuboid environment takes on its own systems of representation and restriction. The black box now re-appears as a tool, an environment that has qualities, that sustains its own ideologies in a similar manner to the proscenium. While it retains the possibility of reconfiguration, this is all too often constrained and mannered. But, most significantly, the black box is seen for what it is: it no longer recedes into an imagined void, but reasserts itself as a site of potentiality. Yet, lest we forget that the material experience of a black box is crafted through means of scenography. Explicitly, the colour and texture of a studio's painted walls is a distinctive agent within a scenographic assemblage. While the colour recedes into normativity, given its sustained relationship with the studio architecture, painting the walls black is a means of place orientation and is, therefore, scenographic.

Scenography beyond stages?

To question the determinist assumption that stages precede scenography is to question a wider underlying symbiosis between stage and scenography. This symbiosis was arguably evident within the tagline for the Prague Quadrennial 2011 (PQ 2011): 'At the still point of the turning world ...'. T. S. Eliot first penned this phrase for the poem *Burnt Norton*, written in 1935, which would later feature as part of the collection *The Four Quartets* (1943). The second passage within Eliot's poem begins with the idiom in question, which figures a range of 'in between' places that exist in our shared global cultures that fall under a number of theoretical positions: whether Foucault's 'heterotopias' or Turner's 'liminoid spaces'. What was self-evident in the selection of Eliot's passage, by Lotker and the PQ team, was the connotation of the still point as an allegory for the timeless ideology of stage as beyond world. Aronson, however, points to the seeming absence of what might be described as a 'stage' in the work presented at PQ2011:

> If set design is understood as the transformation of a stage by material scenery, and if a stage is understood as a designated space that is literally or metaphorically framed within a theatre of some sort, then design – and the stage – was surprisingly absent.
>
> (Aronson 2012: 86)

Given a historical symbiosis between scenography and stage, Aronson implies that a 'post-scenographic theatre' is counter to the spatial and aesthetic methods that theatre-makers have refined since ancient times. Aronson's observations bind scenography to a finite and defined stage.

Whereas Aronson uses the term 'post-scenographic', I contest that what is really under discussion is a provocation for a 'post-stage' scenography. Aronson cites Gob Squad's mixed reality staging for *You're Never Had It So Good* (2011) as an exemplar of a potential post-stage scenography. Gob Squad's performance began with a tour backstage to meet three actors in front of three fixed-position video cameras. The spectators were then led into a theatre auditorium. On a stage, three projection screens displayed (assumed) live feeds of the three backstage locations. The spectators were not invited to return back to these, now projected, locations. Aronson asks, 'where was the performance? Did it exist on the screen? In the space behind the screen? Could the audience even be sure that what they were seeing was not, at least in part, pre-recorded?' (Aronson 2012: 93). The mixed reality methods of Gob Squad, for Aronson, supersede the classical finite stage as a centring principle of scenography. Hans Peter Schwarz relates this fragmenting of spacetime orthodoxies to the critical renewal of scenography: 'Attempts to imagine a new space–time continuum through innovations in media technology ... constitute the system of coordinates underlying the notion of a new scenography' (Schwarz 2011: xv). Similarly, Aronson concludes by stating that scenography 'is no longer defined by the architecture of the theatre or the confines of the stage or the conventional relationship of the spectator and the performer, or the performer to the design' (Aronson 2012: 87). Aronson declares this trend as being symptomatic of the 'dematerialization of the stage' (Aronson 2012: 88).

Aronson's summary of his experiences at the PQ2011 borrows from art critics Lucy Lippard and John Chandler's critique on the dematerialization of art. Like Lippard and Chandler before him, Aronson proposes that the fragmentation of the stage and the breakup of traditional media has provoked a new 'world perspective' that is equally fragmented and resistant to established art forms. The dematerialization of the stage is, for Aronson, a symptom of a mediatized worlding that regularly transcends the old geographies of fixed points and national borders. 'The stage can be understood only if it relates to the spatial and imagistic codes of its society', Aronson concludes.

> And ours is a multitasking society, a culture of the instantaneous, the temporary, the fragmented, the polyvalent, the intangible and ephemeral, the distant and the near. A stage that depicts solidity, linearity, and continuity – in other words, coherence – is not merely a false depiction of the current world, it may be unreadable to a contemporary audience.
>
> (Aronson 2012: 88)

Prior to the practices evident at PQ2011, Hannah and Harsløf position performance design as a symptom of scenography's desire to leave 'the confines of the stage' (Hannah and Harsløf 2008: 12). Aronson's critique on the scenographic qualities of mediated practice is long-standing, arguing that 'projected scenery, and especially film and video, does not work – does not function – on the stage' (Aronson 2005: 86). While noting that there are rare exceptions where the fragmentary experience of intermedia is interwoven within a dramaturgy of place orientation (such as The Wooster Group's focus on adaptation), Aronson's overall argument is that 'such projections and images draw upon a fundamentally different vocabulary from that of the stage; it is not a scenographic vocabulary' (Aronson 2005: 87). Aronson's critique of Gob Squad is potentially more explicitly evident within the mixed reality performances of Blast Theory, particularly *I'd Hide You* (2011).

I am sitting at my computer in 2011 in Liverpool. I log on to a website. I am asked to select a runner who I will then assist in a game of hide and seek. There are multiple runners, each with a video that describes their strategy to winning and their useful attributes (fast runner, quiet, tactical). The game starts. I am presented with a view from the runner's headcam. As they transverse the streets of Manchester, I can see a map with the other runners' location in the corner. The aim is to guide my selected runner using text updates to another runner's location and, upon discovery, click my mouse to earn points. My experience of place orientation is one that is mediated by the webcam feed of my selected runner. I recognize certain areas of the city streets that the runner passes through. They stop and talk to a group of individuals at a streetside bar. While the prominent headgear of the runner is the first point of conversation, the group promptly offers advice on the location of another runner seen earlier. An orientation of place is sustained through the visual and rhetorical references encountered by the runner, along with my own bodily awareness of sitting at my office desk. I am orientated by the relationship between the video stream of the city streets and its graphical representation on the aligned map. While I am sat in my office chair in Liverpool, I am also situated as part of the action in Manchester. My experience of I'd Hide You *is as a gamer and a spectator. The oscillation between these ascribed roles is at times jarring, and at another moments indistinguishable. There are no identifiable representational places that I might otherwise describe as a stage, but there are methods of place orientation in play. I ask myself, 'Is this scenography without a stage?'*

The work of the British mixed reality performance company Blast Theory resists established definitions of a singular finite stage. Instead, there may be multiple sites of action played out in multiple locations. Following Aronson's position on scenography, to describe the networked event of *I'd Hide You* in terms of a stage, or even stages, evokes a potentially analogous relationship. Steve Dixon offers a useful counterargument to Aronson, arguing that 'many theater artists juxtapose live performance and projected media more to excite visceral, subjective, or subconscious audience responses than objective and conscious ones: to appeal to the senses and the nervous system' (Dixon 2008: 336). Dixon's position builds upon the 'haptic visuality' of Marks (2000) and the argument that screen images exist in the timespace of a haptic encounter. Rather than purely an exercise in semiotic interpretation, Marks argues that screen images evoke haptic responses and are spatialized within the moment of reception (with body-to-screen relationships being haptically akin to body-to-stage). Equally, Dixon cites Roberts Blossom, arguing that recorded media on a theatre stage renders time 'as a spatial element' (in Dixon 2008: 336), where recorded media presents a malleability of time that is distinct from the linear time of theatre as lived event. This also echoes Auslander's (2008) argument on the proxy concept of liveness as being a product of pre-recorded media. Indeed, Auslander outlines how liveness is a response to pre-recorded media's ability to isolate time from space, where the two are not necessarily synchronic.

Counter to the space–time ruptures of recorded media, Aronson stresses that theatre is a real-time lived encounter that, given his argument on dematerialization, is predicated on a stage as the locus for place orientation. If scenography is the agent for how stages are crafted (rather than the other way around), this reversal invites an understanding of 'stage' that is arguably inclusive of Blast Theory mixed reality assemblages. Gabriella Giannachi and Steve Benford isolate how the folding of places within mixed reality performance sustains a 'kind of hybrid space' (Giannachi and Benford 2011: 44). A hybrid space of mixed reality echoes Stephen Perrella's argument that the virtual is not another dimension, but 'has folded itself *into* the world' (Perrella 1999: 46; emphasis in original). Deleuze has argued the fold as a method of theorizing how the inbetweenness of spaces sustain dialectical oppositions. The fold sustains an innate tension where oppositional worlds are always in a state of negotiation. A stage is arguably an exercise in folding, of irritating the juxtapositions of worlding that score the porous boundaries of stage and not-stage. Correspondingly, a stage is also a place of transition and transaction; of negotiating place orientation. Sophie Nield approaches a stage as an 'alternative form of border space' (Nield 2008: 144) that stresses how the folding of a stage is enacted and felt. Nield argues that 'the border which is driven through geographical and representational space produces a second border between the body and its visibility to the law. This second border lies between the human and the rights pertaining to the condition of being human' (Nield 2008: 144). Nield observes how systems of discipline (such as theology, law or convention) regulate the placing of bodies. Stages arguably orientate bodies through an enacted spatio-material folding that echoes the oppositional negotiations evident at a land border – of division and inclusion, inside and outside, here and there.

Understanding a stage as a transactional border or fold offers a means of rearticulating what constitutes scenography within Blast Theory's *I'd Hide You*. While there is no discernible singular stage, there is a feeling of togetherness. The various agents of *I'd Hide You* – whether performers or spectator-players, cartography or cityscapes, graphical interfaces or headcams – are connected to one another as part of a wider assemblage. It is the shape and distinctive traits of this assemblage that sustain and demarcate the event of *I'd Hide You* as singular. This sense of togetherness is, in Deleuzian terms, a consequence of the assemblage's 'diagram'. Deleuze argues that an assemblage, while potentially fleeting, sustains a particular diagrammatic order that renders it discernible. If scenography is a crafting of stages through an affective assemblage, scenography's diagram is what gives a stage its orientation. The multiple sites of *I'd Hide You* are mediated through a networked interface that connects and situates the various components as part of a shared assemblage. *I'd Hide You* sustains multiple points of transaction (stages) that are connected through the diagram of a scenographic assemblage. While the mediated networks of HTTP protocols and web browsers are the methods that sustain this assemblage, scenography as place orientation encompasses how these sites of transaction relate to one another within this mediated experience. The scenography of *I'd Hide You* amounts to the diagrammatic orientations of this assemblage, to how these stages of transaction are encountered within a wider feeling of distributed place.

To return to my own experience of *I'd Hide You*, while I was not physically present on the streets of Manchester I was also not not present. Schechner's double negative of acting is equally applicable to the feeling of place orientation that occurs within mediated performances. A similar enacted complication of presence is evident in Foucault's reading of a mirror, where 'it makes this place that I occupy at the moment when I look at myself in the glass at once absolutely real, connected with all the space that surrounds it, and absolutely unreal, since in order to be perceived it has to pass through this virtual point which is over there' (Foucault 1986: 24). Blast Theory's mixed reality performances are full of places and acts of worlding, but also of displacement and, in the Marc Augé (2008) sense, the 'non-places' of super-modernity. I was simultaneously sitting at my desk in Liverpool and running the streets of Manchester. Indeed, an enacted worlding was taking place where my immediate bodily place became folded into a shared encounter of the mediated nexus of *I'd Hide You*. I was within an assemblage crafted from a felt immediacy with a series of distant geographies. Yet, my inhabitation within the game's assemblage rendered a distinct feeling of having been placed: within the game, the nexus of *I'd Hide You* constituted a feeling of place, of worlding. I argue that this distributed encounter of worlding is no less orientating than a perspective stage.

As with Foucault's mirror, I was both within the distributed game place of *I'd Hide You* and outside of the game, simultaneously. My bodily place was complicated by the implication that I was present within the game place too. The mixed reality contexts do not exceed a feeling of place; rather, the diagram of a networked assemblage sustains a particular orientation that shapes a worldly connectedness. As with the placement of a carpet in a town square, a highly visible site of transaction has been crafted, albeit a site that is distributed with no fixed (singular) centre. Depending on your point of orientation (whether running the streets with headgear or sitting on an office chair), participation within the event is shaped by a scenographic diagram. The network of devices – the layout of the browser interface, the colour of the runners' costumes, the routes of the runners within the cityscape – all contribute to a wider assemblage of the scenographic order. Furthermore, in switching the browser off I was no longer orientated by the assemblage; I was no longer proxemic to the encounter of *I'd Hide You*. This reading of Blast Theory's approach firmly positions scenography as that which gives orientation to this transactional milieu. Rather than exceeding stages, *I'd Hide You* sustains multiple stages (as both sites and points of transaction) that are sustained by the diagrammatic orientations of its scenographic assemblage. In arguing how place orientation occurs within a distributed mixed reality event, this also reaffirms bodies as the locus of an individual's encounter of scenographic practice. The beginnings of place orientation remain centred on how a body is oriented towards an event – whether sat in an auditorium or at an office desk, a feeling of place orientation always occurs through the holism of bodily experience.

While a Deleuzian diagram connects potential stage geographies, place orientation as a bodily experience is most explicitly evident when stages are crafted through bodily placement. As part of the PQ2011, I undertook a workshop on 'crowd choreographies' led by the architect Omar Khan. To examine this concept, performance-makers Monika Ponjavic and Marina Radulj proposed that the situation of Ulay and Abramović's *Imponderabilia* (1977) offered a means of effecting crowds. While *Imponderabilia* also signals the proxemics of 'personal space' in the formation of potential stages, the eye contact of Ulay and Abramović sustained a focus that renders the 'border space' of the doorway a stage. Ponjavic and Radulj performed a variation on this situation in the streets of Prague. This same convention is evident when an individual takes a photograph of another in a public place. The line of sight between camera lens and body-subject situates the 'place between' as eventful. Ponjavic and Radulj's intervention evidently shifted the flow of movement. *Imponderabilia*, while exposing social attitudes aligned with personal space, is an act of scenography. The manner in which people responded to Ponjavic and Radulj's line of sight echoes wider cultural conventions aligned with how groups gather around an event. Hall (1968) has argued, as part of the study of proxemics, that there exist (culturally defined) finite distances that demarcate how personal space is policed. In the example of Ponjavic and Radulj, their eye contact extended their shared personal space through means of attentive focus. The learned proxemics of personal space orientated how the public traversed the street, inviting them to change direction or stop. Ponjavic and Radulj's intervention othered the normative rhythms of worlding through bodily presence and eye contact alone. This simple act of focused attention crafted a highly visible site of encounter (a stage-scene). While this is an act of scenography, it is also an act of choreography. Indeed, this example evidences the shared relationship between scenography as a crafting of place orientation and choreography as a crafting of movement. Place orientation and movement are bound to one another – neither preceding the other, yet both effect how the other happens. This reciprocal relationship is what allows the act of choreography and scenography to be understood beyond their constituent 'parts', whether these are gesture or figure, costume or lighting. These sister concepts exist in mutual relation to one another. Scenography is to staging as choreography is to movement. The two theatre-making strategies maintain an ongoing dance of eventual placing.

The examples of *I'd Hide You* along with Ponjavic and Radulj's reworking of *Imponderabilia* offer a less concrete, and potentially more fleshy, reading of how stages are crafted through scenography as sites of transaction. There has, however, been another line of experimental practice that emerged with the twentieth century that sought to transgress stages as a symbol of theatrical orthodoxy. Reviewer Liz Hoggard evokes this line of travel when she described the work of the British immersive theatre company Punchdrunk as having 'no time for stages or even seats' (Hoggard 2013). While framed by an archetypal view of theatrical patronage, Hoggard explains that a 'night in their company doesn't involve a stage, a programme, an ice cream at the interval – or even a seat' (Hoggard 2013). In the immersive context of Punchdrunk, while there are potentially no architectural stages their artistic director Felix Barrett cites the scenographic arguments of Craig as a formative influence:

> What Craig realised was that every single theatrical element—the scenography, the music, the state of

the mind of the audience, the auditorium itself—should be about creating the atmosphere … I just wanted to submerge myself in Craig's stylised, total world. That's why I started Punchdrunk.

(Barrett 2014)

In this regard, the idea of scenography as holistic and atmospheric is evidently fundamental to Barrett's envisioning of the company's immersive approach. Yet, the proposed absence of a stage is demonstrably different to Aronson's argument on scenography has been understood historically. The very notion of stage design, which typically in English relates to set design more so than light or sound, is predicated on a symbiosis between stage and theatrical design. As Aronson has noted, if the stage has dematerialized, how does this impact the practical and intellectual conceptualization of scenography?

To describe Punchdrunk's work as post-stage invites a critique on the symbiotic relationship between stage and scenography – most directly, that there is no division between stage and auditorium because the stage has replaced the auditorium. While the architectural construct of stages as raised or delineated spaces is seemingly absent in immersive works, the stage itself remains – obscured by the fact that the spectators themselves now inhabit the stage. In critical terms, Artaud's call in 1958 for an elimination of the stage echoes the dematerialization of which Aronson speaks:

> So composed and so constructed, the spectacle will be extended, by elimination of the stage, to the entire hall of the theater and will scale the walls from the ground up on light catwalks, will physically envelop the spectator and immerse him in a constant bath of light, images, movements, and noises.
>
> (in den Oudsten 2011: 64)

Artaud's words summarize a trajectory in twentieth-century theatre towards the envelopment of the spectator. This is evident in Schechner's argument for environmental theatre, as well as Appia's proposal for the studio theatre, where artists will reunite 'all the expressions of our social life, and in particular dramatic art, with or without spectators' (cited in Beacham 1988: 278). Appia's proposal for a theatre 'with or without spectators' speaks directly to the ethos of immersive works that companies such as Punchdrunk promote. These provocations are also a critique of the implied privileging assigned to the attentive stage, where those 'on stage' have power over those 'off stage' (inclusive of spectators and production members). While Appia and Tessenow's *Hellerau Festspielhaus* (1911) and many of the postdramatic architectures that followed have often employed defined areas for seating, the legacy of this statement arguably exceeds the idea of a stage-spectator relationship as understood for the majority of the twentieth century.

Punchdrunk's work is, however, institutionally scenography. The use of lights, sound and stage environments is all recognizably scenographic. Moreover, the work of the company is clearly situated as institutionally theatre – a status confirmed by their invitation to become an associate company of the National Theatre. While the classical notion of a distant stage (which is looked upon from a distance) has been challenged and potentially transgressed, a material understanding of scenography has remained relatively stable – albeit operating in different situational contexts. When Artaud spoke of eliminating the stage, he was arguing for new approaches to stage geography that transgressed stage orthodoxies of separation and division – of elevating one group (performers) above another (spectators, production staff). In terms of scenography, Burns recounts how with the dominance of the perspective stage 'acting space was no longer "framed" by the action but by the scenery and the physical boundaries of the stage and proscenium arch' (Burns 1972: 75). Wiles argues that, when paired with music, the perspective stage has 'proved to be one of the most powerful tools of western culture for manufacturing dreams' (Wiles 2003: 207). Subsequently, the methods of scenography were deployed to confirm this worldly distinction and, in turn, would come to signify this division given their prominent association. When Grotowski described scenography as 'superfluous' (Grotowski 1968: 28), the Polish director was arguing against the scenographies that reinforced and made manifest the perspective stage. From the 1600s onwards, scenography had been the agent for an ideological separation of stage from world.

Today, the postdramatic architecture of black box studio theatres seemingly reinforces the idea of a stage as liminoid, to evoke the language of Turner, existing outside of the temporal and geographic logic of their surroundings. Shred of its ideological pairing with the gilded proscenium, Howard describes how a 'plain black box becomes a truly expressive space' (2009: 6). Furthermore, the critic Gaëlle Breton argued that 'Theatre transcends architecture … Once the theatrical spell has been cast, the limits of physical space become irrelevant' (Breton 1989: 4). What is, however, evident in these examples is that, while the notion of a formal theatrical architecture – of raised stages and royal boxes – had been transgressed, the notion of a stage has remained. To return to Schechner's 'special place', the work of Punchdrunk sustains a blurring of the behavioural conventions assigned to stage and auditorium, especially when these physical architectural schemas are absent. Spectators now inhabit a stage or witness a stage action from a position of equivalence, where the scene in the postdramatic black box studio is all-encompassing. It remains crucial that the practical geographies of a stage remain evident within a happening or site-specific performance. The stage is not gone; rather, the auditorium has encompassed it without reaffirming itself as a holistic *theatron*. Stage-scenes remain the place for drama.

Stage-scenes beyond vision

The notion of a stage-scene stresses the withness of scenographics; that these felt orientations only occur due the proximity that comes from being *with* world. This is critically distinct to the ontological division inherent within the concept of the scenic. My critique on the scenic relates to the wider ideological position of stage *as* world. Lehmann outlines how in dramatic theatre a scene is akin to the *finestra aperta* or fixed perspective of painting:

> The dramatic theatre, in which the scene stands for the world, can be compared to perspective: space here is both technically and mentally a window and a symbol, analogous to the reality 'behind'. Like the *finestra aperta* presented by Renaissance painting it offers what might be called an equivalent to the scale of the world, a metaphorical likeness obtained through abstraction and accentuation.
>
> (in Bleeker 2008: 31)

Of course, perspective and scale are significant techniques of scenography. Whether drawn out by the legacies of Barbaro's mistranslation or the formalization of a perspective stage, scenography has been tasked with staging a felt sense of spatial perspective and worldly scale. While the question of scale in scenography is examined further in the next chapter, as Lehmann implies, ideas of scene and perspective are evidently connected. Rancière (2013) applies a similar reading in his review of historical art moments, which he studies as a series of scenes: 'The scene is not the illustration of an idea. It is a little optical machine that shows us thought busy weaving together perceptions, affects, names and ideas, constituting the sensible community that makes such weaving thinkable' (Rancière 2013: xi). The 'optical machine' of Rancière returns to the idea of scene as a means of observation. 'The scene captures concepts at work', Rancière continues, 'in their relation to the new objects they seek to appropriate, old objects that they try to reconsider, and the patterns they build or transform to this end' (Rancière 2013: xi). Rancière's scene does happen in the manner of Stewart's conceptualization, but also stresses that the scene as observation has the capacity to be quantified; of isolating a fragment of experience that allows it to be studied and understood. The boundaries of a scene remain significant, as these present the subject in question as knowable. Whether dramaturgical or scenographic in conception, scenes are rendered attentive by the methods by which they irritate and demarcate an ongoing nexus of worlding. Scenes expose the constructed perceptual borders that score worldly encounters.

It is high summer and I'm visiting the Chelsea Flower Show in 2014. I am consciously aware that the heat is at the forefront of the minds of all I encounter. My light cotton skater dress, bare legs and factor 30 suncream seem inadequate to fully project me from the glare of the sun. Yet, as I traverse the lanes between the individual gardens, I note the discrete techniques employed to demarcate or enact these defined worlds. This feeling of worlding operates beyond the square footage dimensions of the garden plots. Having walked from Sloane Square train station, I'm aware that the Chelsea Flower Show is – in and of itself – a world apart from the wider geographies of the London borough of Kensington and Chelsea. The nexus of the gardens, the being between gardens, forms its own particular sense of place that feels eventful and mundane at the same time. I consider the conditioning of this affective atmosphere as the other patrons pass by me with the general hubbub filtering into my experience of each garden. A garden with high plasterboard walls draws my attention. I stop and orientate myself to a small opening in the wall, peering into a collection of ferns and a stone pathway. I attempt to focus my attention on the distinctive atmosphere of this garden, with the greenness of the ferns scoring the dark grey of the stone. The path draws my attention through the small garden, giving shape to the plot of trees within. It is while I am appearing through this opening that I momentarily feel a cooling breeze. As it disappears, the heat of the sun beats down. I'm drawn to around the corner to regain that felt moment of cooling. I can hear the sounds of running water. As I continue around the tall plasterboard walls, I feel a shift in temperature. A light wind drifts the cooling qualities of the misted water towards me. This affective atmosphere orientates my attention as I move closer to the garden's edge. I look upon a series of waterfalls that sequentially turn on and off. The sounds, textures and temperature all sustain a distinct – yet collaborative – affect in how I am orientated towards this garden. These disparate qualities afford a sense of worlding, a worlding that is discrete from the heat of the sun or the geographies of Kensington and Chelsea. I note that my relationship to this garden is not in terms of its scenic qualities (as a set of aesthetic values), but rather in how I am engulfed by its scenographic orientations. I allow my attention to dwell within the worlding feeling of this cooling garden.

I cite my experience at the Chelsea Flower Show for two reasons. First, it highlights the mutual inter-relationships between gardening and scenography. Second, the conditions of that day isolate how the atmospheric and orientating qualities of the water garden scene exceeded visually conceived notions of border and boundary. My experience also isolates the idea that the scenographics of a garden – the agents of an affective atmosphere – occur within a temporal timeframe that is intrinsic to their capacity to orientate: to guide, focus and render a stage-scene attentive. While identifying gardens as corporal, given that Kant argued that nature as qualifying all artistic tasks, the philosopher considered gardens to be an illusion that '*arranges* nature's *products* beautifully' (Kant 1987: 192; emphasis in original). Yet, if considered as inclusive of the orientating haptics of water vapour, scenes become less 'visual' in conception and instead stress how perceptual worldly borders are porous and negotiable, rather than finite and stable. The scene as unchanging and removed from the wider negotiations of worlding, as its own still life, is arguably challenged when acts of worlding occur without a strict spatialization of stage and not-stage, scene and not-scene. Burns notes that, in the art happenings of Kaprow, 'everyone is liable to be "on-stage" so that there is no possibility of escape to a position from which the theatrical world can be viewed objectively as separate from, contrasting with, or even, complementary to the "real" world, outside the theatre' (Burns 1972: 88). Following the historicism of the picturesque scene and Brook's bare stage, theatre is typically defined as one group viewing a stage-scene from a set distance while another performs. The situational behaviours of a stage have, following Kaprow, shifted as art happenings explicitly collapse the worldings of theatre into the worldings of life. With the increased mediated platforms for exchange in the twenty-first century, Singleton argues that 'the "scène" itself has de-materialized in some forms of performance in which theatre as an artistic product is only an alien precursor to a contemporary performative process and experience' (Singleton 2013: 49). This echoes Aronson's argument on the dematerialization of the stage. The concepts of scene and stage – as evoked by Burns, Singleton and Aronson – are accordingly bound to a politics of demarcation and boundary that proceeds from a vision-centric account of worlding. This approach, however, fails to account for the porous atmospheric orientations that shaped my experiences at the Chelsea Flower Show.

Benjamin argues that the conventions of visual analysis, and of objective 'distance', cannot account for the upheaval of the human perceptual apparatus that has occurred with the onset of mass media. Rather, Benjamin argues that this task is 'simply not solvable by visual means alone – that is to say, through contemplation. They are gradually mastered, on the instructions of tactile reception, by [human's] getting used to them' (Benjamin 1936: 34). Within the history of Western aesthetics, visual approaches to the analysis of art and artifice have established a dominant code for the appreciation and articulation of artistic endeavor. Media theorist Marshall McLuhan (1911–80) argues that the hegemony of the visual has led to a distinct philosophical viewpoint for the organization of sensory experience. In considering worlding in terms of 'visual space', McLuhan suggests experience is defined through the delineation of boundaries and the definition of a fixed point, a centre. These delineated spaces are compartmentalized and labelled. The most explicit example of this is the division of the Aristotelian senses: touch, taste, smell, hearing and sight. Each has its own remit and operates apart from, or possibly in spite of, the others. Visual space, or spacing, is about establishing defined categories with a fixed point and discernible centre. This approach to the organization of our senses is, however, counter to the holistic experience as articulated by phenomenologists such as Maurice Merleau-Ponty (1908–61) and the sensory systems of Gibson. Instead, McLuhan proposes the idea of 'auditory space' as a means of articulating a conceptualization of space in terms of time rather than boundary. As McLuhan writes in 1957:

> the essential feature of sound is not that it has location but that it be, that it fill space. Sound is an envelope. No point of focus; no fixed boundaries; space made by the thing itself, not space containing. It is not pictorial space but dynamic, always in flux; creating its own dimensions moment by moment. It has no fixed boundaries, is indifferent to background the ear favors sounds from any direction, it can experience things simultaneously.
>
> (in Marchessault 2005: 91)

Scenography is not (solely) a sonic art, but McLuhan's observations offer a means of discussing the holistic encounter of scenographics beyond vision. Importantly, this position also affirms scenographics as being time-based.

To paraphrase McLuhan, scenographics operate as an envelope. Yet, it is an envelope with no fixed boundaries, as it exceeds conceptions of pictorial space to embrace the potentiality (of change, transformation, and multiple usages) that are always latent within an affective atmosphere. Scenographics are not bound to the conception of a 'stage image'.

Neher offers possibly the most vehement attack on the notion of a stage image as a principle of theatre-making. Having been a collaborator of Brecht's since childhood, in 1951 Neher declares the visual seduction of a realist image as 'fascist': 'What's to become of thinking if nobody thinks the simplest things? A "stage picture" is always real – that's already implicit in the Nazi term *Bühnenbild*' (in Willett 1986: 75). For Neher, the *Bühnenbild* is a process of reducing thinking by providing a reality beyond reality – of presenting a hermetically sealed representation that bears no direct relationship to the situational geographies from which the spectators pertain. Neher argues that theatre must provide the opportunity for debate, for critique, through a privileging of theatre's materiality over and beyond a strict communication of ideology. Marks articulates a similar tension between the representational power of images and their materiality:

> While optical perception privileges the representational power of the image, haptic perception privileges the material presence of the image. Drawing from other forms of sense experience, primarily touch and kinesthetics, haptic visuality involves the body more than is the case with optical visuality.
>
> (2000: 163)

McLuhan's position on the aural space aligns with Marks' argument on haptic visuality. Each framework seeks to complicate the privileging of vision as the primary means of sensory and critical perception. Similarly, Bloomer and Moore (1977) outline how historically sculptors have sought to understand the three-dimensional in relation to the two-dimensional: preferring to stand at a distance from the object in order to consider its two-dimensional profile above its three-dimensional situation. Bloomer and Moore conclude that the figurative (as defined by vision) had been privileged above the situational (as defined by the bodily). The role of vision as a locus for critical distance – of observing and forming conclusions – has been set at a counterpoint to the bodily, which is framed as subjective.

To return to Neher, the imposition of the stage image as the locus for theatre reception is a structural privileging of (a certain kind of) mind above body. This privileging is evident in how the scenic reduces situational events to quantifiable images. Yet, scenes are also events: moments in time that occur through a materiality. Stage-scenes exceed the strict visual logic of the scenic. While scenes have been codified as discrete images of worlding, I argue that this is a consequence of a visual hegemony that enforces a Cartesian spilt between mind and body, thinking and the situational. My critique on the notion of the scenic is as a structural symptom for how situational events are quantified as images that renders experience objective and measureable. Scenic images are discrete and finite. Scenographics are intangible and affective. In terms of scenography, to argue stages as discrete from scenes is reductive. Scenes define stages and stages shape scenes. Notably, a stage-scene also operates as a place – a situated geography that is encountered and felt. This is discrete from the dramaturgical scene that is symbolically structural and interpretative. The scene in landscape paintings, scene studies and *mise en scène* are all bound to the quantifying tasks of the dramaturgical; of translation and interpretation. In that regard, a stage-scene is a scene that occurs as a situated geography. Scenography only occurs as stage-scenes.

By way of a conclusion, the symbiosis between stage and scenography is a complex weaving of theory and practice disciplined by ideologies of language and experiential repetition. While the notion of the scenic is possibly more finite an idea, the theoretical arguments for a stage render it totalitarian. Stages are inescapable. When I speak of staging, however, I am evoking the potentialities of scenographics. While also bound to notions of the dramaturgical and choreographic, staging denotes the processes of how place is rendered attentive as an operational act of theatre. Removed from the boundaried logic of the finite stage, staging is a crafting that is sequenced and focused on an act of scenographic encounter. While it may exceed the visual logic and ontological division of the scenic, scenography retains the temporal circumstances of staging. The question, therefore, is not whether or not scenography exists without a fixed point, but how the situational act of staging marries with the notion of place orientation. To answer this position, I turn my attention to our inescapable fixed point: that of our own fleshy bodies.

Appia centred his argument for a living art on the holism of bodily experience. This position on spatiality and bodily experience would later feature as a cornerstone of phenomenological critique. Edward Casey argues that place is always mediated through our body, for we are 'always with a body, so, being bodily, we are always within a place as well. Thanks to our body, we are in that place and part of it' (Casey 1997: 214). To feel scenography is to encounter scenography through the act of being bodily. A feeling of place is sensed as a holism, a holism that is of the order of bodies. To render scenography as ontologically distinct or distant from the bodily is to render it sterile and sanitized. As Tschumi points out of architecture, the act of entering a 'building may be a delicate act, but it violates the balance of a precisely ordered geometry … Bodies carve all sorts of new and unexpected spaces, through fluid or erratic motions' (Tschumi 1996: 123). Place orientation begins from a situated bodily centring; finding a spatial resonance and material grounding. Whether invited to look upon (stage-spectator) or look around (immersion), you remain centred by being bodily. Felt orientations *with* and *of* your body are the nexus for any scenographic encounter.

The taxonomy I have centred this chapter around – of scenographic worlding, stage places, post-stage scenography and stage-scenes – is not an argument for a new type of scenography. In critiquing deterministic positions on stage and scenography, my aim is to account for how scenographics are fundamental to theatre and more broadly as acts of staging. The post-stage dichotomy challenges classical stage orthodoxies, but this does not follow that the stage concept has been transgressed. Although the raised platform or the demarcation of an ultra-space is no longer ubiquitous, I argue that the centre point of the stage concept has become less material and more fleshly. The act and experience of drama is now arguably orientated within, towards the bodily and beyond a hegemonic discourse of critical distance and the visual. Whereas previous theatre orthodoxies have seemingly positioned vision as the definitive medium for theatrical reception, the staging experiments of the twentieth century and intermedial practices of the twenty-first confirm a renewed bodily holism as the principal medium for scenographic reception. Whether sat in an auditorium chair or running with fellow participants, scenographies of bodily encounter locate an individual within the drama, the action. While scenography may exist beyond formal stage orthodoxies, it cannot exist without reference to the centring affect of a body. A scenography of feeling is also a scenography of bodily centring.

McLuhan's idea of auditory space sustains a different reading to conventional approaches to the stage-scene and invites a consideration of scenography beyond a finite stage. As in the instance of Blast Theory's *I'd Hide You*, scenography as an event acts as an orientating relational diagram that binds simultaneous stage geographies together. While the invisibility of a fixed point does not dictate the absence of a point (a body), scenography in this context can exceed the ideologies of worlding as vision-based. While Aronson's discord with the lack of a stage or design at the PQ2011 appeared out of sync with its tagline of the 'still point', it may be that there is an underlying assumption to this argument: that all that is scenographic is scenography. Instead, if scenographic and scenography are considered as critically distinct, this invites a potentially different analysis. The argument for critical distinction necessitates that certain practices may align more productively with the notion of scenographic *as opposed to* scenography. The term 'scenographic practice' is familiar, often used in place of 'scenography' without any conscious thought as to whether this denotes something peculiar. The PQ2011 projects that Aronson critiques are scenography, yet they are also scenographic. The broad conceptual remit of scenographics does, nevertheless, imply that these traits can occur in/with other forms of practice that exceed the extra-daily crafting of scenography.

While all scenography is scenographic, not all that is scenographic is scenography.

CHAPTER 6
Scenographic cultures

In his introduction to *Critique of Everyday Life* (1991a), Lefebvre cites an excerpt from *L'Express* from 1956 on the latest trends in New York design that states: 'Kitchens are becoming less like kitchens and more like works of art' (in 1991a: 8). Lefebvre's introduction dwells on how the technologies of capitalist cultures 'replaces the criticism of life through dreams, or ideas, or poetry, or those activities which rise above the everyday, by the critique of everyday life from within' (1991a: 9). The French philosopher and Marxist concludes that the capitalist conception of everyday life 'with all the superior mod cons takes on the distance and remoteness and familiar strangeness of a dream' (1991a: 9–10). Baz Kershaw accounts for this 'familiar strangeness' by reflecting on how acts of performance permeate all aspects of socialization and labour within a post-industrial civil society. Kershaw argues that a conscious fashioning of self shapes how individuals relate to – and sculpt – their lived environments, where

> interior design turns homes into sets, fashion turns clothes into costumes, gourmandism turns food into edible props, tourism turns travel into scene changes, and, in a neat trick in the feedback loop of mediatization, communications turn social exchange into a self-dramatizing set of scenes and scenarios.
> (Kershaw 2001: 206)

Likewise, Böhme argues that the 'attention which is now paid to atmospheres in aesthetic theory has its material background in the fact that staging has become a basic feature of our society: the staging of politics, of sporting events, of cities, of commodities, of personalities, of ourselves' (Böhme 2013: 6). Kershaw and Böhme isolate how acts of staging – of crafting attentive environments – are symptomatic of a wider set of social behavioural practices that equate material cultures with conceptions of human agency and power.

In this chapter, I outline how 'scenographic cultures' are equally evident within the fashioning of places or strategies for consumerism, as well as the staging of political action. I utilize these scenarios to outline how scenographics afford a renewed lens on how stage-scenes are conceptualized and performed within everyday situations. What renders a particular situation scenographic is, I propose, proportional to the high visibility of place orientations that irritate the normative orders of worlding through an active othering. I argue that the worlding irritant of a stage-scene in theatre-making and the othering tactics of scenographics, as evident within acts of interior design or gardening, are one in the same operation. This position echoes the argument taken up by Cathy Turner on dramaturgy. Turner observes that the sociological adoption of dramaturgy also invites a porous exchange with theatre-making.

> If, in a sociological sense, we can discuss the 'dramaturgy' of architecture and event, using theatre terminology to describe everyday life (as the situationists themselves did from time to time), we should be able to discuss the artwork in terms of the way it opens into the everyday, drawing on both the theatrical *and* the sociological use of the term. The 'construction of situations' initially advocated by the situationists might be considered as dramaturgy in this blended or porous sense.
> (Turner 2015: 149; emphasis in original)

I argue that scenographics evoke and sustain the othering traits of constructed situations that, as with the dramaturgical or the choreographic, lends itself to the sociological analysis of place orientation. Essin similarly observes that the term 'scenographic' affords the investigation of a strategic relationship between defined practices and positions: 'I use the adjective "scenographic" to modify the roles played by the New Stagecraft artists – author, critic, activist, entrepreneur, and cartographer – to give contemporary relevance to their activities' (Essin 2012: 6). To investigate this strategic relationship and contemplate the disciplinary porousness of constructed situations, I isolate how scenographics are operationally evident within practices – such as installation art, interior design, marketing, gardening and protest – that exceed the ideological remit of the institutional theatres. As with Essin, I review these practices through modified positions that isolate distinct conceptual tactics – namely scale, behaviour, seduction, curation and activism – in order to argue how scenographics are enacted and sustained. While these tactics are by no means exhaustive, the subheadings and aligned combinations could have been conceived in any manner of ways – i.e. installation art and scenographic activism, interior design and scenographic seduction, and so on. In offering concise accounts on how scenographic tactics might apply to distinct practices beyond theatre, my aim is to expose the underlying othering traits that demarcate situations as scenographic.

Kant might have partitioned the practices covered in this chapter as visual arts, and more precisely as painting. Kant argued that in 'painting in the broad sense I would also include the decoration of rooms with tapestries, bric-à-brac, and all beautiful furnishings whose sole function is to be *looked at*, as well as the art of dressing tastefully (with rings, snuff-boxes, etc.)' (Kant 1987: 193; emphasis in original). The argument for scenographics is, I propose, centred on the potential of *being with* an atmosphere as discrete from *looking at* an object or tableau. The notion of place orientation seeks to highlight how visually conceived objects, such as furnishings and tapestries, also operate as part of a wider assemblage that enact a feeling of place. Furthermore, crucial to the arguments laid forth in this chapter is that place orientations – as well as being highly situational and relational – are conceived in relationship to disciplined orders of knowledge and things.

Ahmed conceives of orientation in terms of proximity and a navigation of otherness (which is both externally and internally enacted). The negotiation of otherness is, for Ahmed, equally tied to how notions of proximity are enacted and disciplined through embodied repetition. The interventional tactics of scenographics proclaim an othering through means of spatial disruption or material intervention, which in turn renders a given situation as attentive: a stage-scene. I argue that these othering tactics of scenographics are equally evident in the art practices of theatre and installation art, as well as the everyday practices of interior design and gardening. Scenographics render highly visible the perceptual borders between illusion and art, ideology and atmosphere. Yet, paradoxically, the high visibility of these traits is collapsed within the repetitions of normative worldings that reframe them as affirming conceptions of individuality or selfhood. In focusing in on worlding irritants, my intention is isolate how the ideological systems of material/body/home fashioning are revealed or scored through scenographics.

I am not the first to note the othering qualities of scenographics. Brejzek suggests that scenography sustains a critical distance from the worlds in which it intervenes. Described as materially and metaphysically 'other', Brejzek argues that scenography's 'otherness … prevents touch and its physical borders clearly separate its constructed perfection and stillness from the unruliness of the world surrounding it' (Brejzek 2011b: 5). Brejzek proposes that the demarcation of scene from world is enacted through a situational othering. In this regard, when I speak in terms of othering as a complication of normative ordering (as an irritant), I do so in relationship to Stewart's claim that the knowableness of a scene exceeds a strict order of representations:

> The question they beg is not what they might mean in an order of representations, or whether they are good or bad in an overarching scheme of things, but where they might go and what potential modes of knowing, relating, and attending to things are already somehow present in them in a state of potentiality and resonance.
>
> (Stewart 2007: 3)

While this process of worlding is interventional, a scenographic trait accounts for how this othering enacts a feeling of worlds (as plural). Moreover, I argue that the processes that form and shape theatrical place orientation discipline how theatre-makers *think through* scenography – be it the spatial and material disciplining of the 1:25 model box or the physical dimensions of lighting equipment. To isolate the othering traits of scenographics is to argue how this perspective is symptomatic of a wider cultural trait towards an enactment of worlding through scene-making.

Installation art and scenographic scale

In *Aesthetics of Installation Art* (2012), Juliane Rebentisch uses the terms 'stage set-likeness' (2012: 167) and 'stage-like' (2012: 170) to outline inherent qualities attributed to the work of installation artists such as Paul Thek and Ilya Kabakov. In particular, the German art philosopher argues that installation art operates between the established categories of the spatial and time-based arts as outlined by Lessing. Adopting the notion that installation art operates like a 'stage set', Rebentisch cites American philosopher Stanley Cavell's understanding of theatre as being predicated on an ontological division of stage from audience, where the 'ontological separation between events on stage and the audience (which is of constitutive importance to theater), essentially distinguishes theater as an *aesthetic phenomenon*' (Rebentisch 2012: 37; emphasis in original). Within this model, Rebentisch suggests that the 'viewer of the installation, like the viewer of a landscape, finds himself [sic] within it; he [sic] moves amid its objects' (Rebentisch 2012: 156). Rebentish concludes that the

> 'total' installation is comparable to a stage set whose fourth wall closes behind the viewer— a 'total' closure that may well feel quite oppressive. It is accessible only from within; it cannot be viewed from some neutral position outside of it.
> (Rebentisch 2012: 157)

The experience and affective qualities of a 'stage set' are, for Rebentisch, representative of the same orientating qualities of installation art.

Crucially, Rebentisch argues that installation art is ontologically indeterminate and is predicated on what I have described as a witness as well as my own position on place orientation. While this book adopts the ontological indeterminism of new materialism, Rebentisch's thesis usefully foresees this framework and considers the situational act of staging as being formative to installation art's ontological condition (her original German-language study was published in 2003 before much of the scholarship on new materialism). Installations are constructed and encountered following the same techniques and processes of scenography: of the relations between objects, the material presence of bodies, or the orientations afforded by the layout's spatial programming. While she adopts the position that theatre occurs on a raised stage apart from its audience, I argue that Rebentisch is evoking scenographics in all but name. I propose that the term 'stage-like' amounts to an observation of the scenographic order, beyond the critical focus of theatricality or performativity. Scenographics accounts for performed acts of place orientation and material othering that can occur in situations ideologically removed from an institutionalized theatre.

Encounters of 'scaled objects' present a useful method from which to review the porous relationships between scenography and installation art. From the discipline of the model box to the encounter of stage scenery, questions of scale are a symptom of scenography's working processes and, often, a prominent mode of encounter. For instance, the vanishing point deployed at the Teatro Olimpico is an exercise in scale manipulation, where visual conceptions of depth are connected to a sense of distance through a perspectival scaling. In *The Model as Performance* (2017), Brejzek and Lawrence Wallen focus on 'size' rather than 'scale' within their critique of the scenographic model box. The pair argue that 'scale itself is less relevant than the dimensional relationship of the viewer to object or space, and the level of immersion achieved' (Brejzek and Wallen 2017: 3). My own usage of 'scale' relates to the othering tactics that come with objects that exceed their signified's normative dimensions. In this regard, scale is derived from a relativeness to human scale and the signified's normative size rather than mathematical ratio. 'Scenographic scale' is when the concept of scale is rendered attentive through means of place orientation. It is, however, Ahmed's account of the disorientating qualities of 'queer objects' that informs my critique of scale as an othering trait of scenographics.

Ahmed concentrates her analysis of queer objects on encounters with tables. The table, for Ahmed, is a locus of philosophical practice that has supported and sustained the act of philosophy throughout history – often as a silent partner. Ahmed's interest in the table begins with Edmund Husserl's (1859–1938) *Ideas* (1913), as the German philosopher recounts the disciplining qualities of his writing table. My own analysis of scenographic scale is spurred by an image of the artist Giancarlo Neri's *The Writer* (2005) on the cover of Ahmed's *Queer Phenomenology* (2006). Situated in a field, Neri's sculpture is that of a chair and table scaled to the size of a building. Ahmed does not make explicit reference to Neri's artwork within her analysis of queer objects. She does, nevertheless, note that queer objects might invite a 're-orientation' through the disciplined normativity that comes with the repetition a certain enacted relationship to, in this instance, tables: 'We normally work "on" the table. The table exists as an "on" device' (Ahmed 2006: 166). Ahmed suggests that table normativity is one of support rather than explicit collaboration, arguing that we do not usually write *with* our tables. The significance of this observation to my own study is that Neri's sculpture challenges a stable relationship to an everyday subject through a change in scale. Neri's table is a conscious act of material othering that subverts and queers the normativity of the subject. Neri's table is scenographic.

In terms of scale, I am interested in how Neri's table is rendered scenographic through an act of orientation that queers any representational readings the sculpture sustains – of the role tables play in our daily lives or as a measure of humanity (both figuratively and metaphysically). I argue that this symbiotically coded sculpture evokes an othering place orientation, which is distantly phenomenological and queer in its encounter. The enormity of the object, coupled with its defamiliarization of an everyday schema, sustains a bodily orientation that complements and exceeds associated contextual readings. This tension is central to understanding the scenographic qualities of this encounter. Neri's table presents an othering orientation that queers the normative orientations that tables typically maintain. Neri's installation invites visitors look up, walk underneath and encounter the place of *this* table, while also pointing to a universal familiarity to *all* tables. Neri's table is an exercise in how scenographic scale works as a means of othering the familiar and, in the Brechtian sense, facilitating a reassessment of the familiar through an orchestrated strangeness. To further isolate this queer condition of scale and its relationship to the scenographic, I now turn to an encounter of an altogether different scale: that of the miniature.

In 2011, at the Performance Studies international (PSi) conference hosted by the University of Leeds, I encountered David Shearing's If anyone wonders why rocks breakdown. *I wait outside a performance studio. David asks me to select a figure from a small table. The figures are rendered in white plastic and are no more than five centimetres in height. Each figure has a particular stance and appearance: some are standing looking out towards a horizon, others are seemingly discussing events with another, and so on. I select a female figure caught in the act of walking. I'm handed wireless headphones that have a voice recounting a poem interspersed with urban sounds. David invites me to step into the studio and place my figure. There are others already exploring this stage place, yet immediately I am orientated towards the floor. Placed throughout the studio are similar white figures to the one I now hold in my hand. I am a giant. I carefully navigate between the select groupings of figures, while the poem and urban soundscape continue. On parallel walls of the studio there two thin regular projections, with heavily blurred videos of what feels like an urban cityscape: loose profiles of streetlights or maybe open windows at night. One of the other giants is watching one of these screens intently. I look down towards her feet. She is very close to some of the figures. I watch with a mild sense of anticipation as the regular shifting of her feet brushes closer to the figures. I can see that other figures have been moved or knocked. I find myself 'correcting' a few at my own feet. I'm not sure this is my role, but I do it anyway – nobody seems to be too concerned. As I move, I place my footsteps carefully. I see a collection of figures apart from the larger groupings. I slowly bend down and place my figure with her new friends. I hope she will be happy here. My giant role concludes with an uncomfortable feeling of a plastic shard under my right foot as I stand. My scale is beyond that of the figures below me, yet I feel responsible and connected. The scenography of* If anyone wonders why rocks breakdown *wants me to care.*

The worlding evident in Shearing's *If anyone wonders why rocks breakdown* is distinct from the worlding of a perspective stage. Yet, unlike Neri's table Shearing's work is institutionally scenography: it has set timeframes, encountered in a theatre studio, performed at a theatre and performance conference, as well as crafting a distinctive affective atmosphere/assemblage inclusive of light and sound that is highly located as a stage-scene. In terms of scenographics, the reality of a scaled miniature object asks the participant to enact an orientation that remains predicated on a proxy stage–auditorium relationship. This proxy relationship is navigated by the relative size of the participant against an implied stage world of the figures. While there is no formal divisional architecture, the enacted distance renders the figures as the site of action, of drama. This negotiation of scales, where the miniature is rendered attentive through scaled detail and the theatrical charge of surrogacy, is also evident in the discipline of the 1:25 model box. Whether in architectural practice or scenography, Brejzek argues that the model box sustains a 'performative quality [that] only unfolds in its dialogue with the viewer's desire to manipulate and play out its inherent narrative proposition' (Brejzek 2011b: 5). What Brejzek isolates as the narrative proposition, I expand into the innate attentiveness and power that derives from scenographic scale. Therefore, I argue that the othering qualities of the scaled object magnify the ideological traits of the subject in question, rendering it extra-daily (or at least extra-ordinary) and attentive.

Bachelard presents a similar position as part of his readings on scale and literary imagination. With a particular focus on acts of imagined miniaturization, Bachelard argues that the 'cleverer I am at miniaturizing the world, the better I possess it. But in doing this, it must be understood that values become condensed and enriched in miniature' (Bachelard 1994: 150). Possession is a consequence of miniaturization for Bachelard. As evident in a model box or in Shearing's installation, the power of miniature scale is potentially a reflected power of possession: where the viewer-participant is dominant through an orchestrated relativeness of size and the imposed attentiveness of the small (in that it invites focused attention). Following Bachelard, the figures are rendered 'on stage' through the reflected power of possession. While the model box is also a tool for the planning of another exercise (that of a 1:1 or 'life-size' scenography), the imposition of these power dynamics is often reflected within the finalized designs. As Bachelard notes, the act of miniaturization paradoxically magnifies the ideologies of the subject while rendering the objects themselves smaller. This same ideological magnification is also evident within Neri's table. The othering trait of an altered scale evidences how the ideological situations of a stage-scene are encountered beyond the institutional theatres. The narratological circumstances of Shearing's figures or Neri's table speak to the dramaturgical scene of *mise en scène*. My argument for scenographic scale, however, exceeds the narratological, where the scaled objects present a reality of their own encounter. What makes Neri's table scenographic is equally what makes Shearing's work scenographic. The two are bound in their exploration of scale as a reality, as a real orientation that is encountered. While Shearing's work is institutionally scenography, Neri's sculpture shares the same scenographic traits as the figures of *If anyone wonders why rocks breakdown*. The encounter of altered scale presents a defamiliarized order of place orientation. The normativity of an object or situation is highlighted through these scenographic interventions. Yet, both Shearing's figures and Neri's table are real – in that their orientation of a viewer's perception is a consequence of a material reality. Whether big or small, these acts of scaling sustain and evoke scenographic orientations.

The proposition of miniature possession also offers a means of rendering the distant possessable. Bachelard recounts how the simple act of looking out on to a landscape presents the onlooker with the ability to possess distant places (trees, houses, buildings, etc.) where they 'offer themselves for our "possession", while denying the distance that created them. We possess from afar, and how peacefully!' (Bachelard 1994: 172). In this instance, Bachelard is recounting how the familiarity of miniaturization, as disciplined through childhood, sustains a projection of this trait on to the distant. The distant is rendered a possessed object through the act of declaring it scaled. However, I argue that Bachelard's reading confirms the politics of the scenic as a quantification of landscape: of rendering landscape a possessable image. Crucially, Bachelard's account of the distant scene and the encounter of real scale isolate how the scenic and scenographics are rendered distinct by the question of withness – of *being with* an environment. What confuses this distinction is that both are equally interventional and charged, albeit in different ways. The scenic sustains a politically passive yet positive charge. The scenographic alludes to a theatrical charge. Whereas the scenic is affirmative in its politics, I maintain the othering of scenographics is a consequence of being with or within an interventional worlding. While the notion of an intervention is always a political act (in that it disrupts, disorders and demarcates the ongoing politics of place), the implication of a scenographic intervention is neither positive nor negative. Of course, in certain quarters, such as architecture, the term 'scenographic' sustains a negative charge. However, I argue that this is a consequence of anti-theatrical rhetoric rather than an innate condition of scenographics. Moreover, the scenic is a passive concept that can nullify its own ideological construction. Bachelard's two examples of how scale is rendered possessable isolate how scenographics necessitate a withness, whereas the scenic maintains a critical distance.

Interior design and scenographic behaviours

Whereas scenographic orientations are explicit and interventional, 'scenographic behaviours' often recede into normativity. I propose that scenographic behaviours are tactics that emerge from the ongoing maintenance of home or interior fashioning. This conflation of material culture with social appearance is inclusive of how an individual or institution performs their relationships to other institutions (country, language, cultural activities, etc.) as well as the display of cultural capital and social status (compliance with fashion trends, hygiene standards, economic status, etc.). I argue that, as with appearance more broadly, these behaviours are disciplined by means of socially mitigated expectations that render highly contrived acts as normative through repetition. In that regard, this relationship has been previously accounted for through the performativity of interior design that, in turn, also affords a conceptual unity between the performativity of self and material cultures. I, however, argue that these utterances are encountered through the orientations afforded by scenographics.

Burns (1972) in her analysis of theatricality, observes how the symbolically loaded and orchestrated stage place is echoed in the culture of what in Britain would be termed the 'front room'. Facing the public street, the typical front room is framed by a large window that acts as a display portal between inside and outside. Burns argues that 'House interiors have become stage sets in which decoration, lighting, furniture, pictures and sometimes even books are chosen not so much for their comfort, convenience or instruction as for their appearance' (Burns 1972: 78). Interior decoration has, since the peak of the British industrial revolution, been seen as a means to perform questions of status (whether social or economic) as part of a ritualized social contract of appearance. The interior house 'setting is seen as designed, consciously or by default, to reveal an image of the owners' (Burns 1972: 78). The placement of chairs or textures of the wallpaper had, in an era of the rising middle classes, become a sign for internal character. This culture of crafting place orientations through material culture reflected a wider emphasis on self-fashioning and self-management brought on by the economic and social changes of the industrial revolution (see Sennett 1977). It is, however, the implication that interior design sustains crafted place orientations that informs my argument for scenographics.

Penny Sparke (2008) begins her analysis of public and private interiors by citing an encounter of a 'scene' within a shopping mall in Calgary, Canada in 2005:

> The scene, which comprised a set of comfortable armchairs carefully positioned on an Oriental-style carpet and accompanied by potted plants, resembled a domestic living room – one, however, that had been removed from its more familiar private environment and repositioned in a public space that was utterly alien to it. Surrounded by enormous plate glass windows, fast-moving escalators and huge structural columns, that miniature scene seemed strangely out of place. What was that private stage set doing in an otherwise public environment?
>
> (Sparke 2008: 9)

Sparke isolates how her encounter with this scene exposed the historical developments that render domestic and public interiors distinct. Sparke argues that the

> dramatic contrast of meanings and values conveyed by their sharp juxtaposition, and the fact that the 'parlour' had been wrenched from its original setting and absorbed within the larger, enveloping space of the mall, caused me to reflect on the relationship between the worlds of the 'private' and the 'public' in the insides of our modern era buildings.
>
> (Sparke 2008: 10)

Interestingly, Sparke employs the language of scenographics and evidently recognizes that this 'sharp juxtaposition' irritated the normative flows of the shopping mall concourse. Equally, within an analysis of the BBC's television show *Changing Rooms* (1996–2004), Sparke situates the labours of the invited designer as focused on projecting the unknowing client's 'inner self' through interior design: 'It endorsed a pluralistic "stage set" approach to interior decoration in which an eclectic range of fantasy environments are created as expressive backcloths in front of which the "inner" lives of their inhabitants can be lived out' (Sparke 2008: 16). In both her analysis of the shopping mall scene and the 'stage sets' of *Changing Rooms*, Sparke isolates the scenographic potential of interior design – a potential that is predicated on the orientations that situate a scene as an intervention and how material assemblages can project, or align with, a crafted sense of self.

Tara Chittenden (2015) relates interior design explicitly to the task of scenography in her analysis of Simon Woodroffe's concept for YO! Home (2012) at the *100% Design London* show. While the founder of the YO! Sushi chain and Yotel Hotels, Woodroffe had previously worked as a roadie and in stage construction for rock bands in the 1980s. Woodroffe's background in stage mechanics informed his idea for *YO! Home* as it 'started by asking what would happen if you used the mechanics of stage scenery to alter an empty room and be able to change it from one thing into the next' (in Lewis 2012: 4). While building on a long history of adaptable living spaces, from Gerrit Rietveld's *Schröder House* (1924) and Kiesler's *Endless House* (1963), Chittenden's analysis of Woodroffe's concept focuses on how scenography (as transformation) isolates how the adaptability of the room's dimensions – including the height of the ceiling – crafts a distinct sense of place orientation, where

> the act of transforming the space also transforms the ambience through the hushed sound of the moving parts, a change to light sources, and reflections in any shiny surfaces – all of these conditions resonate with possible meanings for engaging with the space of flows and designing experiences of living in the apartment.
>
> (Chittenden 2015: 11)

These qualities of an affective atmosphere are rendered felt through their transformation from one state to another. Moreover, Chittenden concludes by observing that 'YO! Home demonstrates a conception of interiors as dramatically activated living spaces and our lives within as theatrically charged' (Chittenden 2015: 12). The 'theatrical charge' that Chittenden describes is, I argue, mediated by the othering trait of scenographics.

The notion that interior design sustains a theatrical charge and, as Sparke outlines, can affirm the fashioning of an 'inner self' is crucial to my own argument on the interventional orientations of scenographics, whether rendered normative or not. Indeed, the idea that the normative worldings of interior design are of the same ontological order of scenographics aligns with a wider culture that collapses economic and social status with material culture. Soja outlines how a thirding of the ontologically real and the contrived, the authentic and the inauthentic, has been conflated in a culture of 'real fake' environments:

> We no longer have to pay to enter these worlds of the "real fake" for they are already with us in the normal course of our daily lives, in our homes and workplaces, in how we choose to be informed and entertained, in how we are clothed and erotically aroused, in who and what we vote for, and what pathways we take to survive.
>
> (Soja 1996: 19)

Soja's argument is that we continually intervene and maintain our environments in a manner that renders them as real as they are fake, as actual as they are contrived. The conflation of material cultures, whether the clothes we wear or the homes we live in, sustains a projected feeling of internal character that is cultivated by scenographic behaviours. The affirmative feeling of being in the 'right place', as enacted by material circumstances, is a shared quality of scenography and interior design. While its 'look' and the semiotic overtones are of distinct interest to this relationship, the feel of an interior design is equally fundamental when considering the othering trait of scenographics. When stepping into a designed stage-scene or room, we (as the audience to this attentive situation) become innately aware that our actions represent an intervention into this ordered environment.

I am visiting a friend in their new home in Exeter, UK. I arrive outside the house in a taxi. I note the house number on the door. I pay the taxi driver and step up to the door. As I knock, I can see through into the front room. I can see maps on the wall and a column of old suitcases precisely placed next to a window table. The ordered yet potentially 'quirky' feeling that this voyeuristic act sustains confirms that I am in the right place. This feels like my friend's home. One of my friends opens the door and invites me in. After some derobing, I walk into the front room. The room has a distinct order. Clean and concise, but also lived in and welcoming. The warm sun spills in through large bay windows. The room has a faint calming scent, potentially the last circulations of incense burned in another room. A sofa with wooden arms is positioned against the longest wall to my left. A chair, upholstered in a different fabric, is situated at a forty-five-degree angle towards a coffee table upon a textured rug. Beyond this is a bookcase. I do not see if these are travel books or otherwise, but I imagine they are a mixture of travel books and Russian novels, given what I know of my friend. The coffee table is made of polished glass with four place mats evidently placed at each corner. The suitcases I saw from outside are now in plain view. They are located next to a window seat that catches the sun in the mid-afternoon. I imagine my friend reading at the window. I ask what the suitcases are for. My friend recounts how each suitcase relates to a particular project that they are currently working on, picking one up as if to show me, and then immediately placing it back down upon the column – slightly off centre (as it had been before). While I do not see inside, the collection of assorted objects and maps on the wall reminds me of the theatre works that I have seen of my friend's and imagine (in a very imprecise way) how each suitcase holds a collection of carefully selected objects – potential props or stimuli – that ties in with my own experiences of their work. I note that the curtains are held to the wall with an ornate rope, with a bow that has been purposefully aligned with the gathered material's centre point. The labour of the room's design, but also its upkeep, is directly evident. Whether viewing the room from outside or entering as a guest, I am invited to project the qualities of this place on to its owners. As with the stage, the designedness of the front room has rendered it a representational site of display, whether intentionally or otherwise. This room has scenographic traits.

While the methods of interior design and scenography are often shared, the two practices sustain distinct ideologies. Whereas everything on stage has a theatrical charge, this same charge can be nullified through conventions of normativity in interior design. Crucially, the 'theatrical' quality of these environments is relational to the visibility of an eventful othering – contrived interventions that orientate how that environment is encountered. As evident in my tour of my friend's house, what was eventful for me was normative for my friend. The interventional affects of scenographics are, in this instance, relative to what is perceived to be normative. Qualified by an individual's durational coexistence within an environment, this normativity is disciplined by a series of learned conventions that positions the interventional designed choices of a carpet texture or bold wallpaper as an act of cultivating home. While this assemblage of objects and orientations is explicitly crafted, the interventional qualities of this crafting are nullified through an ideology of home-making, of fostering a home as a reservoir for self-dwelling. In this regard, the assemblage of home operates as an extension of self (as habitus), as well as a manifestation of a projected self that can be observed by others.

Jane M. Jacobs and Susan J. Smith connect the act of self-fashioning and the maintenance of home within a special issue on 'rematerializing home'. The geographers argue that if we did away with the home/housing binary and attended instead to an assemblage of dwelling then we would capture the dispersed and variant logics of value and valuation that actively constitute not only the field of meaning, experience and practice that is called 'home' but also the house that is the locus of its performance.

(Jacobs and Smith 2008: 518)

Home-making as an 'assemblage of dwelling' evokes the same vein of new materialist thinking that informs my own position on how scenography happens as an affective atmosphere. Consequently, the assemblage of interior design arguably operates under the same situational conditions of scenography. The textures, spatial programming and orchestration of the environment are all charged with an attentiveness that renders them highly visible to the 'tourist' or visitor. While this visibility recedes with time, the same is the case for when scenographies are installed as 'permanent' exhibitions or features of a building. What at first is highly visible recedes with the prolonged duration of relative experience. Subsequently, all interior designs arguably begin as scenography only to recede into normativity with time.

Whether conceptualized as a scenography or not, scenographics in interior design are an agent for how material cultures evoke a theatrical charge that renders attentive an object's relationship to other objects, as well as other bodies. Scenographics operate as loci for orientating and projecting relationships between otherwise independent objects that reorder these into an eventful assemblage. In turn, these assemblages of objects are conflated with the immaterial conditions of the environment (inclusive of scent, light and sound) to form a distinctive affective atmosphere. While interior design is an exercise in place orientation, the theatrical charge that results from a culture of attentive display renders scenographics as central to how interior design is encountered as an affective stage-scene. The difference is one of duration. Interior design, while not as slow as built architecture, operates at a different speed to the stage-scene of scenography. Homes are places for sustained dwelling and, correspondingly, the interventional qualities of a change in a wall colour or the position of lighting fixtures fades as time passes. Whereas theatre occurs as art time following Blau (1982), our own homes typically occur as lifetime. My visit to my friends' home in Exeter was, from my point of view, eventful: it had qualities that I have come to associate with art time (as distinct and demarcated). Moreover, my presence invites a tour of their interior design choices. While these choices sustain a normative quality due to their sustained familiarity, the act of introducing me to these choices highlights the interventional quality of the carpet or lamp to my friends, if only momentarily. The encounter with the interior design of their home is not extra-daily for my friends. The theatrical qualities of their design choices have receded with time.

To conclude this brief study of scenographic behaviours, it is the epistemological double negative of how interior design is, on one hand, recognized as a constructed and highly contrived material culture and yet, on the other hand, is positioned as authentic or self-sustaining that divorces it from scenography. Interior design is operationally theatre (it is a staging, a performance). Scenographics act as an irritant that are always present in interior design and yet the interventional quality of this trait is deemed authentic (as a crafting) and normative (as a behaviour). Home interiors are reflective of character in the same manner that body fashioning has become conflated with a performance of internal character. Following the Romanticist ideologies of 'self as immanent in appearance' (Finkelstein 1991), the post-industrial social person attends to their body in line with ideological forces (whether economic, labour relations or moral positions) that affirm a performed social order as normative. This mantra also extends to home fashioning. Burns argues that in 'private life people take great pains to select the right background for major consequential acts, for love, quarrelling or parting; for we are all too conscious of the effect of congruities and incongruities' (Burns 1972: 79). These relationships between place and action are designed, whether explicitly in terms of home interiors or geographically by being in the 'right place' for a life event. A performance of home, at least in part, occurs through the othering traits of scenographics. Whereas Burns describes these as 'stage-set like', in positioning the cultural practices of interior design as scenographic, this focuses in on how place orientation features as a part of our daily lives. While theatricality signals the dualism of thing and thing as representation of other, recognition of how scenographics intervene and shape place orientations focuses on how crafted atmospheres also observe their own social history as an act of material othering. The act of interior design, whether undertaken by professional interior designers or by the homeowners themselves, is an act of the scenographic order. While I would still hesitate to describe these individuals as scenographers, given the politics of this term, the practice of interior design is no less scenographic.

Marketing and scenographic seduction

The commercial shop window is undoubtedly a site of scenographics. The field of 'visual merchandising' exposes and exploits the seductive qualities of scenographics. While mannequins and graphic representations of products are overtly visual in their conception, the crafting of consumer experiences and the field of visual merchandising encompasses all aspects of a shop's atmosphere: inclusive of scent, sound, graphics, and spatial programming. Mattila and Wirtz argue that 'consumer responses to a physical environment depend on ensemble effects (configurations)' (Mattila and Wirtz 2001: 274). Similarly, management theory and marketing psychology has adopted the model of 'environmental aesthetics', as outlined by Rachel Kaplan and Stephen Kaplan (1982). This is closely aligned with notions of 'gestalt theory' that considers the various stimuli that comprise a store's design as part of a holistic experience of perceptual environments. New materialist notions of assemblage and affective atmospheres stem from a similar vein of thought, albeit not focused exclusively on human-orientated encounters of finite situations (a room) or design principles. For example, environmental aesthetics and gestalt theory provide the basis for studies on the use of feng shui and classical music to cultivate 'atmospheric harmony' (Garaus 2017) for commercial profit. Accordingly, techniques for gestalt within store design are representative of the same orientating qualities that define affective atmospheres. The crafting and composition of a store's atmosphere employ a number of explicit scenographic methods for orientation, such as directed lighting or a soundscape. If marketing is an act of orientating attentiveness through atmospheric interventions, then the practices of visual merchandising are predicated on scenographic manipulations. Visual merchandising is scenographic.

'Scenographic seduction' relates to the application of scenographics to manipulate the potential of an affective atmosphere to inform decision-making. This process is equally applicable to how the 'fictive' worldings of literature feel possible, if not plausible. Whether the high level of detail within the hotel rooms of Punchdrunk's *The Drowned Man* (2013) or the colour palette of Taymor's *The Lion King*, these enacted theatrical atmospheres move beyond the schema of the possible to enact felt situations that materially affirm speculative worlds as convincing, credible, seductive. Yet, the seductive potential of scenographics and their ability to craft holistic atmospheres extend beyond questions of representational verisimilitude. Management academics John Deighton and Kent Grayson describe seduction as the 'interactions between marketer and consumer that transform the consumer's initial resistance to a course of action into willing, even avid compliance' (Deighton and Grayson 1995: 660). Seduction in this instance denotes how processes of persuasion cultivate changes to an atmosphere that affects an individual's behaviours or attitude towards an idea. Following this line of thought, Juliet Rufford has described scenography as 'seductive design' (Rufford 2018). Adopting Hal Foster's argument on the political economy of design, Rufford argues that scenographics have the capacity to become co-opted by capitalism as a commodifying tactic that subverts and disempowers critical thinking. Den Oudsten notes a similar position when outlining the potential for a shared origin between the marketplace and theatre, 'where the convincing merchant would display his articles with just that extra bit of flair' (den Oudsten 2011: 2). This crossover is evident when those aligned or practised within the crafts of scenography apply their labour to commercial merchandising or as a medium for propaganda.

The notion of scenographic seduction, I propose, extends beyond the tactics of consumer capitalism. As part of the Allied war effort in the 1940s, theatre designers were recruited to craft inflatable tanks to misdirect the attentions of Axis pilots. Megan Garber outlines how this group of recruited artists 'staged a series of, basically, "traveling shows": elaborate plays designed to intimidate and/or confuse the Axis. Its members put their theatrical skills to use, engaging in "playacting," designing "soundscapes," and creating "set-dressing"' (Garber 2013). The scenographic techniques of soundscaping and set dressing were employed as means of place orientation and material surrogacy to seduce the Axis reconnaissance pilots and change their behaviours. Likewise, Laura Levin recalls how the American military in 2003 employed a television production designer, George Allison, to conceive a 'setting' for their television broadcasts from Iraq. With multiple screens and a soft-focus map of the world situated behind a lectern, Levin suggests that Allison's staging of American surveillance and intelligence techniques sought to adopt the spectacle or grammar of the television show's speculative technologies and imagined environments to persuade a global audience of their projected power. Levin concludes that 'who better to prop up the illusion of self-sufficiency and military might than a scenic designer who cut his teeth working on glitzy TV shows' (Levin 2014: 1). In this regard, scenographic seduction conflates disparate material practices, such as visual merchandising and the military application of inflatable tanks or television production techniques, to isolate the affirmative capacity of scenographics to persuade and convince. This affirmative potential is, consequently, approached as a locus for how material cultures deploy scenographics as both means of display (of communication) and seduction (of attraction and immersion).

I am looking for somewhere to eat in Guildford, UK. Along with my partner, we walk down a familiar street and see a new restaurant that has either just opened or we had not noticed it before. The restaurant is called Thaikhun. As we enter, I note immediately that this Thai restaurant has gone to significant lengths to cultivate a feeling of a street food vendor in Bangkok. To my right is a row of aeroplane seats that have been repurposed as dining chairs. To my left is wall of items on shelves seemingly awaiting purchase and yet they are rusted, disused or unattended. All of the chairs are evidently repurposed (or appear to be repurposed) from a previous usage: in a school, a church, a meeting room. The room is long and narrow with no external windows, aside from those behind me looking out on to the street. As we are taken to our seats, we progress further down into the narrow room, with the light from the street windows being replaced by the low glow from hanging lanterns. As we sit, the multifaceted qualities of this restaurant's crafted atmosphere act upon my senses. The table has differently patterned plastic wipe-clean material upon its surface to the other tables in our area. We have been sat in the only section of the restaurant that has other guests already in attendance. I can see a couple enjoying a bowl of noodles and I hear a group of friends gossiping about their day. At the end of the restaurant, I can just about see the open kitchen. The smells of Thai cuisine fill the air. While I have not been to Bangkok, the experience reminds me of a street vendor I visited in Taipei (Taiwan). In particular, I cannot avoid inspecting the assorted objects that adorn the three levels of shelving that continue for the length of the wall I am facing. Above them are a series of weathered road signs and general commercial signage. I look closer at one of the signs. I see that the uneven edges and gaps caused by flaking paint or peeling stickers are illustrative – in that the whole sign, inclusive of wear, is an image that has been glued on to a hardwood board. Moreover, the sign is evidently only recently constructed and has never been 'outside'. The sign is a surrogate object. Indeed, having been writing this chapter earlier that day I consider the implications of this sign as a seductive object – an object that persuades me of an idea, an idea that I already knew to be a construction (I am in Surrey, not Bangkok), and yet, upon revealing its own material assemblage, I am reminded of the broader act of seduction at hand. I am reminded that the highly crafted atmosphere of Thaikhun is intentional and purposeful. Crucially, the underlying message to which it pertains (that food cultures emerge from an environmental context as much as a culinary one) is all-encompassing, and yet it is also a message that I am happy to be seduced by. The atmosphere of the restaurant affirms the Gesamtkunstwerk *of the contemporary-themed restaurant. I am immersed within the Thai-ness of Thaikhun through methods of seduction that are scenographic in conception and execution.*

The scenographics of Thaikhun sought to evoke a particular atmosphere to persuade my partner and me of the food's authenticity, while also affirming the restaurant as an extra-daily or 'special' place. The immersive qualities of Thaikhun act as evidence for the seductive qualities that Deighton and Grayson attribute to decision-making, as well as the gestalt feeling central to Kaplan and Kaplan's environmental aesthetics. Yet, my experience of Thaikhun's scenographic orientations was qualified by their othering qualities. While the old dusty TV or the road signs were familiar on one level, on closer inspection they were equally out of place: the objects and the assemblage of the restaurant were a clash between 'authentic' textures (such as the toilets constructed of breeze blocks, with unconcealed cooper plumbing tubes for taps) alongside the 'inauthentic' construction methods of the digitally printed road signs. The Thaikhun afforded a surrogate experience of a Bangkok street food restaurant. The scenographics of the assorted chairs and the distance from daylight were all designed to seduce myself, as diner, that I was eating in Bangkok – yet with full knowledge that I was in Guildford. This epistemological double negative of surrogacy is crucial to unpicking the othering that scenographics afford. Rather than dismissing this experience as inauthentic, the seductive qualities of the atmosphere and the level of detail undertaken exceed strict orders of knowledge (of authentic and inauthentic) to focus on the real orientations that these assemblages, and the corresponding affective atmosphere, evoke within the diner. Thaikhun immersed my partner and me within the crafted atmosphere of a Bangkok street market to seduce us into a feeling of gestalt alignment – of being in the 'right place'. What is more, the scenographics of this Thai restaurant in Guildford made explicit the methods and techniques that sustain a feeling of place. Thaikhun provides an example of how scenographics draw attention to how constellations of place are crafted and encountered.

The scenographic qualities of the themed restaurant and the experience of dining are articulated by Joshua Abrams (2013). Abrams cites a textbook on restaurant design that suggests it is 'often said that restaurants are at least 50 per cent theater' (Walker 2011: 53). This is explicitly evident in Abrams' discussion on the Catalan chef Ferran Adrià, who 'conceived the meal as event, introducing the move indoors as a theatrical "interval" and shifting focus to both scale and the ways in which the surroundings were a crucial component of it' (Abrams 2013: 9–10). Adrià introduces elements of decontextualization, irony, spectacle and performance in order to fully immerse the diner within the event of the meal. Abrams argues that this constitutes a 'scenography of surprise [that] produces an active engagement for the diner, who becomes a co-producer in the dramaturgy of the meal' (Abrams 2013: 10). The notion that the co-relationships between participant, place and dramaturgy might afford a distinctly active engagement is also crucial to practices of immersion. My experience of Thaikhun in Guildford was equally immersive in its conception. While geographically removed from the Bangkok streets it references, the alignment of cuisine and atmosphere was evidently crafted to sustain a synergy between food and environment. Unlike the 'scenography of surprise' that Abrams cites as central to Adrià's dining experience, the assemblage of the Thaikhun restaurant was contextual and affirming in its orientation of my dining experience. What is more, my experience of Thaikhun was explicitly focused on an enacted worlding that exceeded the learned cultural signifiers that I have come to associate with Guildford and its surrounding geography. The all-encompassing qualities of a crafted atmosphere seemingly afford a potential environment in which to seduce, or persuade, individuals by any message otherwise entrenched. This is fundamental to the marketing tactics as outlined by Kaplan and Kaplan.

The conflated geographies of the Thaikhun are a reminder that the othering tactic of surrogacy is often paramount to understanding how scenographics are recognized. Scenographic surrogates signal the theatrical charge of an object or situation in reference to a learned system of interpretation. Accordingly, a scenographic surrogate exploits the interpretative processes related to the dramaturgical scene of *mise en scène*. Burns isolates this tension as the difference between a chair and a chair on stage, where the 'chair is real but it represents a more real chair in the real world' (Burns 1972: 82). The chair in the restaurant, along with wider notions of interior design, may suggest qualities through placement or through its selection (often chairs have not been made by their owners), yet it is also a very real chair. On the stage, a theatrical charge renders a chair an attentive object and heightened symbolic vehicle. The chair is to be examined, considered and analysed. Besides, the inflection remains that the chair has been placed, deliberately, and that the chair's positioning as much as its material construction is all open for discursive analysis. Burns confirms this line of thought, arguing that:

Places and settings are therefore not seen merely as neutral backcloths for asocial action. They are perceived in relation to the individual in such a way that action is at the same time contained by the setting and is the container of it.

(Burns 1972: 81)

In highlighting how interior design is bound to an inferred personality or character trait (of its inhabitants/owners/crafters), Burns isolates how scenographics disrupt the normativity of a room to render it an attentive place. This process is crucial to the seductive qualities of the restaurant or any other commercial space. In orchestrating the scenographics of the commercial environment, the fields of visual merchandising and restaurant design isolate how scenographics seduce through their capacity to be all-encompassing. This trait is crucial to how immersive environments more broadly are constructed for the purpose of rendering an individual complicit to the political geography in which they reside.

Gardening and scenographic curation

I am sat at home writing this chapter on a sunny day in mid-April in 2017. The window from my home office looks out on to a garden that I share with my partner. I can see from the window my partner planting flower cuttings that we had bought earlier that day at a local garden centre. She clears an area in the seedbed that runs the length of the garden path. She plants a cutting every thirty centimetres or so, being careful to ensure that the gaps between the bulbs are even. I recall a conversation we had earlier when selecting the cuttings in question. They are lavender. My partner's intention is that, when returning home from work, the scent from the lavender will afford a distinct welcoming atmosphere (my partner and I enjoy its scent). Furthermore, in positioning the cuttings along the path her plan is that the flowers brush against our coats as we return home, scenting the material. This gentile scenting will then act as a signifier for home when accidentally smelled at work or when we pick up our coats in the morning. There is a plan and an intention to this garden design. I watch as she gets out the lawnmower to cut the grass, being sure to render the edges between the seedbeds and grass as clean and precise as possible. There is a care and precision that goes into the planning of the garden's future design (the flowers are not yet in bloom), as well as the crafting of the grass to appear ordered and well kept. As I look upon the garden, I can see the labour that she has put into its plan and upkeep. The concise quality of the garden's order is in direct relationship to her intervention, her work and decision-making. I realize that the act of gardening and the decision-making that this act engenders is scenographic in intention and execution. I note that this crafting of scenographic orientations is also curatorial in purpose. My partner has conceptualized and executed a distinct curatorial plan that will afford a shift in the orientations that our garden sustains. My partner's plan and actions are an act of scenographic curation.

As with notions of performance before it, curation has arguably been adopted as a post-disciplinary concept that has become potentially borderless and applicable to all areas of contemporary culture. Art historian Mika Tokumitsu aptly summarizes this in an article for New Republic magazine entitled 'The Politics of the Curation Craze': 'Blogs are curated. So are holiday gift guides. So are cliques, play lists, and restaurant menus. "Curated," a word that barely existed forty years ago, has somehow come to qualify everything in our lives' (Tokumitsu 2015). Tokumitsu observes how professional curators have witnessed this expansion occur from the sidelines, with many taking either negative or agnostic positions on the subject. Unlike performance, the critical expansion of curation occurred outside of the academic remit of curatorial practice. In particular, the adoption of curation has coincided with the increased focus on social media platforms that seemingly reward the collection of 'things' as much as the content itself. This focus on the agency of collecting has driven the uptake of curation as a social practice. Yet, the framework of the curatorial is as an imposition as well as a task. To consider gardening as a form of curating is to consider how humans, whether for nutriment or subjectivities, cultivate the material structures of 'nature'. The garden operates as a locus for arguing how scenographics are enacted within the orchestration of one of our most basic tasks. Moreover, the garden sustains a similar set of dialectical tensions to the theatre, which equally signposts and exposes the orienting capacity of scenographics as an interventional crafting of place. Gardens, like scenographies, are rendered peculiar by their capacity to score how place is constituted.

In the chapter entitled 'Garden Thinking and the Baroque Pastoral' (2017), Will Daddario traces how Italian playwrights of the 1600s often appropriated the 'rural space' of the public garden to stage events where the mind is unfettered by regulation or institution. Daddario argues that 'the garden was a crucial pastoral site, a merger of the sacred, the divine, the rural, and the urban' (Daddario 2017: 23). Daddario's proposed 'garden thinking' exploits the dialectical tensions between inside and outside, rural and urban, nature and art.

> Not only do the meanings of gardens bloom through the labor of dialectical thinking; the garden also exists as dialectical space, as thought-made-spatial, insofar as its entire existence hinges on the differentiation and epistemic exclusivity between inside and outside, between the manicured landscape within the wall, hedge, or fence and the natural, unkempt terrain beyond.
>
> (Daddario 2017: 24)

In particular, Daddario focuses on how the dialectical place of the garden invites a particular form of spatial practice that seemingly welcomes a distinctive mode of dwelling (as, following Heidegger, both a mode of thinking and being in situ). Indeed, Daddario relates the ordering of an argument to the order of gardening, where 'the artist cultivates ideas from seed, arranges them in rows so that neighboring ideas can inform one another, and eventually presents the assortment of individual ideas as a whole' (Daddario 2017: 24). For Daddario, the material circumstances of a garden and the act of gardening are representative of a mode of thought that is peculiar to the negotiation of the dialectical tensions it sustains.

In terms of scenographics, Daddario details how ornamental gardening is called topiary, which stems from Aristotle's *topoi* as 'a place where different items can be arranged in an order than will aid in their subsequence recollection' (in Daddario 2017: 25). Topiary work or art today is most often associated with the clippings of a bush to resemble something other than a bush through a sculpting of its form alone. It can, however, also apply to the crafting of garden mazes or any 'living' architectural feature that has been wrought to take on a particular shape or profile. Vitruvius employed the term *topiarius* to denote the task of a gardener. Interestingly, this term was also applied to the design of interior landscape frescoes within Roman villas. These same frescoes would have applied the perspective techniques associated with *skenographia*. The capacity for the *topiarius* to apply to gardening and frescoes stresses how Roman culture adopted landscape as a commodity, which could be shaped and orientated to human needs. It also stressed how the dialectical situation of the garden sustained a shared, if critically removed, condition of dwelling to that of the theatre – where both were sites that sustained moments of reflection through a crafting of distinctive place orientations. Kant, however, aligned gardening with painting. Recognizing that, while gardening is corporeal, the philosopher suggested that, 'like painting, this beautiful arrangement of corporeal things is given only to the eye, because the sense of touch cannot provide a presentation of intuition of such a form' (Kant 1987: 192–3). Kant argued that landscape gardening is conceived *with* nature's products, but *for* the appreciation of the human eye more so than bodily sensations. While this aligns with the first adoption of scenography as painterly perspective, the argument for scenographics seeks to complicate this partitioning and consider how visually conceived practices also affect through a wider atmospheric feeling that gardens undoubtedly sustain.

My aim for 'scenographic curation' is not as an exclusive or unique quality of scenographics. Rather my intention is to stress how these orientations are crafted outside of an institutional definition of scenography. Given the expansive remit of curation, all scenography is an exercise in curating place orientations. Yet, the distinction between crafting and curating reveals a potential point of focus. If scenography is a crafting (that proceeds from a wright-ing rather than a write-ing), then the curation of scenographics is rendered peculiar to this process, as it results from another method or process of assemblage. Crucially, the underlying focus of gardening is not the formation of scenographies. While I could describe a garden as scenography (in how it orientates an interventional feeling of place), this would be to isolate the orientating qualities of scenographics that are then conceptualized as scenography. Scenography will always be scenographic. Gardens, on the other hand, become scenographic. Scenographics are not a formative quality of gardening. Scenographics result from the orientating qualities that the curation of a garden sustains and provokes. The placement of seedbeds shifts the place-orientating qualities of a defined garden. As the plants grow and flower, new scenographics emerge. Scenographics in this instance are a consequence of gardening. What scenographic curation isolates is how these future orientations are taken into account when planting and conceiving the spatial programming of a garden.

Scenographic curation results in interventional and highly visible orientations. This is distinct from the normativity that is typically assigned to interior design, or what I have termed 'scenographic behaviours'. However, these two loose headings – of behaviour and curation – share many of the same qualities and issues of ideology when applied to home fashioning (which for the purposes of this argument is inclusive of gardens). While these practices overlap and intersect with one another, curation is approached as an explicit negotiation of the interrelationships between discrete things, as well as the atmosphere that these assemblages maintain. Scenographic behaviours apply to gardening in that a garden is maintained through acts of management and cultivation, which are behavioural and ongoing in execution. Scenographic curation relates explicitly to the decision-making processes and human agency that assemble scenographics in the manifestation of a particular atmospheric quality. It is the notion of responsibility – more so than the interpretative contexts of 'writing' to which I would assign the dramaturgical – that denotes the quality of scenographic curation; where the care of curation is tied to a human agency. Consequently, scenographic curation is representative of questions of 'intention' that are typically assigned to the human agent within the conception and encounter of a scenographic environment.

Protest and scenographic activism

Essin defines 'scenographic activism' as recognition of the 'significant contributions made by [stage] designers in creating activist theatre, performance produced to provoke a desired response from their audience that forwards specific sociopolitical goals' (Essin 2012: 97). Focused on how scenographies can be crafted to enact the political agendas of social justice movements and trade unions, Essin cites the techniques for scenographic activism as being inclusive of the 'strategic arrangement of space (often in a manner than minimizes divisions between performers and spectators) and visual interpretations that prompt spectators to connect critically and/or affectively with a performance' (Essin 2012: 97–8). Crucially, Essin focuses her definition on the political reading of stage designers' work as distinct from their political beliefs or associations. In terms of scenographics as an agent for place orientation, my own approach to scenographic activism adopts the underlying potential that Essin describes (to articulate, provoke or enact political change through the methods of scenography). However, I look to apply this to a broader conceptualization of protest practices to argue how these events are enacted through means of scenography. In particular, I propose that the interventional and orientating traits of scenographics afford and sustain the temporal displacements that occur through acts of occupying powerful geographies (sites charged with power and authority). Scenographics irritate the worldings of power and are uniquely suited to score the political ruptures that acts of protest enact. From the use of masks and costumes to the act of occupying a street or room, scenographic activism is arguably a familiar and vital component that shapes how contemporary democratic politics are conducted. To evidence my claim that scenographics are integral to contemporary protest practices, I return to an example that affords distinctive yet connected arguments on the significance of scenographics to protest; namely, the Occupy movement's deployment of tents outside St Paul's Cathedral between 2011 and 2012.

I am at a conference in Las Vegas in 2012. I am with a number of architects and scenographers discussing notions of performative architecture. After a long session, we go to a bar. A news programme on the television details how the ongoing protests outside St Paul's Cathedral are developing. Behind the reporter, I can see a collection of tents that are situated on the paved area outside of the cathedral. I know this place. I have been there many times before. Yet, the tents have altered the qualities of this place. Whereas once I have known this area as a passage or a meeting point, now it operated as a site of contestation and political thought. A colleague turns to me and observes how the tents occupied the 'space' of St Paul's in a manner that reminded her of the land art projects of 1960s, which we had been discussing earlier. Yet, my colleague was quick to state that the Occupy Movement itself was no doubt unaware of this. Two thoughts spring to me immediately. The first is that, even if they are unaware of the potential reference, this act of political orientation is no less effective. The second is that I know one of the protesters living in the tents outside St Paul's – Ronan McNern. I know Ronan because he had been a PhD researcher studying scenography at Leeds with me. I had seen him being interviewed on Sky News only a few days before. I turn to my colleague and suggest that they may be more aware of the scenographic potentials of the protest than we give credit. Beyond questions of representation, the tents occupied the historical space of power that is St Paul's through their physical presence and the orientations that these afford. I cannot help but be reminded that the first skēnē was a tent, a temporary structure, which altered how theatrical space was crafted and understood. The protests at St Paul's were equally radical in their reordering of space, of power. The interventional capacity of scenographics to other and irritate the spaces of power was, to my mind, encapsulated within the tents that occupied St Paul's. Often deemed superficial or trivial, I realize that scenographics have the potential to other spaces of power, and in doing so enact speculative politics.

The notion that scenographic orientations were evident within Occupy the London Stock Exchange's (OccupyLSE) use of tents – as well as New York or at Tahrir Square as part of the Arab Spring – positions these interventions as political and serious. Likewise, this carries with it the idea that the interventional qualities of these orientations enact and affirm politics, which, in the very act of occupying, further speculate positions on how power and space are interrelated. In *Campsite: Architectures of Duration and Place*, Charlie Hailey (2008) considers the act of camping through Heidegger's notion of *Einbruch* – of breaking *into* space. Whereas *Räumen* (clearing space) and *Einräumen* (making room) seek to 'make space' along with *Raumgeben* (giving space), *Einbruch* is an act of disrupting the normative contexts and situations of place. Notably, this term also translates as 'burglary' or 'irruption'. Hailey argues that breaking 'in effect relinks and refastens camp to place' (Hailey 2008: 9). He continues:

> We might understand this refastening as a process that works back from place to camp. In this sense, camp reifies the abstractions and ideas of place through the camper's mental and often physical reconstruction of place. Through sitting and breaking, camping becomes one of many possible materializations of place.
>
> (Hailey 2008: 9)

This notion that camps simultaneously intervene and materialize place is a shared condition of scenography. As potentially one of the other possible strategies for the materialization of place that Hailey implies, the act of camping and scenography both complicate and 'break into' the established flows and norms of a place. With 'space' being representative of how powerful ideologies are rendered real through their appropriation of place, Hailey's approach to the camp as breaking into space presents an apt framework for understanding the scenographics of the tents outside St Paul's. This notion of interrupting the flows of power/space has, however, previously been accounted for within the utterances of the performative.

Hannah considers the political potential of scenographics when arguing the performative qualities of the *Journée des Barricades* ('Day of the Barricades') in Paris in 1588. Reflecting on how the revolutionary protest against King Henry III (1551–89) of France led to the spontaneous construction of street blockades from materials requisitioned from the immediate area, Hannah argues that 'the barricade – an unstable and ephemeral architecture, originally built as a communal act of camaraderie and defiance – presents a powerfully performative concept' (Hannah 2009: 108).

The legacy of the *Journée des Barricades* has remained within the lexicon of French rebellion, with the 1968 May protests a poignant example. Cars were overturned and trees uprooted to form temporary borders that both disrupted civic action and inscribed the protesters' dissatisfaction upon the physical fabric of Paris. Nevertheless, the power that Hannah assigns to the barricade's performative traits are, I argue, qualified by scenographics: in the manner that the barricade 'takes place' in a literal sense as a temporary intervention that serves to emphasize the structure's dual status as both an instigator of action (in its denial of passage) and as a consequence of action (a protest). The barricade orientates encounters of place through intervention. It reveals how ideologies of space (and power) are ever-present within our public streets, disrupting the orders of flow and law. In situational terms, the barricade is scenographic. While Hannah assigns the power of this act with the performative, I propose that it is useful to consider how the notion of scenographics applies and isolates the othering trait intrinsic to this act of place orientation. Subsequently, the barricade is potentially the characteristic example of scenographic activism: that which irritates the politics of worlding through an act of place orientation.

While barricades explicitly reorder flows of power/space through resistance, the tents adopted by OccupyLSE disrupted as much through persistence as resistance. Tents were, arguably, the first method of scenography. The Greek *skēnē* afforded an architecture of refuge, while also being a highly visible intervention that othered the spatial politics of its immediate surroundings. Similarly, the OccupyLSE protesters' tents enacted a means of spatial disruption, which in turn unsettled – or called attention to – how power and space are bound to one another. Yet, the function of the tent as refuge remains, as the occupancy of the tents was crucial to this protest strategy. Returning to the notion of *Einbruch*, the act of taking refuge implies a direction of travel and motion – of breaking *into* space or at least breaking *away* from another space. Hailey argues that this underlies the transient 'space of breaking' that 'combines continually localized arriving with the expansiveness of concurrent departure' (Hailey 2008: 9). A recurring theme within the news reports of OccupyLSE's protest was whether or not the tents were themselves occupied at night. The *Guardian* reported that an unnamed spokesperson for the protesters stated:

> While it is quite possible that not every tent is occupied every night, we try to keep vacancy to a minimum and operate a sign-in/sign-out system to help ensure this happens. The camp attracts thousands of people every day. We do not expect all the people who are expressed through this movement to be able to stay overnight.
> (in Jones and Walker 2011)

The impact of the tent's political agency is, in this instance, tied to the potential for humans to be dwelling inside. Of course, this was crucial to maintain for the protest. Authorities would have had no hesitation in removing the tents from the location otherwise. The complication exists in how the tents sustained a highly transient population. Much like Schrödinger's cat, the tents were simultaneously populated and unpopulated at the same time. This potential was both politically performative and situationally scenographic.

In *Notes Toward a Performative Theory of Assembly* (2015), Butler argues the significance of human bodies to protest and the political potential of alliance through spatial–bodily relationships. Considering how mass protest groupings reorientate and complicate systems of power through the interventional act of being with place, Butler reviews the performative power of alliance through mass transition (as with a march) or through the occupying of public space with human bodies. To argue this point, Butler adopts the political theorist Hannah Arendt's notion of the 'space of appearance'. Arendt argues that space brings about politics, where

> it is the space of appearance in the widest sense of the world, namely, the space where I appear to others as others appear to me, where men [*sic*] exist not merely like other living or inanimate things but make their appearance explicitly.
> (Arendt 1958: 199)

The performative alliance of human groupings is, therefore, bound to the 'space in-between' bodies where 'any action takes place in a located somewhere, it also establishes a space that belongs properly to alliance itself' (Butler 2015: 73). It is the capacity of bodies and materiality to enact a 'space of appearance' that scores the political potential of performative alliance. The togetherness and complicitness, of *being with others*, is sustained through a proximity that is manifest within that place, at that moment. Scenographic activism isolates the witness of alliance that enacts politics through the capacity of bodies being both *of and with* place.

While Butler focuses on the performative alliance of bodies, Brejzek looks to stress how – in the example of how social media had been adopted by flash mobs to form and enact alliances – these 'virtual scenographies' act as an orientating architecture. Brejzek describes the occurrence of a flash mob as enacting a 'pervasive scenography', where 'the mob ruptures the urban mesh for a brief moment by its stillness, thus transforming the public space into a pervasive scenography of physical presence and virtual communication' (Brejzek 2010: 118–19). The notion that human groupings co-opt their surroundings for political or performative purpose drills down to the core issue at hand. While scenographics are neither true nor false in execution, their affects are qualified as such through a set of aesthetic politics that quantify these actions in relationship to established norms. Turner summarizes this position, arguing that the situational potentials of theatre can speculate and perform alternative worldings that afford insights into a new or future politics:

> While the theatre does not present a perfected world, it does make a world out of it: these tensions are held within some kind of tangible whole. The dramaturgical experiment inherent in such a theatre might not offer an image of the world that anyone would seek to emulate or reconstruct, but it opens up new possibilities, in a potentially exhilarating confirmation that a reinvented space is possible, perfect or otherwise.
> (Turner 2015: 192)

The potential for assemblages of bodies and objects – whether tents and barricades, flash mobs and their surroundings – to enact speculative or renewed politics through the very act of being with place is decisive to the performative power of alliance that Butler identifies within mass acts of protest. Scenographic activism, following this model, can enact speculative politics through the potential of place orientation to reorientate how bodies and materials, power and place, relate to one another.

To conclude this chapter on scenographic cultures, I return to the words of Brecht and the reality of illusion:

> The illusion created by the theatre must be a partial one in order that it may always be recognized as illusion. Reality, however complete, has to be altered by being turned into art, so that it can be seen to be alterable and be treated as such.
> (in Willett 1964: 219)

The idea of theatre offering a method for isolating and recognizing how reality is constituted evidently applies beyond a theatrical paradigm. Brecht's position is that the illusionary frame of theatre exposes how other institutions and social orders are equally illusionary, albeit politically distanced from theatricality. Indeed, the sustained and linguistic bias against the theatrical across the English-speaking world arguably acknowledges the 'threat' posed by theatricality. Systems of social power are more often than not predicated on the assumption that disciplined behaviours and cultural institutions are not viewed as constructions, which have become normative through repetition and discipline. The methods of scenography are, following this position, labelled deceptive. While Schechner has declared that in the twenty-first century 'people as never before live by means of performance' (Schechner 2013: 28), to describe an event as 'stage-managed' is to imply it lacks political sincerity. Equally, to frame an outfit as 'costumey' is to suggest that it is either out of character or poorly constructed. These negative readings frame how scenographic cultures are discussed to trivialize their impact and potentiality to reveal, enact and represent wider orders of power. This position is arguably a consequence of the Romanticist ideology that positions stability as a moral and political necessity. Acts of resistance to appearance normativity – whether rendered though acts of costume or other forms of scenographic intervention – are understood in relation to the Romanticist ideology of stability. While, as anthropologist Daniel Miller (2010) points out, the conventions associated with the stable internalized 'Western self' are not universal, in English-speaking cultures appearance normativity is assessed against structures of authenticity that in neo-liberal cultures become tradeable commodities. Theatricality is the counterpoint to the disciplined, as Benjamin terms it, 'cult value' of authenticity as stable and normative. To embrace the critical duality of theatricality as a ubiquitous condition of codified appearance reveals, and potentially destabilizes, the ideological constructs of normativity that underlie how power is identified and negotiated in everyday life. In large post-industrial societies, where there are significantly more strangers than acquaintances, the agents of theatricality are accordingly dangerous and require active policing. A scenographic trait is one of those agents.

Whereas slow architecture pertains to monumentality, fast architecture is scenographic.

CHAPTER 7

Scenographic architecture

For modernist architectural critics such as Kenneth Frampton, 'scenographic' is a byword for bad architecture. Brejzek outlines Frampton's position that conflates the anti-theatrical rhetoric of Plato and Romanticism with a misreading of scenography as anti-spatial:

> To Frampton, the colourful, playful and eclectic façades of postmodernist architecture, rich with formal references and direct quotations, were mere surface, superfluous and inauthentic and motivated by cynicism ... Frampton understands the 'scenographic' not as inherently spatial (perspectival) but as a continuation of the painting of the *skene* with no purpose other than decoration.
>
> (Brejzek 2015: 26)

With a clear lineage to the first adoption of scenography, Frampton's scenographic is taken to pertain to the descriptive in architectural decoration. Scenographic architecture consequently accounts for frescos and façades that for modernist architects – as summarized by Adolf Loos's manifesto 'Ornament and Crime' originally published in 1908 – were excessive with no material function. 'Façade' in this instance is a loaded term. While accounting for the external features of a building, 'façade' also denotes concealment and disguise. Modernist critiques of the façade are critiques of the façade's scenographic tendencies - its theatrical charge and othering qualities. The notion of the scenographic in architecture has, subsequently, come to be associated with descriptive design that is surface-orientated or physically flimsy. Typically, this will centre on figurative images that are removed from the situational affects of architecture. Loos and Frampton's arguments were for architectures that went beyond descriptive decoration. Yet, as Böhme observes, the concepts and working focus of scenography evidently relate to contemporary architectural theory:

> Recognition of the space of physical presence as the actual subject matter of architecture moves perilously close to stage design. The latter has always known that spaces it creates are spaces of atmosphere. And stage design has always made use not only of objects, walls, and solids, but also of light, sound, colour, and a host of other conventional means: symbols, pictures, texts.
>
> (Böhme 2006: 406)

The holistic premise of scenography lends itself to the event-based theoretical positions of architects – whether Tschumi or Juhani Pallasmaa – that position the act of architectural encounter as being formative to any design process. Nevertheless, the term 'scenographic architecture' for most architects currently reads as wholly descriptive and is typically taken as a symptom of all that is bad in architecture.

Given the negative connotations associated with the term, in this chapter I offer a renewed reading of scenographic architecture following scenography as place orientation. In particular, my proposal is centred on the interventional qualities of scenographics and how these traits take place *alongside-and-with* pre-existing architectures and geographies. My argument for scenography as place orientation is predicated on the idea that the othering traits of scenographics craft orientations from ongoing situations of place.

Therefore, scenographic architecture is an intervention with place: it is not a replacement or a surrogate for another place. Scenographics following this reading are also not anti-description. Description is a condition of how the material crafting of a stage-scene is *read*: a condition that is of the order of the dramaturgical scene. The stage-scene of scenographic architecture exists side by side with the dramaturgical scene, where the descriptive and the figurative perform a codified reading that is potentially independent of the geography in which it is situated. The interventional qualities of scenographics are partially encountered through an interpretative matrix where materials, textures and placements are rendered symbolically other; as contextually 'out of place'. I argue that what connects the scene of scenography and the dramaturgical scene is that they are both interventional: each scene is an instance of orientation, of shaping how a place is encountered. Scenographic architecture will sustain stage-scenes that can be figurative as well as critical and embodied. In that regard, I review the idea of scenographic architecture with a distinct focus towards the explicitly temporal. While no architecture is permanent, scenographic architecture will sustain a distinctive temporality through a distinctly faster rhythm to the long-term experiences of 'slow architecture'. I propose that the 'fast architecture' of scenographics is evident in the othering qualities of *trompe l'oeil* as well as the surrogate structures of Potemkin villages. It is with the notion of a fast architecture that I begin.

Fast architecture

It's a sunny day in June 2016 and I am walking through the University of Surrey, where I work. As part of a wellbeing event, I see that two bouncy castles have been hired and placed on a central field. I had been writing a draft of this chapter earlier that day. I reflect on how two inflatables are situated within the grounds of the university through their material (inflated plastic) and the use of guy ropes that anchor it to the ground. My head turns to consider the contrast with the brick and plate-glass buildings nearby. The bouncy castles are transitional and provisional, yet also playful and symbolically 'other'. I observe students using the elastic qualities of this architectural environment to jump around. I note that, while this scenario is not institutionally theatre, it could be described as scenographic. First, the placement within the field denotes an act of staging: consideration has clearly been given to how people will move between the castles, while also how the castles themselves occupy the field's 'centre stage'. Second, the inflated materiality of these temporary environments situates them as a form of eventual architecture: an architecture that is for 'the now'. Third, these structures perform a schema for 'castle'. They evoke a learned symbolic signifier for the castle concept that, in turn, juxtaposes the seriousness of fortification against the playfulness assigned to a child's party (the context in which bouncy castles are most ready associated). I note that, while they are bouncy castles, they are not a castle in the sense of Balmoral. As situated objects, the pair denotes a duality that is intrinsic to the politics of theatricality, as they are neither a castle nor are they not not a castle. Yet, fundamental to my experience of these castles is that they are also interventional. I am fully aware that these structures and the behaviours they sustain are a temporary fixture at this locale. I conclude that – whether in terms of ideology or situation – the bouncy castles are scenographic.

My example of the bouncy castles encapsulates a number of positions concerning the notion of scenographic architecture. For individuals such as Svoboda, the term 'scenographic' evokes a perspectival or interventional quality; for others, like Frampton, it sustains an anti-theatrical bias that renders it trivial or superficial. From a situational position, bouncy castles afford behavioural orientations that result from its material qualities. They are also, from an ideological position, encountered in relationship to their temporary status and potential for material surrogacy. The bouncy castles are an event architecture that operates as an active othering of how normative architectural encounters are contextually understood. The culturally assigned playfulness of the bouncy castle disguises the interventional qualities of this situated architecture that renders it 'not-serious'. Seriousness in architecture is all too often bound to an inferred or explicit monumentality. Fast architecture is a counterpoint to the monumentality imposition. Fast architecture situates scenographic traits within a temporal dimension that complicates the reading of scenographic as fixed pictorial surfaces or 'merely' decor. Whereas slow architecture pertains to sustained monumentality, fast architecture evokes scenographic modes of orientation and scores the ongoing processes of worlding.

Slow architecture is the bastion of monumentality. In 1922, Appia outlined how conceptions of monumentality are 'intended to stimulate [people's] admiration rather than their gratitude' (in Beacham 1993: 137). Pallasmaa stresses that architecture's monumental qualities are derived from its capacity to act as both a measure and a reminder of the passing and event of time: 'Architecture emancipates us from the embrace of the present and allows us to experience the slow, healing flow of time … [Buildings] enable us to see and understand the passing of history, and to participate in time cycles that surpass individual life' (Pallasmaa 2005: 52). Pallasmaa's focus on the 'healing flow of time' is tied to the capacity of architecture to exceed (or recede from) human perceptions of time. Chris Salter, however, identifies the interrelationship between monumentality and slowness within architecture's capacity to pertain to the representative power of sculpture, where 'architecture manifests the sculpture's yearning for objects materialized at monstrous size' (Salter 2010: 81). Moreover, Krauss's (1979) adoption of 'architecture' and 'not-architecture' to map the expanded field of sculpture exemplifies how notions of slow architecture discipline and regulate their surroundings through material persistence. In particular, Krauss details how the matrix point of not-architecture recognizes that sculpture can exists *alongside* architecture and yet remain qualified by this architecture's monumentality, its resolve. This position arguably conceptualizes architecture as an expression of human perseverance and power. Kant articulates a similar line of thought when categorizing the 'plastic arts', which he saw as inclusive of sculpture and architecture.

> *Sculpture* is the art that exhibits concepts of things corporeally, as they *might exist in nature* (though, as a fine art, it does so with a concern for aesthetic purposiveness). *Architecture* is the art of exhibiting concepts of things that are possible *only through art*, things whose form does not have nature as its determining basis but instead has a chosen purpose, and of doing so in order to carry out that aim and yet also with aesthetic purposiveness.
>
> (Kant 1790: 191; emphasis in original)

Fundamental to Kant's critique is the determining factor of 'nature' and how plastic arts evoke or depart from this criterion. Yet, the idea that architecture persists whereas sculpture is figurative (of nature in Kant's model) and/or mobile is crucial to how these differentiations have been positioned in opposition. The persistence of slow architecture is the agent for the political power apportioned to monumentality: of authority through endurance. As a manifestation of assigned human power and ideological persistence, the politics of slow architecture are aptly summarized within the history of theatre architecture.

In *Places of Performance: The Semiotics of Theatre Architecture* (1989), Carlson outlines how theatre buildings have been adopted as civic monuments. Acting as symbols for a civil society as well as a platform for debate, Carlson argues that the civic relationship to theatre relates to figures such as Voltaire (1694–1778) aligning the politics of the Enlightenment with the symbolic potential of 'prestige' buildings. Carlson argues that Voltaire 'encouraged the development of both monumental theatre as civic centres of culture and private theatres as locations of refined, intimate recreation' (Carlson 1989: 52). While the relationship between theatre building and civic identity was 'totally absent in the medieval and Renaissance concepts of theatrical space' (Carlson 1989: 68), Carlson does compare the civic monument of the Greek *theatron* in Athens – with its views upon the city below – with the vantage point afforded by the Eiffel Tower in Paris. Carlson observes that both are 'mechanisms for presenting to their users a striking panorama of artificial and natural space' (Carlson 1989: 62). Of course, the *theatron* was originally a temporary appropriation of landscape (a hillside) that over time became a stable 'site' for theatrical practice. Likewise, the Eiffel Tower was a temporary exhibition structure for the 1889 World's Fair to showcase advances in the application of wrought iron within bridge construction. The potential for these viewpoints to be rendered symbolic of power, and assigned prestige due to their physical reordering of how public space is observed, informs how theatre buildings are appropriated and conceived as civic architecture today. Crucially, the explicit formative temporality of the *theatron* and the Eiffel Tower as first conceived evidences how architecture becomes adopted by systems of power to evoke and sustain a sense of social permanence. While evidently symbolic of power (be that of nation, monarchy or theology), the appropriation of these architectures as civic monuments scores how architecture is conceptualized in terms of monumentality – as a witness to the past and a connection to the future that extends the ideas of human power (or powerful ideas) throughout time.

Fast architecture enacts interventions *with* place; it emphasizes encounters of 'the now'. Whereas slow architecture sustains a sense of *passing through* human perceptions of time (of linking past into present to promote the future), fast architecture stresses the act of *taking place* in the present moment. It exists as a manifestation of an event's situational geographies that explicitly cites itself as fleeting, in – to borrow from Peggy Phelan (1993) – a 'state of disappearance'. Scenography is fast architecture *par excellence*. As explicitly interventional and temporary, scenographics score the intersections between the persistence of slow architectures (such as a street or courtyard) with the situational, material and technological interventions (such as raised platform accented by a focused light beam) that render a normative place eventual. Indeed, Salter has argued that the eventual contexts of scenography can prototype and experiment with architectural ideas. Salter suggests that architecture 'seems to have historically needed the theater to assist in pushing conceptual and structural boundaries – to practice scenography on the stage in order to carry it over into the urban wild' (Salter 2010: 84). Salter cites diverse examples to evidence his point, from the theatre architecture of Palladio to the early scenographies of the design studio Diller + Scofidio (now Diller Scofidio + Renfro).

Following this position, the first experiments in architecture could arguably be understood as instances of fast architecture. Vitruvius cited the origin of architecture as a co-option of fallen trees, the sculpting of caves or the intimation of bird nests (see Gwilt 1874: 32). In particular, Vitruvius traced the transition between the temporary materials of wood to the durational materials of stone. Similarly, Hailey (2008) outlines how many cities were originally established as Roman camps (*castra*): whether York, Manchester or Vienna. These camps then became 'permanent' in relationship to the immobility of heavier, more durable architectures that emerged with time and the socio-economic benefits that come with settling. While origin arguments are always problematic, these examples highlight how fast architecture can manifest methods and ideas that are then adopted and implemented within the design and execution of slow architecture.

From the use of velvet ropes to form a queue to the elastic qualities of bouncy castles, the slow architectures of monumentality are scored by acts of fast architecture. I argue that these material practices sustain interventional place orientations and, consequently, are scenographic in conception and execution. Céline Condorelli offers a similar observation in her approach to 'support structures'. Whether manifest as conceptual ideas or physical systems for support, Condorelli considers the practice of architectural scaffolding as an explicit articulation of how the temporality of support structures score the duration and fragility of slow architecture along with the ideas these monuments represent:

> Scaffolding and other forms of support appear as temporary even though they might be there for a very long time, as if a state of need could only be comprehended as momentary and passing, like illness, which is something one (hopefully) recovers from.
>
> (Condorelli 2009: 21)

Equally, Condorelli argues that the very existence of the temporary scaffold, of the support structures, 'unconsciously remind[s] us of the muddle of the world which we don't like, and what we are trying to preserve is the ideologic, the purity in the sense of its autonomy, its ideality' (Condorelli 2009: 21). Monumentality pertains to an ideology that co-opts architecture as the literal manifestation and persistence of human ideas. The passing context of the scaffold – as that which occurs to sustain to the monumental – also serves to highlight the need for support. It is a sticking plaster that will fall away; a crucial part of a healing process; and a sign of the structure's temporal fragility.

Sylvia Lavin, in *Kissing Architecture* (2011), offers a re-reading of architectural experience in terms of the topographic and durational circumstances of a 'kiss'. With particular reference to the installation artist Pipilotti Rist's media projections upon the surfaces of found architectural walls, Lavin argues that a 'kiss offers to architecture, a field that in its traditional forms has been committed to permanence and mastery, not merely the obvious owner of sensuality but also a set of qualities that architecture has long resisted: ephemerality and consilience' (Lavin 2011: 5). Moreover, Lavin extends this position to consider how projected surfaces operate in union with, but as discrete agents from, architecture.

> Kissing confounds the division between two bodies, temporarily creating new definitions of threshold that operate through suction and slippage rather than delimitation and boundary. A kiss performs topological inversions, renders geometry fluid, relies on the atectonic structural prowess of the tongue, and updates the metric of time. Kissing is a lovely way to describe a contemporary architectural practice.
>
> (Lavin 2011: 5–10)

This model of architectural experience as an ongoing negotiation of discrete material agents that operate together, yet remain ontologically distinct, is tantamount to the orientating potential of scenographics. While Rist's projections are undoubtedly scenographic, the whole atmospheric encounter – or what Lavin describes as a kiss – affords interventional place orientations that are also scenographic in formation and affect. Lavin's kiss isolates how scenographic orientations result from the overlap and interrelationships between slow and fast architectures. If scenographics score encounters of world through means of irritating conceptual and practical borders (between ideas, objects and situations), then the kiss of Rist's installation and the support structure of scaffolding both arguably intervene and irritate the worlding normativity of slow architecture *in the manner of* scenographics. Scaffolds and projected kisses are understood in relation to their scenographic intervention – irritating the neat perceptual borders between building and street, inside and outside, slow and fast.

The temporality of scaffolding and the kiss of projected media highlight how scenographics exists alongside-and-with slow architectures. It also serves to exemplify the distinction between scenographics and the anti-theatricality assigned to the scenic. Scaffolding is as politically real as slow architecture, albeit existing for a different timeframe. Correspondingly, the kiss of projected media intervenes in the manner of a worlding land border than renders the slippage between perceptual states as highly visible. Böhme, however, observes that among the architectural professions the bias against scenography is also an enactment of disciplinary hierarchies. Böhme asks:

> Should the architect learn from the stage designer and perhaps even develop a new awareness of [their] art? Hasn't the architect always looked down upon the stage designer as a younger [sibling] or even as a frivolous disciple of his own art? ... That will not happen.
>
> (Böhme 2006: 406)

The last statement is telling. A refusal to embrace the cross-pollination of scenography and architecture is predicated upon a systematic distrust that scenography is not serious or authentic. This anti-theatricality is also evident in the early arguments for performance art in the 1970s as being systematically discrete from the assigned inauthenticity of theatre. Interestingly, architectural communities have readily embraced the notion of 'performative architecture'. Branko Kolarevic describes performative architecture as that which can 'respond to changing social, cultural, and technological conditions [and in which] culture, technology, and space form a complex active web of connections, a network of interrelated constructs that affect each other simultaneously and continually' (in Salter 2010: 84). While Kolarevic's usage is broad in its conception, the term is also used to navigate around an assigned anti-theatricality and evokes von Hantelmann's (2010) critique on the overuse of 'performative' to describe a potentiality for movement or 'stage-like'. Furthermore, the adoption of 'performative' within architecture has been co-opted into questions of automation and robotics, more so than the passive utterances of 'slow architecture'. Akin to von Hantelmann's observations that performative art is readily acknowledged as a defined genre of practice (in ignorance of the position that all art is performative), performative architecture typically operates as a discrete field of practice rather than a critical framework on how all architecture performs.

While the positive embrace of scenographic architecture is less common, there are a number of positions that seek to consider the architectural qualities of theatrical place orientation. Architectural critic Gray Read argues that Brook's famous statement on a bare stage is predicated on an act of architecture, where 'Brook's work as a theatre director is architectural. He creates a place and atmosphere, a situation, where the creative imagination of both actors and spectators can flourish' (G. Read 2013: 3). Read's analysis is centred on Brook's usage of a carpet to demarcate a stage within African townships: 'The carpet almost magically empowered actors to construct an imaginary elsewhere within the intense presence of townspeople gathered together, an elsewhere that was not exactly superimposed on the architecture of the town, but there nonetheless' (G. Read 2013: 3). Whereas Read defines Brook's act of manifesting a stage-scene as architectural, I argue that it is only architectural in so much that it is scenographic: as a crafting of interventional place orientations. The slippages described by Read between the carpet and the slow architectures that demarcate the township – along with the implied social geographies of the street in which the performance takes place – are enacted and understood in relationship to the orientating qualities of scenographics. If scenographics enact an othering of place, then the placement of the carpet as an act and the corresponding reordering of its immediate geographies are only understood as architectural through an active othering of place orientation. The carpet is an intervention that irritates the monumentality of the surrounding slow architectures. The carpet is an enactment of fast architecture. The carpet is scenographic.

The description of scenography as 'architectural' is, Rufford argues in her book *Theatre and Architecture* (2015), relational to wider criticisms of scenography's theatrical charge as a commodification of architecture. Rufford focuses on Frampton's notion of 'tectonics' to recognize that the 'reason Frampton wants to distance architecture from the mimetic arts, and from scenography in particular, is that, historically, the tendency towards visual effects in architecture has coincided with an emphasis on architecture as commodity' (Rufford 2015: 17–18). Influenced by Heidegger's distinction that architecture is ontological rather than representational, Frampton argues tectonics as the corporeality of architecture: how buildings are felt and encountered. Rufford argues that, while some scenographic practices do operate as a commodity

(as a means of seduction), she stresses that this is not universal. For a production entitled *Henry 8: A Sexual Sermon* (1994), Rufford outlines how Dorita Hannah's 'critical scenographic practice' exposed the ideologies that frame a black box studio. Hannah's design scheme identified all the scuffs, scratches and irregularities of the studio the performance was due to take place in. Hannah then proceeded to smear each of these marks with white paint, which in turn was covered with layers of flaking black paper. The performance designer outlined that the aim was to

> reference the corrupt regime of Henry VIII, a syphilitic king who carved a smooth white swathe through the dark, diseased space in which the audience sat like members of his court, reminding us that, as onlookers, we are always complicit with history's events.
> (Rufford 2015: 19)

Rufford argues that Hannah's scenographic interventions 'thus critiqued residual attitudes in theatre and architecture that treat built form as a dumb container' (Rufford 2015: 19), with the suggestion being that the tectonics of the black box were scored by Hannah's scenographic interventions. Moreover, the reciprocity of architecture and its capacity to shape events, and equally be shaped by events, is exposed through this scenographic scoring upon the walls of the studio. The scenographics of the white paint act to other and complicate the monumentality of the studio, which in turn renders the previously normative history of the walls as attentive.

While I agree with Rufford's analysis, the qualities that Frampton defines as tectonics I would align with slow architecture (both situationally and ideologically). The critique of scenographics as commodifying stems, I argue, from how these techniques are deployed, which is distinct from the underlying qualities they evoke. As outlined in the previous chapter, while scenographics can be seductive, this tactic results from their capacity to persuade or convince through an all-compassing atmosphere of orientations: tactics that are exploited by commercial marketing as well as theatre-makers. While these orientations can recede with normativity, scenographics commodify insomuch that they also expose and reveal how these processes of commodification are enacted. Furthermore, I propose that the distinction between slow and fast architecture can be conceptualized in relationship to the high visibility of scenographics. In particular, slow architecture does not exceed experiences or necessarily even perceptions of time. Yet, slow architecture is normative in its relationship to its situational geographies. While the normativity of slow architecture is relative to an individual's social history within a particular locale (the Eiffel Tower is normative for those who see it every day, but eventual for the tourist), this monumentality is scored by the interventional qualities of scenographics – as that which alter how architectures are orientated, inhabited or experienced. Whereas slow architecture pertains to monumentality, fast architecture is scenographic.

Trompe l'oeil and scenographic propaganda

Fast architecture applies to all manner of architectural interventions that enact a temporal othering: of skewing, reordering or disrupting perceptual encounters with slow architecture. Yet, the first adoption of scenography into English is as a method of perspective drawing, which is discrete from the affective atmospheres of place orientation. *Trompe l'oeil* is perhaps the most explicit manifestation of a scenographic perspective as understood within architectural practice. In French, *trompe* means 'deceive' and *l'oeil* is 'the eye'. *Trompe l'oeil* is an exercise in evoking a semblance of depth upon a two-dimensional surface. This painting technique is associated with the practices of optical illusion and forced perspective. The relationship between *trompe l'oeil* and theatre-making is most often cited in relationship to Vitruvius. The first adoption of scenography is strongly tied to the techniques of *trompe l'oeil*, whether through the works of Sebastiano Serlio or Inigo Jones. Wiles argues that the

> art of trompe l'oeil scene-painting was developed, to enhance the proposition that the stage was a two-dimensional mirror. Greek scene painters developed the art of perspective to create depth – not the single-point perspective beloved of renaissance princes but a looser form that satisfied spectators in all parts of the auditorium.
>
> (Wiles 2003: 212)

While technically an illusion, *trompe l'oeil* is often assessed in relationship to its capacity for optical realism. The anti-theatrical framing of *trompe l'oeil*, alongside its potential for spectacle, situates this technique as a variation on scenographic practice within architectural discourse. While Frampton positions all forms of architectural ornamentation as scenographic, *trompe l'oeil* represents the *par excellence* of the anti-spatial within Frampton's reading of scenographic: the semblance of space without the potential for action, inhabitation and spatial experience. The notion of a scenographic perspective within architecture is, consequently, aligned with the curation of illusion: of anti-spatial 'fictive' worldings.

My positioning of *trompe l'oeil* as a scenographic method invites a discussion on the interrelationship between conceptions of the scenic and the scenographic. *Trompe l'oeil* is operationally scenic in the same way that a landscape painting seeks to quantify the argument for conservation or, in theological terms, isolate the otherworldliness of 'divine' creation. Whereas the concept of the scenic has been allied with that which is ideologically 'positive', the scenographic, through its relationship to theatre-making, has been charged as deceptive. The illusionism in landscape painting has been historically codified as a celebration of nature or divinity through artistic expression (which in turn is deemed 'god-given'). Loos' critique of ornamentation in architecture evokes a similar set of ideologies that privilege the assigned purity of a *tabula rasa*. Indeed, Loos cites the pseudo-theological aims of many modernist practices that situate material cultures as a cleansing of the human through 'better' design: 'Freedom from ornament is a sign of spiritual strength' (Loos 1971: 24). Framed by the anti-theatrical bias of Platonic- and Puritan-influenced Romanticist philosophies, the illusionistic qualities of scenographics are codified as lacking intellectual depth or, following Plato, an exercise in repetition without reference to the otherworldliness of the divine. The illusionary context of *trompe l'oeil* thereby presents a useful case study in which to isolate the ideological charges of the scenic from the interventional orientations of scenographics.

The dual encounter of scenographics and scenic politics as articulated by *trompe l'oeil* were evident within a district council scheme for 'virtual shops' in County Fermanagh, Northern Ireland. In June 2013, the 39th G8 summit was due to meet at the five-star hotel Lough Erne Resort in County Fermanagh. The local district council, in preparation of this event, committed to a scheme of 'tidying' the surrounding villages and towns. As part of this scheme, abandoned shopfronts were fitted with *trompe l'oeil* posters that covered the entirety of shops windowpanes. If passing the building at speed in a motor vehicle (as many G8 delegates would be), the shops may appear to be thriving sites of commercial enterprise. The *trompe l'oeil* depicted vibrant interiors filled with customers and produce. A BBC article isolated the staged qualities of these 'fake shops'. The article recalls the *trompe l'oeil* of a surrogate butcher's shop in the town of Belcoo and how

> you can almost smell the meat in the window – rashers of succulent bacon, plump bangers, juicy steaks, hams fit for a Tudor banquet. But clues tell you it's not quite as it should be. There's no name on the frontage. The door of the shop appears ajar but there's no glimpse of a tail-wagging terrier, head cocked for a stray piece of luncheon meat.
> (BBC 2013)

The branding scheme for these 'new' shops was overtly conscious of the theatrical charge these *trompe l'oeils* sustained. In Fivemiletown, there was a 'Virtual Fivemiletown Deli' and 'Flavour of Tyrone: Virtual Travel Agents' along with 'Old Heritage Antique'. The use of the term 'virtual' within two of the names is telling. In nearby Belcoo, there were an unnamed butcher's and a stationery store. Chief executive of the district council, Brendan Hegarty, defended the scheme, outlining how it

> was aimed at undeveloped sites at the entrance to the town and then right throughout the county in terms of the other towns and villages, looking at those vacant properties and really just trying to make them look better and more aesthetically pleasing.
> (BBC 2013)

Hegarty's statement implies that it was the scenic qualities of *trompe l'oeil* – of the charged connotations of the picturesque or painterly – that provided the motivation for this scheme. It is, however, the scenographic traits of these crafted interventions within the economically deprived towns of County Fermanagh that, I argue, isolates how worldings are curated and staged within townships more broadly.

While overtly political in its conception, the *trompe l'oeil* deployed by County Fermanagh District Council was evidently an interventional technique that sought to augment the lived normative geographies of County Fermanagh for a set period of time. The *trompe l'oeils* were eventful and interventional in their application. In this regard, the *trompe l'oeils* are scenographic in that they operate as a worlding irritant. The posters disrupted the normative worldings of County Fermanagh and, in doing so, exposed how shopfronts operate as sites of attentive sites more broadly. The worlding of the *trompe l'oeils* is understood in relation to the worldings that occur when shopfronts are curated and designed to display produce for a potential customer. Whether the configuration of mannequins or the ordering of fruit baskets, these are acts of staging that are of a scenographic order. Nullified by repetition and ubiquity, the staged shopfront is a scenographic act that is as normative as the slow architectures that encase them. The interventions of the *trompe l'oeils* in County Fermanagh, however, expose the theatrical charge of these material cultures. The *trompe l'oeils* are evidently a surrogate – an enactment of the Other – that sustains an active othering of place. For instance, the orientations of the butcher shop *trompe l'oeil*, with its semblance of depth through the inclusion of an open door, invites the onlooker to perceive a projected interior that equally feels welcoming and familiar. Yet, the *trompe l'oeil*'s worlding is predicated on its surrogate status: it is not not a butcher shop. The orientations of welcoming and familiarity are simultaneously disruptive and estranging. Unlike the ideological charge of the scenic, the scenographic traits of *trompe l'oeil* are what situate this technique as an interventional, rather than normative, exercise in place orientation. Consequently, my analysis of *trompe l'oeil* offers two conclusions on the status of scenographic architecture. First, that *trompe l'oeil* represents a distinction between that which is scenography and scenographic. The *trompe l'oeil* of County Fermanagh are not scenography, yet they are scenographic. Second, the scenic qualities of an event or practice do not exclude it from being scenographic.

Potemkin villages and scenographic placemaking

The potential for scenographics to complicate a politics of place, as well as othering how place is encountered, is directly evident within another typical example of scenographic architecture. The term 'Potemkin village' first emerged in Russia. Prince Grigory Potemkin was a first minster and lover of Empress Catherine II in the late 1700s. The tale of the Potemkin village is most often connected with Catherine's decision to tour the provinces. Potemkin is said to have ordered the construction of façades to mask the downbeat architecture that Catherine would pass by in her carriage. The tale concludes with the idea that Catherine completed her journey under the impression that her subjects lived in well-kept housing and relative prosperity. This political application of scenographics is explicitly related to the propaganda noted in County Fermanagh for the G8 summit. However, the Russian scholar Aleksandr Panchenko has argued that the façades where known to be 'fake' and were considered more in terms of decoration by Catherine and her courtiers:

> Potemkin did in fact decorate the city and settlements, but never hid the fact that they were decorations. Dozens of descriptions of the journey to New Russia and Tauride have been preserved. In none of these descriptions made in the actual course of events is there a trace of 'Potemkin villages,' although the decorativity is recalled constantly.
>
> (in Manovich 1995)

Nevertheless, in the nineteenth century the tale of the Potemkin village came to be associated with political deception through scenographic techniques. Michael David-Fox observes how the notion of the façade operated as a central metaphor for Western Europeans when recounting Russian politics. As exemplified by the Marquis de Custine's book *La Russie en 1839* (1843), David-Fox argues that, for Custine, 'the vast empire was nothing but a gigantic "theater," on whose stage Russians were less interested in being civilized than making Europeans believe they were so' (David-Fox 2012: 20). The notion that the Potemkin village is politically deceptive is crucial to this adoption. Indeed, this same metaphor is applied in the twentieth century to Soviet-era coverups of poor social wellbeing and infrastructure. In this usage, the notion of a Potemkin village exceeds its scenographic origin and becomes shorthand for state-led misdirection. Consequently, the notion of a Potemkin village operates as an explicitly scenographic enactment of 'placemaking' that focuses on the capacity of scenographics to seduce, as well as affirm, orientations of place.

Placemaking, or place-making, has a distinct history from scenography. While there are numerous shared traits, the argument for placemaking has been centred on the social order of architecture. Lynda H. Schneekloth and Robert G. Shibley define placemaking as 'the way in which all human beings transform the places they find themselves into the places where they live' (Schneekloth and Shibley 1995: 1). If placemaking focuses on a 'living place', then the extra-daily interventions of scenographics render place eventful or attentive. This is not to be confused with Tschumi (1996) notions of 'event space' as a precept for conceiving and experiencing architecture. The eventful interventions of scenography stress its peculiar temporality, and interventional qualities, as fast architecture. The act of placemaking, however, is a *de facto* part of an everyday practice of dwelling. As outlined by de Certeau, everyday practices are conditioned by adopted attitudes towards a particular place (be it a home, a public garden or a university) as disciplined by selected social behaviours, language and memories. Heidegger equally observed how dwelling is a psychophysical process, where '[t]o dwell, to be set at peace, means to remain at peace within the free, the preserve, the free sphere that safeguards each thing in its essence' (Heidegger 1971a: 246; emphasis in original). However, Schneekloth and Shibley's call for a return to the 'lost principles' of placemaking is a response to the lack of social engagement in urban planning. Schneekloth and Shibley argue that modernist architects and town planners rarely considered how memory and identity are intertwined *as* place.

Adopted as a policy strategy, placemaking aims to engage with community groups and facilitates collective approaches to urban planning. In focusing on scenography as place orientation, the 'life places' of placemaking and sequenced 'event places' of scenography are discrete. Scenography is not a 'place', but what renders place eventful through interventional means (i.e. the placing of a carpet in a town square to craft a stage or the focusing of a spotlight to direct attention). While scenography is never 'natural' or strategically normative, scenographics can become normative through sustained repetition. This distinction is centred on the interventionist quality of scenographics as a trait of place orientation that is removed from, or qualified by, the daily social practices of placemaking. 'Scenographic placemaking' is, therefore, concerned with how the practices of urban development are rendered eventful or attentive through scenographic traits that expose the underlying material and social constructions of place.

The Potemkin village is the epitome of scenographic placemaking. Contemporary variants on the Potemkin village, while still applied to economic and political deception, are inclusive of structures and even whole towns that exemplify how placemaking policies are enacted within contemporary urban areas. This includes the construction of Thames Town in China and Junction City in the USA. The first, Thames Town, is based on the archetypal architecture of a European town. Originally designed as a functioning suburb of Shanghai, after proving unpopular it now hosts Chinese tourists wanting to experience Western townships without travelling to Europe. The town includes a one-to-one interpretation of a church in Bristol, as well as cobbled streets. The second example, Junction City, is a military training facility at Fort Irwin, California. What makes this facility scenographic is that it has been constructed to train combatants for exercises in the Middle East. It therefore includes a layout and built structures that echo the characteristic architecture of the region, such as single-storey buildings, Arabic graffiti and the domed structures synonymous with a mosque. In that regard, Thames Town and Junction City are scenographic in the same manner that themed entertainment parks are also scenographic, whether Disneyland or medieval fairs. They are all experienced with the knowledge that, though constructed from durable and lasting materials, the architecture is performing *in-place-of* another architecture, even if the signified architecture is itself fictive (i.e. the Sleeping Beauty Castle). Yet, the persistence of these surrogate architectures positions them as monumental, in situational terms, while being politically scenographic. This tension is a defining trait of scenographic placemaking, being both politically real and contrived at the same time.

In terms of placemaking, the scenographics of the Potemkin village are arguably increasingly present within contemporary urban cities. While the usage of *trompe l'oeil* on construction sites is possibly the first example that comes to mind, media theorist Lev Manovich argues that the cityscapes of cinema also operate as a form of Potemkin village. Citing the technological smoothness between place and actor synonymous with the Hollywood movie, Manovich argues that the filmic representation of cityscapes allows a degree of immersion for the viewer within a politically contrived cinematic space:

> Accordingly, the space no longer acts as a theatrical backdrop. Instead, through new compositional principles, staging, set design, deep focus cinematography, lighting and camera movement, the viewer is situated at the optimum viewpoint of each shot. The viewer is 'present' inside a space which does not really exist. A fake space.
>
> (Manovich 1995)

Essential to this position is that the manner in which we encounter the street is informed by how cityscapes are signified and assimilated within media and art practice. As Debord argued in 1957, what 'alters the way we see the streets is more important than what alters the way we see painting' (in Bishop 2006: 100). The act of placemaking is, on one hand, a material process that involves the construction of architecture and, on the other hand, is a political charging of place through the spatial imaginary. For instance, an economically 'underperforming' district of a megacity can be rendered 'desirable' through a combination of material interventions *and* advertising. The two work hand in hand to 'regenerate' a place within the cultural imagination. How we imagine cites to be, therefore, is fundamental to how these same cities are experienced.

In *The Condition of Postmodernity* (1989), David Harvey cites the travel writer Jonathan Raben's book *Soft City* (1974), which defines 'city' as a nexus of experiences that conflates rationalism with subjective experience. Harvey argues that Raban's city was 'more like a theatre, a series of stages upon which individuals could work their own distinctive magic while performing a multiplicity of roles' (Harvey 1989: 4–5). Harvey concludes that, due to the realities of scale, 'the city is somewhere where fact and imagination simply *have* to fuse' (Harvey 1989: 5; emphasis in original). Soja's argument for thirdspace and the conceptual thirding of spatial imaginaries isolates this same concern. Urban cities are experienced in relationship to the tacit knowledge and subjectivities that come with having lived within these places, as Raban confirms: 'The city as we imagine it, the soft city of illusion, myth, aspiration, nightmare, is as real, maybe more real, than the hard city one can locate in maps and statistics' (Raban 1974: 10). Harvey's assessment of Raban focuses on how the postmodern condition has fused the strict ontological binaries of real–fake and authentic–imagined to reveal how place was always, to borrow from Massey, a constellation of subjective and empirical experiences that come with architectural inhabitation. This interrelationship has been exploited within town planning through the notion of placemaking.

My proposal for scenographic placemaking borrows from Harvey's assessment and is partly a critique of how placemaking policies are implemented as interventional and disruptive, yet can also be affirming and eventful. The examples of Thames Town and Junction City exemplify how scenographics reveal and highlight the ongoing constructions of place as material *and* ideological. What this approach does not afford in and of itself is a strategy for investigating how placemaking is conducted. Performance scholar Stuart Andrews stresses the need to consider an ethics of placemaking. In particular, Andrews is critical of private landowners who co-opt artistic labour and practice in order to gentrify urban areas and raise its commercial potential – pushing up rents, ousting businesses and even displacing the artists themselves:

> If artists and organisations are to engage in placemaking, it is critical they focus on their own creative exploration of place, and on making and showing art and performance in dialogue with place and community. Placemaking that combines a short timescale with limited interest in artistic exploration is problematic, as it may attempt a quick-fix to a physical place rather than a more considered engagement.
>
> (Andrews 2016: 13)

The policy-driven contexts of placemaking is, as with scenographics, a contentious crafting of place through social or architectural interventions. What scenographic placemaking highlights – with the notion of the Potemkin village as an explicit example – is how these policies irritate and intervene with the human-perceived normativities of place. The worlding of a particular location is always in motion, always open and equipped for change. The human dimension, however, complicates the rhythm of this change as the slow architectures of place are invested with social and political meaning, whether personal or collective. This position is symptomatic of what renders slow architecture monumental. It is very possible that the Potemkin villages of Thames Town and Junction City will become monumental through a human perception of time that positions them as having always been thus; that their very persistence imbues them with memory, meaning and, in political terms, power. Scenographic placemaking offers a tactic for reviewing how monumentality is enacted through architecture and, more precisely, how places are fashioned through the material and political interventions.

To conclude, Frampton's scenographic architecture focuses on the seductive capacity of scenographics to signify and mediate an order of representations that exceeds the geo-material condition of the architectural situation itself. This is an argument that I would ascribe to the aesthetic politics of the scenic. Frampton's notion of tectonics seeks to capture the corporeality of architectural experience. My own argument for scenographics does not contend nor disagree with the notion of tectonics. Indeed, this line of thought is also present within Pallasmaa's position on architecture as tactile and, while Frampton does not qualify tectonics in terms of the temporal, Tschumi's argument on event-space. Scenographics are predicated on how material interventions other and reorder the normativities of place that slow architecture undoubtedly recede into. In conceptualizing scenographics as fast architecture, the intention is to align conceptions of scenographic architecture with the second adoption of scenography. Frampton's critique of the scenographic is tied to the representational schemas and diagrammatic emphasis of the first adoption. This renewal of scenographics within architectural theory also draws attention to the capacity of these traits to score the epistemologies of architectural assemblages. From scaffolding to projected media, fast architecture is, on the one hand, the most mobile and flexible aspect of an architectural assemblage and, on the other hand, affords a conceptual mechanism for unpicking how place is constituted more broadly. If slow architecture is a manifestation of human power, then fast architecture is a reminder of the temporality of power, a temporality that is often rendered transparent through ideology. Moreover, the ontological indeterminism of scenographics allows them to simultaneously enact the commodifying tactics that Frampton critiques, as well as reveal these very same tactics. As with performatives, the morality or 'realness' of any political or social promise that a Potemkin village or *trompe l'oeil* might enact exceeds the materiality of these scenographic assemblages alone. Scenographics only deceive insomuch that the politics they enact are deceptive.

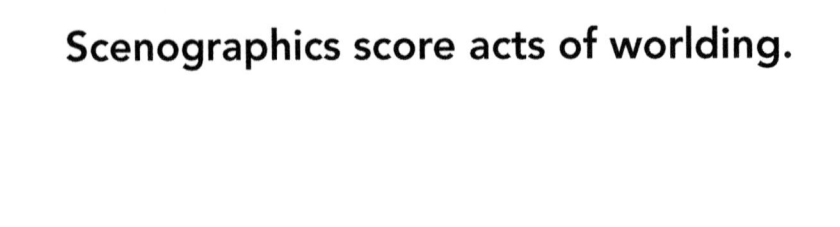

Scenographics score acts of worlding.

Conclusion

This book was conceived as a celebration of scenography. From the outset, my intention was to map the significance of scenography to theatre-making and argue what scenographic traits afford. The notion of scenographics arose as a conceptual bridge that binds this dual imperative. Indeed, it was not my initial aim to propose an overarching theory or consolidate this perspective within a particular term. My objective had been to resist the introduction of new terms and instead focus on refining the established lexicon. Yet, the plurality afforded by the term 'scenographics' and its complementary potential alongside the traits of performatives, the dramaturgical and the choreographic afforded a framework that isolated the diversity of orientating stimuli I sought to defend. Similarly, my adoption of place orientation emerged from a mapping of how scenographic practices evoke attentive places or scenes through interventional methodologies, exceeding strict definitions of vision or spatiality.

My implementation of Ahmed's twofold approach to orientation opened out the study into the structural conditioning that is inherent to the affirmative act of othering. The proposal that scenographics are only known through their potential for othering is bound to a negotiation of normativity. This conceptual positioning renders scenographics as qualified by the learned orthodoxies of theatre practice, material cultures, social appearance and aesthetic politics. Nevertheless, the othering of scenographics also orientates action through the potentiality that comes with an affective atmosphere. Scenographies are potentiality machines that remain radically open to change, multiples usages and transformative experiences. The next stage of this exercise is, I foresee, to further refine how scenographics operate within this porous conceptual landscape and whether or not a strict isolation of these traits is requisite. This task comes with a series of challenges and opportunities.

One of the first challenges I sought to complicate was the *tabula rasa* metaphor that I saw as all too often limiting the potential of scenographics; namely, that this ideology also confirms the deterministic position that stages precede scenography, positioning the concept and practice of scenography as supplementary – rather than formative – to theatre-making. Laura Levin summarizes the underlying ideologies that render scenography 'additional' by arguing how world is conceived as removed from human. Building on the notion of a totalizing 'world picture' that renders all 'nature' knowable and divisible from human, Levin suggests that this 'ground plan, conceived of as "picture", helped to render the world calculable and knowable so that it could be put more readily at the disposal of the human subject' (Levin 2014: 7). Levin's argument aligns with Neher's critique of the 'stage image' as reductive and imposing of a set ideology. Likewise, I argue that scenography exceeds the imposed authorship of a stage image. The notion of a stage image evokes the politics of the scenic that, as Levin ascribes of the world picture, renders 'the world' as *for* humans: as receptacle, commodity and resource. Scenography is a crafting of place orientations that exceed the strict authorial contexts of a stage image and the codifications that come with systems of aesthetics politics, such as *mise en scène*. Subsequently, a scenography of orientation operates as a critique of how aesthetic politics have governed the reception and critical engagement of stage-scenes. As summarized by Fried, the position that the art of painting or sculpture is manifested in its totality in each passing moment – rendering it timeless – represents a discrete ontology of experience from place orientation. Fried's argument resists a temporal dimension within its reception flattening the artwork's multiple orientations into discrete quantifiable images. Levin argues that to overcome the split between human and world, 'the figure standing at a distance would need to become the ground, to see himself [*sic*] as of, and not just in, the world' (Levin 2014: 8). Scenographics are manifest in the potential of material cultures to evoke worlding thresholds that happen in time. Moreover, the potentiality of scenographics is predicated on their temporal witness: of their capacity to evoke and sustain action through means of proxemic orientation. It is this difference of *being with* scenographics and *looking upon* scenic images that renders the crafting of scenography as discrete from the logocentrism of *mise en scène*.

The treatment of a lived event *as-if-it-were* a picture-scene is, I argue, the locus of *mise en scène*. My own position is that the critical future of *mise en scène* will be with film. It better suits the textual focus of film criticism and the isolation of the screen as the point of film reception. The scenographics of filmmaking are captured within the critical and experiential contexts of cinematography – which is inclusive of light balance and camera lens as well as editing methods – as well as production design. Film scenographies, I argue, exist in the situational architectures of encounter – whether a cinema, living room or at a computer desk. In these scenarios, place orientation is governed by the conditions of these environments and their association with the *mise en scène* of the film. The act of selecting a sofa and positioning it in a particular orientation to the screen, and then turning the lights off ready for the film to start, is a scenographic act. This composed and designed environment orientates the experience of the situation. With the advent of mixed reality technologies such as augmented vision and virtual reality headsets, there is capacity for the scenographies of place orientation to collapse into the *mise en scène* of film. The relationships between gaming and film production will, I predict, necessitate a reframing of film beyond the screen in the same manner that theatre practice and criticism challenged the dogma of proscenium arch in the twentieth century. In this way, film will be engaged in an active theatring as it returns to the principles of a *theatron*, where the place of seeing and the action are encountered in unison, albeit now mediated through computation. Scenography will be crucial to this return. As with the mixed reality performances of Blast Theory, the crafting of multiple stages that constitute a distributed performance will remain centred on the bodily situation of the spectator, participant, gamer. This shift in filmic encounter will confirm the distinction between the dramaturgical analysis of *mise en scène* and the place orientations of scenography. Scenography is not *of* film. Scenography is of theatre.

Throughout this book I offer accounts of how scenography orients acts of theatre. Yet, I have not included any images of scenography. I sought to highlight that scenography can only fully be understood as a richness of lived materiality and the orientations that proceed from this experiential context. What this book does offer is a framework for communicating scenography's affects: whether on humans, objects or human-objects alike. Nonetheless, the scenographic order does exist in how you are reading this text. Whether an office or a bedroom, a library or a park, the material situation of your immediate environment will orientate how you encounter these words. The words themselves are conditioned by the manner in which they are encountered. Circumstances of temperature, mood or time of day will all affect the relationship between text and reader. I wish you a sunny day. The manner in which you have chosen to position your body in relationship to this text, whether on a screen or in your hand, is a crafting of place orientation. To understand the broad conceptual imperatives that I have aligned within the notion of scenographics, it is useful to consider how these imperatives 'take place' as part of everyday life. The potentiality of a scenographic trait is tied to how places, bodies and materials coalesce as felt assemblages that orientate and complicate the perceptual borders of landscape, architecture and stage-scenes.

I challenge you to consider the orientating qualities of a stage-scene in the same manner that you encounter a land border. The felt reality of standing at a land border draws a heightened state of attention to how the secondspaces of cartography become felt thirdspaces of nationhood. This quality of nationhood is enacted as a feeling that emerges from the repetition and legal enforcement of ideologies (awareness of national relations and histories) and biometric laws (the assignment of bodies with a particular nation and the privileges/restrictions that this carries with it). Stage-scenes and land borders are equally disciplining. They invite or request a heightened state of appearance that isolates underlying ideologies through an act of place orientation. Next time you are standing at a land border, consider the orientating qualities of this encounter and its relationship to the felt qualities of being on stage. Stage-scenes and land borders isolate the negotiation of worlding through an interrelationship of disciplined physical and ideological orientations. Scenographic orientations isolate how worlding borders are made, felt and witnessed. Consequently, scenography is a crafting of how these worlding thresholds are encountered and negotiated.

My provocation that scenographics score acts of worlding is bound to relative normativities that become obscured through their repetition and enforcement. The difficulty of this position exists in how normative situations of world are qualified as such. As noted in my discussion on interior design, the maintenance and durational experience of being with scenographics can render them normative over time. My position on how interior design is formatively scenographic is critically distinct to how I conceive the ongoing cultivation of private gardens, which become scenographic through their encounter. This distinction is again relative to the contextual and ideological situations that these practices are presented within and to their (human-orientated) intended purpose. One of the challenges for scenographics is how this relational framework exists in tandem with – and perceptible through – the repetitions of normativity. In that regard, I have adopted the notion of irritation as a way of negotiating how the hypertrophic traits of scenographics reveal and evoke perceptual orders of world. Importantly, scenographics do not alter or transform worlding thresholds in and of themselves. Rather, scenographic traits other, complicate and irritate a slicing of worlds that is ever present yet goes unseen and unconsidered. Scenographics are agents for revealing acts of worlding.

The critical capacity and future of scenographics challenges the centrality of design orthodoxies and the designer as the locus for a scenographic enactment. *Scenography Expanded* (2017), edited by McKinney and Palmer, includes a range of well-devised and critically astute essays that 'demonstrate an expansion and a rethinking of traditional notions of scenography and point the way towards defining and discussing a new field' (McKinney and Palmer 2017: 19). In this regard, the material and overall arguments correspond with my own analysis of how the second adoption of scenography has embraced its place-orientating capacity beyond the strict aesthetics of the picturesque, the hegemony of the visual and embraced the potentiality of a scenographic trait. Yet, many of the contributions follow a recognizable orthodoxy in considering the role of the designer or design as being formative to scenography in/as performance. McKinney and Palmer note the need for a critical framework that cultural geographers or architects might adopt, seeing the collection as 'a first step that we hope will work to stimulate further exploration of expanded scenography; to examine not simply what it is, but what it does and how it does it' (McKinney and Palmer 2017: 19). This focus on what scenography does – as discrete from what it is – has been the underlying motivation of this book. My argument for scenographics focuses on the capacity of interventional place orientations to afford and evoke action, to shift how a place is encountered that is explicitly eventful in its effect. I have sought to evidence how these orientations are present in tasks and practices that are removed or contextually beyond the orthodoxies of theatrical design – be they political protests, marketing or placemaking. Yet, what I have not discussed is the processes of making scenographics or scenography. The role human- (and potentially non-human-) orientated design plays within the formation of scenographics remains a distinct opportunity, especially when considering the intersections between the varied practices that enact scenographic orientations.

In my introduction, I outlined how my adoption of the term 'beyond' signalled my own intention to reconsider scenography's role within theatre-making. My argument that scenography is a task of all theatre-makers and is formative to all acts of theatre is the accumulation of this cyclical investigation – of the return as implied by Kiesler (1926) and outlined by Bhabha (1994). Indeed, the ambition of Kiesler's manifesto 'The Theatre is Dead' has afforded a critical focus throughout. In particular, it has not been my aim to conceptualize a new form or type of scenography.

Rather my intention has been to map how the established lexicon relates to the practical and conceptual tasks of contemporary theatre-making. The distinction between an institutional and operational understanding of theatre has been applied in order to map the intersections and politics that come with cultural historicisms, alongside the opportunities afforded by practice. Blast Theory's *I'd Hide You* is situationally no less theatre than Ex Machina's *Needles and Opium*. Notions of postdramatic theatre and the frameworks of performance theory have broadened the scope of theatre to exceed strict institutional definitions. Yet, these frameworks have also been applied to resist a porous understanding of theatre. Notions of performance have replaced theatre in certain quarters to avoid any representational politics that may complicate the assigned authenticity of a staged event. As most evident within discourses of architecture, my own approach to scenographics aims to transgress these assigned politics in order to isolate and understand how the ontologies of experience are equally qualified by acts of speculation as well as empirical conditions. Nevertheless, these speculative acts – whether theatre, performance, interior design or protest – are also real acts that are played out to real affects. Scenographics as interventional acts of place orientations negotiate this ontological schism.

Last, I invite readers to consider the overall progress and future of scenography. Within this book I have taken the position that it is useful, on the one hand, to resist the borderless territory of post-disciplinary perspectives, such as performance or curation, in order to argue the specificity of scenography. On the other hand, I have outlined how the orientating potential of scenographics sustains post-disciplinary traits and critical affordances that exist within all manner of artistic practices and acts of social appearance. Consequently, I argue that acts of theatre isolate the worlding expressions of scenographics, which in turn complicate orders of world. Scenographics have the potential to enact speculative worlds that afford new insights into what it means to be worldly or how to be *with* worlding orientations. It is this potential that opens out the study and practice of scenography into the borderless disciplinary position occupied by performance studies. Yet, I return to that question of specificity. The imperative for specificity is not, in the conventional sense, a drive to define and render a concept as uncontested. Rather, my intention is to invite those unfamiliar with the concepts and practical remit of the second adoption to gain confidence in how scenography might apply and usefully complicate their own work. This is crucial if scenography is to emerge as an equal partner alongside its sister theatre-making strategies of dramaturgy and choreography. In going beyond scenography, I have challenged the orthodoxy that scenography is exclusively *for* designers. While this position has been politically useful in the past, if scenography is to be fully recognized as a vital and formative task of theatre-making, then the exclusivity of design needs to be contested and transgressed. I challenge you to be confident in how this porous scenography opens out its critical and practical possibilities. Let's take the opportunity to enact and imagine a renewed scenographic rhetoric of potentiality.

Bibliography

Abrams, J. (2013) 'Mise en plate: The scenographic imagination and the contemporary restaurant'. *Performance Research* 18.3: 7–14.

Ahmed, S. (2006) *Queer Phenomenology: Orientations, Objects, Others*. Durham, NC and London: Duke University Press.

Alberge, D. (2017) 'David Hare: classic British drama is "being infected" by radical European staging'. *Guardian Online*. Accessed 29/01/17 from www.theguardian.com/stage/2017/jan/29/david-hare-classic-british-drama-infected-radical-european-staging

Allain, P. and Harvie, J. (2006) *The Routledge Companion to Theatre and Performance*. London and New York: Routledge.

Anderson, Benedict. (1991) *Imagined Communities: Reflections on the Origin and the Spread of Nationalism*, 2nd edition. London: Verso.

Anderson, Ben. (2009) 'Affective atmospheres'. *Emotion, Space and Society* 2.2: 77–81.

Andrews S. (2016) 'Placemaking demystified'. *International Arts Manager* 12.2: 12–13.

Arendt, H. (1958) *The Human Condition*. Chicago: University of Chicago Press.

Aristotle (1966) *Aristotle's Ars Poetica*, ed. R. Kassel. Oxford: Clarendon Press

Aronson, A. (1981) *The History and Theory of Environmental Scenography*. Ann Arbor: UMI Research Press.

Aronson, A. (1984) 'American scenography'. *TDR: The Drama Review* 28.2: 3–22.

Aronson, A. (2005) *Looking into the Abyss: Essays on Scenography*. Ann Arbor: University of Michigan Press.

Aronson, A. (ed.) (2012) *The Disappearing Stage: Reflections on the 2011 Prague Quadrennial*. Prague: The Arts and Theatre Institute.

Aronson, A. (ed.) (2018) *The Routledge Companion to Scenography*. London & New York: Routledge.

Artaud, A. (1970) *The Theatre and its Double*, trans. V. Corti. London: John Calder.

Augé, M. (2008) *Non-Place: Introduction to an Anthropology of Supermodernity*. London: Verso Books.

Auslander, P. (2008) *Liveness: Performance in a Mediatized Culture*, 2nd edition. London and New York: Routledge.

Austin, J. L. (1962) *How to do Things with Words*. Oxford: Oxford University Press.

Awasthi, S. (1974) 'The scenography of the traditional theater of India'. *TDR: The Drama Review* 18.4: 36–46.

B. N. (1967) 'Current and forthcoming exhibitions'. *Burlington Magazine* 109.770: 318–21.

Bachelard, G. (1994) *The Poetics of Space*. Boston: Beacon Press.

Balme, C. (1997) 'Beyond style: typologies of performance analysis'. *Theatre Research International* 22.1: 24–30.

Barba, E. (1985) 'The nature of dramaturgy: describing actions at work'. *New Theatre Quarterly* 1.1: 75–78.

Barba, E. and Savarese, N. (1991) *The Dictionary of Theatre Anthropology: The Secret Art of the Performer*. London: Routledge.

Barbieri, D. (2017), *Costume for Performance: Materiality, Culture and the Body*. London: Bloomsbury.

Barrett, F. (2014) 'Inspiring innovators: Felix Barrett, founder of Punchdrunk, credits Edward Gordon Craig with shaping our understanding of theatre today', ed. I. Lloyd. *Intelligent Life: Economist Magazine*, September/October. Accessed 20/02/17 from http://recoagulation20.rssing.com/chan-11171830/all_p19.html

Barthes, R. (1977) *Image, Music, Text*, trans. S. Heath. London: Fontana Press.

Baugh, C. (2005) *Theatre, Performance, and Technology: The Development of Scenography in the Twentieth Century*. Basingstoke: Palgrave Macmillan.

Baugh, C. (2010) 'Brecht and stage design: the *Bühnenbildner* and the *Bühnenbauer*'. In J. Collins and A. Nisbet (eds), *Theatre and Performance Design:*

A Reader in Scenography, 188–203. London: Routledge.

Baugh, C. (2013) *Theatre, Performance and Technology: The Development and transformation of Scenography*, 2nd edition. Basingstoke: Palgrave Macmillan.

BBC (2013) 'When is a shop not a shop?' *BBC News Magazine Monitor*, 7 June. Accessed 10/09/15 from www.bbc.co.uk/news/blogs-magazine-monitor-22819331

Beacham, R. C. (1988) '"Brothers in suffering and joy": the Appia–Craig correspondence'. *New Theatre Quarterly* 4.15: 268–88.

Beacham, R. C. (1993) *Adolphe Appia: Texts on Theatre*. London: Routledge.

Beacham, R. C. (1994) *Adolphe Appia: Artist and Visionary of the Modern Theatre*. Reading, UK: Harwood Academic Publishers.

Beacham, R. C. (2013) 'Otium, opulentia and opsis: setting, performance and perception within the mise-en-scène of the Roman house'. In G. W. M. Harrison and V. Liapis (eds), *Performance in Greek and Roman Theatre*. Leiden and Boston: Brill.

Benjamin, W. (1968) 'The work of art in the age of mechanical reproduction'. In H. Arendt (ed.), H. Zohn, (trans.), *Illuminations*, 217–52. New York: Schocken Books.

Bennett, J. (2009) *Vibrant Matter: A Political Ecology of Things*. Durham, NC and London: Duke University Press.

Bhabha, H. K. (1994) *The Location of Culture*. London and New York: Routledge.

Birch, A. and Tompkins, J. (eds) (2012) *Performing Site-Specific Theatre: Politics, Place, Practice*. Basingstoke: Palgrave Macmillan.

Bishop, C. (ed.) (2006) *Participation*. London: Whitechapel Gallery.

Blau, H. (1982) *Take Up the Bodies: Theater at the Vanishing Point*. Champaign: University of Illinois Press.

Bleeker, M. (2008) *Visuality in the Theatre: The Locus of Looking*. Basingstoke: Palgrave Macmillan.

Bloomer, K. C. and Moore, C. W. (1977) *Body, Memory, and Architecture*. London: Yale University Press.

Böhme, G. (1993) 'Atmosphere as the fundamental concept of a new aesthetics'. *Thesis Eleven* 36.1: 113–26.

Böhme, G. (2006) 'Atmosphere as the subject matter of architecture'. In P. Ursprung (ed.), *Herzog and Meuron: Natural History*, 398–407. London: Lars Muller Publishers.

Böhme, G. (2013) 'The art of the stage set as a paradigm for an aesthetics of atmospheres'. *Ambiances: International Journal of Sensory Environment, Architecture and Urban Space*, 10 February. Accessed from http://journals.openedition.org/ambiances/315

Bourriaud, N. (2002) *Relational Aesthetics*. Dijon: Les Presses du Réel.

Brack, K. (ed.) (2010) *Katrin Brack: Bühnenbild, Stages*. Berlin: Theater der Zeit.

Bradby, D. (1991) *Modern French Drama 1940–1990*, 2nd edition. Cambridge: Cambridge University Press.

Bradby, D. and Williams, D. (1988) *Directors' Theatre*. New York: St Martin's Press.

Brejzek, T. (2010) 'From social network to urban intervention: on the scenographies of flash mobs and urban swarms'. *International Journal of Performance Arts and Digital Media* 6.1: 109–22.

Brejzek, T. (ed.) (2011a) *Expanding Scenography*. Prague: The Arts and Theatre Institute.

Brejzek, T. (2011b) 'Space and desire'. In T. Brejzek, W. Greisenegger and L. Wallen (eds), *Space and Desire: Scenographic Strategies in Theatre, Art and Media*, 4–9. Zuurich: Zurich University of the Arts.

Brejzek, T. (2015) 'The scenographic (re-)turn: figures of surface, space and spectator in theatre and architecture theory 1680–1980'. *Theatre and Performance Design* 1.1–2: 17–30.

Brejzek, T. and Wallen, L. (2017) *The Model as Performance: Staging Space in Theatre and Architecture*. London: Bloomsbury.

Breton, G. (1989) *Theaters*. New York: Princeton Architectural Press.

Brook, P. (1968) *The Empty Space*. Harmondsworth: Penguin.

Brown, A. L. (1984) 'Three and scene-painting Sophocles'. *Cambridge Classical Journal* 30.1: 1–17.

Brown, R. (2010) *Sound: A Reader in Theatre Practice*. Basingstoke: Palgrave.

Burian, J. M. (1970) 'Josef Svoboda: theatre artist in an age of science'. *Education Theatre Journal* 22.2: 123–45.

Burian, J. M. (1971) 'Art and relevance: the small theatres of Prague, 1958–1970'. *Educational Theatre Journal* 23.3: 229–57.

Burian, J. M. (1973) 'Post-war drama in Czechoslovakia'. *Educational Theatre Journal* 25.3: 299–317.

Burian, J. M. (1974) *The Scenography of Josef Svoboda*. Middletown. CT: Wesleyan University Press.

Burian, J. M. (2002) *Modern Czech Theatre: Reflector and Conscience of a Nation*. Iowa City: University of Iowa Press.

Burns, E. (1972) *Theatricality: A Study of Convention in the Theatre and in Social Life*. London: Longman.

Bury, J. (1975) 'VELKÁ BRITÁNIE'. *Prague Quadrennial services page*. Accessed 12/08/15 from http://services.pq.cz/en/pq-67.html?itemID=122&type=national

Butler, J. (1990) *Gender Trouble: Feminism and the Subversion of Identity*. New York: Routledge.

Butler, J. (2015) *Notes Toward a Performative Theory of Assembly*. London and Cambridge, MA: Harvard University Press.

Butterworth, P. (2005) *Magic on the Early English Stage*. Cambridge: Cambridge University Press.

Carlson, A. (1977) 'On the possibility of quantifying scenic beauty'. *Landscape Planning* 4.1: 131–72.

Carlson, A. (1979) 'Appreciation and the natural environment'. *Journal of Aesthetics and Art Criticism* 37.3: 267–75.

Carlson, M. (1989) *Places of Performance: The Semiotics of Theatre Architecture*. New York: Cornell University Press.

Carlson, M. (1996) *Performance: A Critical Introduction*. New York and London: Routledge.

Carlson, M. (2002) 'The resistance to theatricality'. *SubStance* 31.2–3: 238–50.

Carp, S. (2010) 'Worlds beyond history'. In K. Brack (ed.), *Katrin Brack: Bühnenbild, Stages*, 20–23. Berlin: Theater der Zeit.

Carter, L. (2016) 'Interview: lighting designer Lucy Carter'. *Almeida Theatre*. Accessed 22/09/16 from www.almeida.co.uk/interview-lighting-designer-lucy-carter

Carter, P. (2015) *Places Made After Their Stories: Design and the Art of Choreotopography*. Crawley: UWA Publishing.

Carver, G. (2013) 'Between nothing and everything: the summit of Mount Everest'. *Performance Research* 18.3: 15–18.

Casey, E. S. (1997) *The Fate of Place: A Philosophical History*. Berkeley and London: University of California Press.

Chaudhuri, U. (1997) *Staging Place: The Geography of Modern Drama*. Ann Arbor: Michigan University Press.

Chittenden, T. (2015) 'When is a bedroom not a bedroom? Bringing a space of flows to the design of apartment interiors in YO! Home'. *Journal of Interior Design* 40.4: 1–15.

Collins, J. and Nisbet, A. (eds) (2010) *Theatre and Performance Design: A Reader in Scenography*. London: Routledge.

Condorelli, C. (2009) *Support Structure*. Berlin: Sternberg Press.

Corner, J. (ed.) (1999) *Recovering Landscape: Essays in Contemporary Landscape Architecture*. New York: Princeton Architectural Press.

Craig, E. G. (ed.) (2009) *On the Art of the Theatre*, ed. F. Chamberlain. London: Routledge.

Crandell, G. (1993) *Nature Pictorialized: 'The View' in Landscape History*. Baltimore: Johns Hopkins University Press.

Crone, B. (2013) 'Curating, dramatization and the diagram: notes towards a sensible stage'. In J.-P. Martinon (ed.), *The Curatorial: A Philosophy of Curating*, 207–14. London and New York: Bloomsbury.

Curtin, A. (2010) 'Defining and reconstructing theatre sound'. In J. Collins and A. Nisbet (eds), *Theatre and Performance Design: A Reader in Scenography*, 218–29. London: Routledge.

Curtin, A. and Roesner, D. (2015) 'Sounding out "the scenographic turn": eight position statements'. *Theatre and Performance Design* 1.1–2: 107–25.

Curtis, S. (2016) *The Designer: Decorator or Dramaturg?* Platform Papers 46. Redfern, NSW: Currency House Inc.

Daddario, W. (2017) *Baroque, Venice, Theatre, Philosophy*. Basingstoke: Palgrave Macmillan.

David-Fox, M. (2012) *Showcasing the Great Experiment: Cultural Diplomacy and Western Visitors to the*

Soviet Union, 1921–1941. Oxford and New York: Oxford University Press.

Davis, T. C. (2003) 'Theatricality and civil society'. In T. C. Davis and T. Postlewait (eds), *Theatricality*, 127–55. Cambridge: Cambridge University Press.

Davis, T. C. and Postlewait, T. (eds) (2003) *Theatricality*. Cambridge: Cambridge University Press.

de Certeau, M. (1984) *The Practice of Everyday Life*, trans. S. Rendall. Berkeley and London: University of California Press.

Deák, F. (1973) 'The agitprop and circus plays of Vladimir Mayakovsky'. *The Drama Review: TDR* 17.1: 47–52.

Deighton, J. and Grayson, K. (1995) 'Marketing and seduction: building exchange relationships by managing social consensus'. *Journal of Consumer Research* 21.4: 660–76.

Deleuze, G. (1994) *Difference and Repetition*, trans. P. Patton. London and New York: Bloomsbury.

Deleuze, G. (1988) *Spinoza: Practical Philosophy*, trans. R. Hurley. San Francisco: City Lights Books.

Deleuze, G. (2006) *Two Regimes of Madness: Texts and Interviews 1975–1995*, ed. D. Lapoujade, trans. A. Hodges and M. Taormina. New York and Los Angeles: Semiotext(e).

den Oudsten, F. (2011) *space.time.narrative*, Farnham: Ashgate.

Diamond, E. (1996) *Performance and Cultural Politics*. New York and London: Routledge.

Dixon, S. (2007) *Digital Performance: A History of New Media in Theater, Dance, Performance Art, and Installation*. Cambridge, MA: MIT Press.

Doležel, L. (1998) *Heterocosmica: Fiction and Possible Worlds*. Baltimore, MD: Johns Hopkins University Press.

Dorney, K. and Gray, F. (2014) *Played in Britain: Modern Theatre in 100 Plays 1945–2010* (Version 001). iPad application software, developed by V&A Publishing. Accessed 01/09/15 from http://itunes.apple.com

Dundjerovic, A. (2003) 'The multiple crossings to the far side of the moon: transformative mise-en-scène'. *Contemporary Theatre Review* 13.2: 67–82.

Eckersall, P. (2006) 'Towards an expanded dramaturgical practice: a report on "The Dramaturgy and Cultural Intervention Project"'. *Theatre Research International* 31.3: 283–97.

El-Tayeb, F. (2011) *European Others: Queering Ethnicity in Postnational Europe*. Minneapolis: University of Minnesota Press.

Eliot, T. S. (1943) *The Four Quartets*. San Diego: Harcourt.

Entwistle, J. (2000) *The Fashioned Body*. Cambridge: Polity Press

Essin, C. (2012) *Stage Designers in Early Twentieth-Century America: Artists, Activists, Cultural Critics*. New York and Basingstoke: Palgrave Macmillan.

Filmer, A. (2013) 'Disrupting the "silent complicity" of parliamentary architecture'. *Performance Research* 18.3: 19–26.

Finkelstein, J. (1991) *The Fashioned Self*. Cambridge: Polity Press.

Fischer-Lichte, E. (2008) *The Transformative Power of Performance*, trans. S. I. Jain. London and New York: Routledge.

Fischer-Lichte, E. and Wihstutz, B. (eds) (2013) *Performance and the Politics of Space: Theatre and Topology*. London and New York: Routledge.

Foucault, M. (1986) 'Of other spaces'. *Diacritics* 16: 22–7.

Fried, M. (1967) 'Art and objecthood'. In M. Fried (1998), *Art and Objecthood: Essays and Reviews*, 148–72. Chicago and London: University of Chicago Press.

Garaus, M. (2017) 'Atmospheric harmony in the retail environment: its influence on store satisfaction and re-patronage intention'. *Journal of Consumer Behaviour* 16.3: 265–78.

Garber, M. (2013) 'Ghost army: the inflatable tanks that fooled Hitler'. *Atlantic* Accessed 01/02/16 from www.theatlantic.com/technology/archive/2013/05/ghost-army-the-inflatable-tanks-that-fooled-hitler/276137/

Gardner, L. (2009) 'Bright spark: the rise of the lighting designer'. *Guardian*. Accessed 03/02/17 from www.theguardian.com/stage/theatreblog/2009/feb/16/stage-lighting-design

Geertz, C. (1973) *The Interpretation of Cultures*. New York: Basic Books.

Giannachi, G. and Benford, S. (2011) *Performing Mixed Reality*. Cambridge, MA: MIT Press.

Gibson, J. J. (1966) *The Senses Considered as Perceptual Systems*. Oxford, England: Houghton Mifflin.

Goffman, E. (1958) *The Presentation of Self in Everyday Life*. Chicago: Anchor Books.

Goodwin, J. (ed.) (1989) *British Theatre Design: The Modern Age*. London: Weidenfeld & Nicolson.

Graue, M. (1984) 'West German scenography'. *The Drama Review: TDR* 28.2: 77–101.

Greenberg, C. (1961) *Art and Culture*. Boston: Beacon Press.

Greenblatt, S. (1980) *Renaissance Self-Fashioning: From More to Shakespeare*. Chicago: University of Chicago Press.

Gress, E. and O'Horgan, T. (1970) 'An interview with Tom O'Horgan on aspects of the contemporary theater'. *Leonardo* 3.3: 341–9.

Grotowski, J. (1968) *Towards a Poor Theatre*. New York: Routledge.

Grotowski, J., Wiewiorowski, T. K. and Morris, K. (1967) 'Towards a poor theatre'. *Tulane Drama Review* 11.3: 60–65.

Gwilt, J. (1874) *The Architecture of Marcus Vitruvius Pollio: In Ten Books*, London: Lockwood.

Hailey, C. (2008) *Campsite: Architectures of Duration and Place*. Baton Rouge, LA: Louisiana State University Press.

Hall, E. T., Birdwhistell, R. L., Bock, B., Bohannan, P., Diebold, Jr, A. R., Durbin, M., et al. (1968) 'Proxemics [and comments and replies]'. *Current Anthropology* 9.2–3: 83–108.

Hammond, S. H. (1857) *Wild Northern Scenes; or, Sporting Adventures with the Rifle and the Rod*. New York: Derby & Jackson.

Hann, R. (2017) 'Debating critical costume: negotiating ideologies of performance, appearance and disciplinarity'. *Studies in Theatre and Performance*. Accessed 09/04/18 from www.tandfonline.com/doi/full/10.1080/14682761.2017.1333831

Hannah, D. (2008) 'State of crisis: theatre architecture performing badly'. In A. Aronson (ed.) *Exhibition on the Stage: Reflections on the 2007 Prague Quadrennial*, 41–9. Prague: Arts Institute.

Hannah, D. (2009) 'Constructing the barricade: an urban performance building between the archive and the repertoire'. In D. Cross and C. Doherty (eds), *One Day Sculpture*, 108–14. Bielefeld, Germany: Kerber Verlag.

Hannah, D. and Harsløf, O. (eds) (2008) *Performance Design*. Copenhagen: Museum Tusculanum Press.

Hannah, D. and Mehzoud, S. (2011) 'Presentation/representation/re-presentation'. In T. Brejzek (ed.), *Expanding Scenography*, 102–13. Prague: Arts and Theatre Institute.

Harman, G. (2016) *Immaterialism: Objects and Social Theory*. Cambridge: Polity Press.

Harvey, D. (1989) *The Condition of Postmodernity: An Enquiry into the Origins of Cultural Change*. Cambridge, MA and Oxford, UK: Blackwell.

Harvey, D. (1993) 'From space to place and back again: reflections on the condition of postmodernity'. In J. Bird, B. Curtis, T. Putman, G. Robertson and L. Tickner (eds), *Mapping The Futures: Local Cultures, Global Change*, 2–29. New York and London: Routledge.

Heathfield, A. and Jones, A. (2012) *Perform, Repeat, Record: Live Art in History*. Bristol: Intellect.

Heidegger, M. (1927) 'Being and time: introduction'. In D. F. Krell (ed.) (2011), *Martin Heidegger: Basic Writings*, 1–40. Routledge Classics Series. London and New York: Routledge.

Heidegger, M. (1971a) 'Building dwelling thinking'. In D. F. Krell (ed.) (2011), *Martin Heidegger: Basic Writings*, trans. A. Hofstadter, 239–56. Routledge Classics Series. London and New York: Routledge.

Heidegger, M. trans. Hofstadter, A. (1971b) 'The thing'. In M. Heidegger, *Poetry, Language, Thought*, trans. A. Hofstadter, 163–80. New York: Harper Colophon Books.

Hill, L. and Paris, H. (eds) (2006) *Performance and Place*. Basingstoke: Palgrave Macmillan.

Hoggard, L. (2013) 'Felix Barrett: the visionary who reinvented theatre'. *Guardian*, 14 July. Accessed 17/01/15 from www.theguardian.com/theobserver/2013/jul/14/felix-barrett-punchdrunk-theatre-stage

Horswell, J. (ed.) (2004) *The Practice of Crime Scene Investigation*. Boca Raton, FL: CRC Press.

Howard, P. (2002) *What is Scenography?* London: Routledge.

Howard, P. (2009) *What is Scenography?* 2nd edition. London: Routledge.

Innes, C. (1993) *Edward Gordon Craig*. Cambridge: Cambridge University Press.

Irwin, K. (2008) 'The ambit of performativity: how site makes meaning in site-specific performance'. In H. Hannah and O. Harsløf, *Performance Design*, 39–62. Copenhagen: Museum Tusculanum Press.

Jacobs, J. M. and Smith, S. J. (2008) 'Living room: rematerializing home – guest editorial'. *Environment and Planning A* 40.3: 515–19.

Jays, D. (2017) Dangerous dreams: the mind-blowing world of designer Bunny Christie – in pictures. *Guardian*, 4 September. Accessed 04/10/17 from www.theguardian.com/stage/2017/sep/04/bunny-christie-designs-in-pictures-curious-incident-of-the-dog-in-the-night-time-ink

Jones, S. and Walker, P. (2011) 'Occupy London activists deny claims that few tents are occupied at night'. *Guardian*. Accessed 10/01/17 from www.theguardian.com/uk/2011/oct/25/occupy-london-tents-night

Joy, J. (2014) *The Choreographic*. Cambridge, MA: MIT Press.

Kant, I. (1790–1987) *Critique of Judgment*, trans. W. S. Pluhar. Indianapolis and Cambridge: Hackett Publishing Co.

Kantor, T. (1961) 'My idea of the theatre'. In J. Collins and A. Nisbet (eds), *Theatre and Performance Design: A Reader in Scenography*, 211–24. London: Routledge.

Kaplan, R. and Kaplan, S. (1982). *Humanscape: Environments for People*. Ann Arbor, MI: Ulrich's Books.

Kaye, N. (ed.) (1996) *Art into Theatre: Performance Interviews and Documents*. London and New York: Routledge.

Kennedy, D. (1993) *Looking at Shakespeare: A Visual History of Twentieth-Century Performance*. Cambridge: Cambridge University Press.

Kennedy, D. (2001) *Looking at Shakespeare: A Visual History of Twentieth-Century Performance*, 2nd edition. Cambridge: Cambridge University Press.

Kennedy, D. (2003) *Oxford Encyclopedia of Theatre and Performance*. Oxford: Oxford University Press.

Kennedy, D. (2010) *The Oxford Companion to Theatre and Performance*. Oxford: Oxford University Press.

Kershaw, B. (1999) *The Radical in Performance: Between Brecht and Baudrillard*. New York and London: Routledge.

Kershaw, B. (2001) 'Dramas of the Performative Society: theatre at the end of its tether'. *New Theatre Quarterly* 17.3: 203–11.

Kiesler, F. (1926) 'The theatre is dead'. *Little Review* 11.2: 1.

Kirby, M. (1984) 'International scenography: an introduction'. *The Drama Review: TDR* 28.2: 2.

Kirschenblatt-Gimblett, B. (1998) *Destination Culture: Tourism, Museums and Heritage*. Berkeley: University of California Press.

Kirshenblatt-Gimblett, B. (2004) 'Performance studies'. In H. Bial (ed.), *The Performance Studies Reader*, 43–56. London and New York: Routledge.

Krauss, R. (1979) 'Sculpture in the expanded field'. *October* 8.1: 30–44.

Krell, D. F. (ed.) (2011) *Martin Heidegger: Basic Writings*. Routledge Classics Series. London and New York: Routledge.

Lavender, A. (2016) *Performance in the Twenty-First Century*. London and New York: Routledge.

Lavin, S. (2011) *Kissing Architecture*. Princeton, NJ and Oxford: Princeton University Press.

Lefebvre, H. (1991a) *The Production of Space*, trans. D. Nicholson-Smith. Oxford: Blackwell.

Lefebvre, H. (1991b) *Critique of Everyday Life*, vol. 1, trans. J. Moore. London and New York: Verso.

Lehmann, H.-T. (1997) 'From logos to landscape: text in contemporary dramaturgy'. *Performance Research* 2.1: 55–60.

Lehmann, H.-T. (2006) *Postdramatic Theatre*, trans. K. Jürs-Munby. London: Routledge.

Lessing, G. E. (1766) *Laocoon*. Boston, MA: Roberts Brothers.

Levin, L. (2014) *Performing Ground: Space, Camouflage and the Art of Blending In*. Basingstoke: Palgrave Macmillan.

Loos, A. (1971) 'Ornament and crime'. In U. Conrads (ed.), *Programs and Manifestos on 20th-Century Architecture*, 19–25. Cambridge, MA: MIT Press. Originally published 1908.

Lotker, S. (2009) 'PQ2011 call', *PQ2011 Facebook page*. Accessed 17/09/15 from www.facebook.com/notes/pq/pq-2011/132959362117/

Lotker, S. and Gough, R. (2013) 'On scenography: editorial'. *Performance Research* 18.3: 3–6.

Loxley, J. (2007) *Performativity*. London and New York: Routledge.

McAuley, G. (1999) *Space in Performance: Making Meaning in Theatre*. Ann Arbor: University of Michigan Press.

McCormack, D. (2013) *Refrains for Moving Bodies*. Durham, NC and London: Duke University Press.

McEvilley, T. (1986) 'Introduction'. In B. O'Doherty, *Inside the White Cube: The Ideology of the Gallery Space*, 7–12. Berkeley and London: University of California Press.

McKinney, J. (2015) 'Scenographic materialism, affordance and extended cognition in Kris Verdonck's ACTOR #1'. *Theatre and Performance Design* 1.1–2: 79–93.

McKinney, J. and Butterworth, P. (2009) *The Cambridge Introduction to Scenography*. Cambridge: Cambridge University Press.

McKinney, J. and Palmer, S. (2017) *Scenography Expanded*. London: Bloomsbury.

McNamara, B. and Monk, M. (1972) 'The scenography of Meredith Monk'. *TDR: The Drama Review* 16.1: 87–103.

Macgowan, K. (1923) *The Theatre of Tomorrow*. London: T. Fisher Unwin, Ltd.

Macgowan, K. and Jones, R. E. 1923. *Continental Stagecraft*. London: Benn Brothers Ltd. [Originally published 1922, New York: Benjamin Blom, Inc.]

Machon, J. (2012) *Immersive Theatre: Intimacy and Immediacy in Contemporary Performance*. Basingstoke: Palgrave Macmillan.

Mackey, S. (2016) *Performing Places project website*. Accessed 03/04/16 from http://crco.cssd.ac.uk/489/1/index.html

Manovich, L. (1995) 'To lie and to act: Potemkin's villages, cinema and telepresence'. *Ars Electronica 1995 catalog*. Accessed 12/09/15 from http://manovich.net/content/04-projects/010-to-lie-and-to-act-potemkin-s-villages-cinema-and-telepresence/08_article_1995.pdf

Marchessault, J. (2005) *Marshall McLuhan*. London: Sage.

Marks, L. C. (2000) *The Skin of the Film: Intercultural Cinema, Embodiment, and the Senses*. Durham, NC: Duke University Press.

Martinon, J.-P. (ed.) (2013) *The Curatorial: A Philosophy of Curating*. London and New York: Bloomsbury.

Massey, D. (2005) *For Space*. London and New York: Sage.

Mattila, A. S. and Wirtz, J. (2001) 'Congruency of scent and music as a driver of in-store evaluations and behavior'. *Journal of Retailing* 77.2: 273–89.

Miller, D. (2010) *Stuff*. Cambridge: Polity Press.

Monks, A. (2010) *The Actor in Costume*. Basingstoke: Palgrave Macmillan.

Morgan, M. H. (1914) *Vitruvius: The Ten Books on Architecture*. Cambridge, MA: Harvard University Press.

Nancy. J.-L. 1997) *The Sense of the World*, trans. J. S. Librett. Minneapolis: University of Minnesota Press.

Nield, S. (2008) 'Siting people: power, protest, and public space'. In A. Birch and J. Tompkins (eds) (2010), *Performing Site-Specific Theatre: Politics, Place, Practice*, 219–32. Basingstoke: Palgrave Macmillan.

O'Connor, A. (2002) 'Local scenes and dangerous crossroads: punk and theories of cultural hybridity'. *Popular Music* 21.2: 225–36.

O'Doherty, B. (1986) *Inside the White Cube: The Ideology of the Gallery Space,*. Berkeley and London: University of California Press.

Oddey, A. and White, C. (eds) (2006) *The Potentials of Space: The Theory and Practice of Scenography & Performance*. Bristol: Intellect.

Orr, J. (2013) 'Edinburgh Fringe review: *Missing*'. *A Younger Theatre blog*. Accessed 12/09/15 from ww.ayoungertheatre.com/edinburgh-fringe-review-missing-gecko-theatre-pleasance/

Oxford English Dictionary (n.d.) 'Scenography, n.' *OED Online*. Oxford University Press, September 2016. Accessed 24/11/16 from www.oed.com/view/Entry/172236?)

Pallasmaa, J. (2005) *Eyes of the Skin: Architecture and the Senses*. Chichester: Wiley.

Palmer, S. (2015) 'A "chorégraphie" of light and space: Adolphe Appia and the first scenographic turn'. *Theatre & Performance Design* 1.1: 31–47.

Panofsky, E. (1991) *Perspective as Symbolic Form*. New York: Zone Books.

Pavelka, M. (2015) *So You Want to Be a Theatre Designer?* London: Nick Hern Books.

Pavis, P. (1992) *Theatre at The Crossroads of Culture*. New York and London: Routledge.

Pavis, P. (2003) *Analyzing Performance: Theater, Dance, and Film*. Ann Arbor: University of Michigan Press.

Pavis, P. (2012) *Contemporary Mise en Scène: Staging Theatre Today*, trans. J. Anderson. London: Routledge.

Pearson, M. and Shanks, M. (2001) *Theatre/Archaeology: Disciplinary Dialogues*. London and New York: Routledge.

Pérez-Gómez, A. and Pelletier, L. (1992) 'Architectural representation beyond perspectivism'. *Perspecta* 27.1: 20–39.

Perrella, S. (1998) *Hypersurface Architecture*. London: Architectural Design.

Phelan, P. (1993) *Unmarked: The Politics of Performance*. London and New York: Routledge.

Polieri, J., Goff, G. and Goff, M, (1968) 'Le livre de Mallarmé A Mise en Scène'. *TDR: The Drama Review* 12.3: 179–82.

Pradier, J.-M. (1995) 'Ethnoscénologie, manifeste'. *Théâtre/Public* 123.2: 46–8.

Pradier, J.-M. (2001) 'Ethnoscenology: the flesh is spirit'. In G. Berghaus (ed.), *New Approaches to Theatre Studies and Performance Analysis*, 61–81. Tubingen: Max Niemeyer Verlag.

Příhodová, B. (2011) 'The specificity of scenography: a Czech contribution to the theory of scenography'. In C. M. Billing and P. Drábek (eds), *Czech Stage Art and Stage Design*. Prague: Muni Press.

Raban, J. (1974) *Soft City*. London: Harvill Press.

Radosavljević, D. (2013) *Theatre-Making: Interplay Between Text and Performance in the 21st Century*. Basingstoke: Palgrave Macmillan.

Rancière, J. (2013) *Aisthesis: Scenes from the Aesthetic Regime of Art*, trans. Z. Paul. London: Verso.

Read, A. (2013) *Theatre in the Expanded Field: Seven Approaches to Performance*. London: Bloomsbury.

Read, G. (2013) 'Introduction: the play's the thing'. In M. Feuerstein and G. Read (eds), *Architecture as a Performing Art*. Farnham and Burlington, VT: Ashgate.

Rebentisch, J. (2012) *Aesthetics of Installation Art*. Berlin: Sternberg Press.

Reid Payne, D. (1993) *Scenographic Imagination*, 3rd edition. Carbondale and Edwardsville: Southern Illinois University Press.

Reid Payne, D. (1994) *Computer Scenographics*. Carbondale and Edwardsville: Southern Illinois University Press.

Reynolds, D. and Reason, M. (2011) *Kinesthetic Empathy in Creative and Cultural Practices*. Bristol: Intellect.

Rewa, N. (2009) *Design and Scenography: Critical Perspectives on Canadian Theatre in English*. Toronto: Playwrights Canada.

Roth, M. (2000) 'Szenographie – zur Entstehung von neuen Bildwelten'. *ARCH +* 149–50: 84–5. Accessed 09/04/15 from www.archplus.net/home/archiv/artikel/46,356,1,0.html

Roy, S. (2012) 'Gecko's *Missing* – review'. *Guardian*, 6 May. Accessed 12/09/15 from www.theguardian.com/stage/2012/may/06/gecko-missing-amit-lahav-review

Rufford, J. (2015) *Theatre and Architecture*. Basingstoke: Palgrave Macmillan.

Rufford, J. (2018) 'Scenography and the political economy of design'. In K. Kipphoff and S. Graffer (eds), *Anthology of Essays on Contemporary Performance*. Oslo: Vigarorlaget.

Said, E. (1978) *Orientalism: Western Conceptions of the Orient* [reprinted 1995]. London and New York: Penguin.

Salter, C. (2010) *Entangled: Technology and the Transformation of Performance*. Cambridge, MA: MIT Press.

Schechner, R. (1968) 'Six axioms of environmental theatre'. *The Drama Review: TDR* 12.3: 41–64.

Schechner, R. (1985) *Between Theater and Anthropology*. Philadelphia; University of Pennsylvania Press.

Schechner, R. (1988) *Performance Theory*. New York and London: Routledge.

Schechner, R. (1992) 'A new paradigm for theatre in the academy'. *The Drama Review: TDR* 36.4: 7–10.

Schechner, R. (2000) 'Theatre alive in the new millennium'. *The Drama Review: TDR* 44.1: 5–6.

Schechner, R. (2013) *Performance Studies: An Introduction*, 3rd edition, ed. S. Brady. London and New York: Routledge.

Schlemmer, O. (1926) 'Theater (Bühne)'. In W. Gropius (ed.), A. S. Weinsinger (trans.) (1961), *The Theatre of the Bauhaus*. London: Eyre Methuen.

Schneekloth, L. H. and Shibley, R. G. (1995) *Placemaking: The Art and Practice of Building Communities*. New York: Wiley.

Schwarz, H. P. (2011) 'Foreword'. In F. den Oudsten (2011), *space.time.narrative*, ix–xix. Farnham: Ashgate.

Sennett, R. (1977) *The Fall of Public Man*. London: Penguin.

Serlio, S. (1611) *Five bookes of architecture: translated out of Italian into Dutch and out of Dutch into English*, trans. R. Peake. *Archive*. Accessed from https://archive.org/details/firstbookeofarch00serl

Shearing, D. (2014) 'Scenographic landscapes', *Studies in Theatre and Performance* 34.1: 38–52.

Singleton, B. (2013) 'Mise en scène'. *Contemporary Theatre Review* 23.1: 48–9.

Soja, E. (1989) *Postmodern Geographies: The Reassertion of Space in Critical Social Theory*. London and New York: Verso.

Soja, E. (1996) *Thirdspace: Journeys to Los Angeles and Other Real-and-Imagined Places*. Oxford and Maldon, MA: Blackwell Publishing.

Southern, R. (1957) *The Seven Ages of Theatre*. London: Faber and Faber.

Sparke, P. (2008) *The Modern Interior*. Chicago, IL: University of Chicago Press.

Spier, S. (ed.) (2011) *William Forsythe and the Practice of Choreography: It Starts from Any Point*. London and New York: Routledge.

Stanger, A. (2014) 'The choreography of space: towards a socio-aesthetics of dance'. *New Theatre Quarterly* 30.1: 72–90.

Stewart, K. (2007) *Ordinary Affects*. Durham, NC and London: Duke University Press.

Stewart, K. (2011) 'Atmospheric attunements'. *Environment and Planning D: Society and Space* 29. 3: 445–53.

Stewart, K. (2014) 'Tactile Composition'. In P. Harvey and E. Casella (eds), *Objects and Materials*, 775–810. New York and London: Routledge.

Svoboda, J. Morris, K. and Munk, E. (1966) 'Laterna magika'. *Tulane Drama Review* 11.1: 141–9.

Taper, B. (1996) *Balanchine: A Biography*, 2nd edition. Berkeley and London: University of California Press.

Taylor, D. (2016) *Performance*. Durham, NC and London: Duke University Press.

Tokumitsu, M. (2015) 'The politics of the curation craze', *New Republic*, 24 August. Accessed from https://newrepublic.com/article/122589/when-did-we-all-become-curators

Townsend, D. (1997) 'Picturesque'. *Journal of Aesthetics and Art Criticism* 55.4: 365–76.

Tripney, N. (2015) 'What the BAC fire has taught us about the value of theatre'. *The Stage*, 4 April. Accessed 12/09/15 from www.thestage.co.uk/features/2015/bac-fire-taught-us-value-theatre/

Tschumi, B. (1996) *Architecture and Disjunction*. Cambridge, MA: MIT Press.

Tuan, Y.-F. (1977) *Space and Place: The Perspective of Experience*. Minneapolis: University of Minnesota Press.

Turner, C. (2010) 'Mis-guidance and spatial planning: dramaturgies of public space'. *Contemporary Theatre Review* 20.2: 149–61.

Turner, C. (2015) *Dramaturgy and Architecture: Theatre, Utopian and the Built Environment*. Basingstoke: Palgrave Macmillan.

Turner, C. and Behrndt, S. (2008) *Dramaturgy and Performance*. Basingstoke: Palgrave Macmillan.

Turner, V. (1982) *From Ritual to Theatre: The Human Seriousness of Play*. New York: Performing Arts Journal Publications.

Unruh, D. (1991) 'Postmodern issues in design: part III: the problem with costumes'. *Theatre Design and Technology* 27.4: 27–32.

von Arx, S. (2015) 'Framing the unknown'. Edward Gordon Craig Lecture at the Royal Central School of Speech and Drama, 18 May.

von Hantelmann, D. (2010) *How to Do Things with Art*. Dijon: JRP Ringier/Les Presses du Réel

Wagner, R., (1993) *'The Art-Work of the Future' and Other Works*, trans. W. Ashton Ellis. London: University of Nebraska Press.

Walker, J. R. (2011) *The Restaurant: From Concept to Operation*, 6th edition. Hoboken, NJ: Wiley.

Webster, N. (1913) *Webster's New International Dictionary*, ed. W. Torrey Harris and F. Sturges Allen. Cambridge, MA: G. & C. Merriam. Accessed 13/10/15 from www.websters1913.com/

Wickham, G. (1974) *The Medieval Theatre*. Cambridge: Cambridge University Press.

Wiles, D. (2003) *A Short History of Western Performance Space*. Cambridge: Cambridge University Press.

Willett, J. (ed. and trans.) (1964) *Brecht on Theatre*. New York: Hill and Wang.

Willett, J. (1986) *Casper Neher: Brecht's Designer*. London: Methuen.

Youngblood, G. (1970) *Expanded Cinema*. New York: E. P. Dutton.

Index

Abramović, Marina 9, 12, 90
Abrams, Joshua 110
acting, double negative of 12, 89
action art 29
activism, scenographic 100, 113–17
Adorno, Theodor 80
Adrià, Ferran 110
aesthetics: environmental 108, 110; minimal 74; picturesque 135; politics of 23; relational 73; of the scenic 47; sensory 2; Western 67, 94
Ahmed, Sara 33–4, 36, 37, 100, 101–2, 133
Allain, Paul 39
Allison, George 109
Anderson, Benedict 20, 67, 81
Andrews, Malcolm 26
Andrews, Stuart 129
anti-theatricality 31, 123; *see also* theatricality
Appetecchia, Enzo 74
Appia, Adolphe 7, 9, 11, 12, 25, 37, 42, 54, 61, 71, 72, 75–6, 77, 83, 84, 86, 91, 95, 121
Arab Spring 114
architecture: barricades as 114; built 107; choreography of 61; civic 121–2; corporeality of 124; dance 7; dramaturgy of 99; effect of bodies on 95; eventual 120; exhibition 28; fast 16, 120, 122–5, 127, 129–30; fictive 128; foam 71; landscape 22–3, 134; monumental 120–2, 125, 129; vs. 'not-architecture' 62, 121; orienting 116; and Performance Design 64; performative 19–20, 114, 123; postdramatic 91; postmodernist 119; reciprocity of 19–20, 124; of refuge 115; scenographic 11, 16–17, 60, 104, 119–20, 123, 125, 126, 127, 129, 136; and scenography 3, 6, 12, 19, 45, 122–3, 124; sculpture and 62, 121; situated 120; situational 134; slow 16, 107, 120–1, 122, 123, 124–5, 126, 129–30; stage 28, 48, 81; vs. stage design 12; study of 13, 32, 45, 61; theatre 43, 69, 74, 83, 87, 92, 121, 122; time-based qualities of 59; as visual art 31; *see also* Potemkin villages; skene houses; *trompe l'oeil*

Arendt, Hannah 115
Aristotle 17, 21, 40, 41, 112
Aronson, Arnold 39, 51, 58, 64, 87–8, 91, 96
art: action 29; *art serene* 12; living 83, 95; plastic 121; scenic 7; visual 31; *see also* architecture; installation art; performance art; sculpture
'Art and Objecthood' (Fried) 30
Artaud, A. 91
art theory 30
The Artwork of the Future (Wagner) 57
assemblages 16, 22, 36, 67, 89, 116; affective 76, 82; architectural 130; of dwelling 106; enacted 70; of interior design 106; mixed reality 88; of theatrical design practices 77
atmospheres 80, 99; affective 20–1, 27, 37, 67, 68, 70, 73, 105; holistic 108; personal/impersonal 37; restaurant 109–10; staged 71, 72
audience engagement 72, 133
audience reception 72, 133
Auslander, P. 88
Austin, J. L. 10, 29
auteur 58
authenticity 136; assigned 34–5, 123; assumed 10; concept of 34; of food 109; politics of 36; structures of 117
Autoren-Gestalter 58

BAC 74
Bachelard, Gaston 82, 103–4
Balanchine, George 60–1
Ballets Russes 60
Balme, Christopher 54
Barba, Eugenio 9, 59, 63, 70
Barbaro, Daniele 40–1, 92
Barrett, Felix 90–1
barricades 114–15
Barthes, Roland 37, 61
basic-orienting systems 33
Baugh, Christopher 5, 6, 7, 25, 42–3, 44, 46, 58, 60, 61, 69

behaviors, scenographic 104, 106, 113
Behrndt, Synne 59, 61
Bell, Simon 23
Benford, Steve 88
Benjamin, Walter 34–5, 93–4, 117
Bennett, Jane 16, 76
Bhabha, Homi 1, 2, 135
black box studio 86, 91–2
Blast Theory 16, 88, 89–90, 96, 134, 136
Blau, Herbert 69–70, 107
Bleeker, Maaike 67, 74
blocking 19, 21, 57, 68, 75, 76
Bloomer, Kent C. 37, 94
Blossom, Roberts 88
bodily experience 90, 95–6
Böhme, Gernot 12, 20–1, 68, 70, 71, 80, 99, 119
Bouffes du Nord theatre 85
Bourriaud, Nicolas 73
Brack, Katrin 71
Bradby, David 52–3, 56
Brecht, Bertolt 43, 45–6, 68, 116
Brejzek, Thea 4, 31, 40, 57, 100, 103, 116, 119
Breton, Gaëlle 92
Brook, Peter 8–9, 31, 57, 85–6, 93, 124
Brown, A. L. 21
Brown, Ross 47
Bühnenbauer ('stage builder') 39
Bühnenbild 45–6, 94
Burian, Jarka 43, 51, 56, 72
Burns, Elizabeth 31, 76, 91, 93, 104, 106, 110–11
Bury, John 56
Butler, Judith 10, 115–16
Butterworth, P. 5, 47, 53, 57, 72, 85

Callow, Simon 13
capitalism 108
Carlson, Allen 26, 27, 28–9
Carlson, Marvin 2–3, 10, 21, 121
Carp, Stefanie 71
carpet 89, 104, 106, 107, 124, 128
Carter, Lucy 71
cartography 19, 79, 89, 134
Casey, Edward S. 95
Cavell, Stanley 101
Chandler, John 87
Changing Room (television show) 105
Chelsea Flower Show 92–3

Chittenden, Tara 105
chora 70
choreographers 3, 15, 51, 57, 60–1, 64
choreographic traits 28, 61
choreography 4, 8, 15, 20, 28, 48, 51, 58, 60–1, 63, 67, 70, 73, 75, 77, 136; crowd 90; *see also* dance
Christie, Bunny 79, 82
cinema: cityscapes of 128; influence of 8–9
cinematography 128, 134
Computer Scenographics (Payne) 4
Condorelli, Céline 122
conservation movement 26–7, 125
consumer capitalism 108
Corner, James 22–3, 27
costume(s): clothes as 99; design of 41, 42, 47, 48; on the Ghost Train 35; in *The Lion King* 20; in *Needles and Opium* 52; and place orientation 21, 48; as scenography 2, 3, 4, 5, 6, 15, 32, 39, 41, 42, 46–9, 51, 56, 64, 70, 72, 73, 76, 90, 113, 116; in theatrical design 14, 19, 39, 41, 42; theatricality of 31
County Fermanagh 125–6
Craig, Edward Gordon 5, 7, 9, 24, 42, 43, 48, 54, 61, 69, 70, 72, 75, 84, 86, 90–1
Crandell, Gina 26
Critique of Judgment (Kant) 26
Crone, Bridget 32, 81
cultural capital 104
culture, capitalist 99
cult value 34, 117
curation 44, 55, 81, 100, 136; of illusion 125; scenographic 112–13
curatorial stage 81
Curtin, Adrian 47

Daddario, Will 112
dance 9, 28, 48, 60–1, 77; modernism in 61; *see also* choreographers; choreography
dance architecture 7
dancers 9, 58, 60, 69, 74
David-Fox, Michael 127
Davis, Tracy C. 10, 29
de Certeau, Michel 22, 24, 70, 127
Deighton, John 108, 109
Deleuze, Gilles 16, 35, 67, 70, 85, 88–9
den Oudsten, Frank 30, 31, 42, 45, 46, 58, 69, 72–3, 108
design: of action 55; architectural 4, 7, 13, 119, 122, 123; 'better' 125; costume 41, 42, 47, 48; descriptive

119; European practices of 17, 41; exclusivity of 136; exhibition 55, 58; game 32; garden 32, 111, 112; graphic 61; lighting 42, 48, 52, 71, 74; orthodoxies of 7, 135; performing/performance 7, 14, 58, 87; political economy of 108; production 59, 75, 134; restaurant 110, 111; scenography and 6, 7, 12, 21, 58, 124, 135; set 2, 6, 7, 13, 14, 16, 31, 42, 44, 47, 48, 53, 67–8, 71, 77, 79, 87, 91; sound 14, 41, 47, 74–5, 76–7; spatial/material 13, 45, 46; stage 2, 6, 7, 12, 14, 39, 41, 42, 47, 49, 56, 61, 91, 113, 119, 123; for the stage 14; store 108; theatre/theatrical 2, 6, 7, 13, 14, 19, 31, 39, 40, 41, 42, 44, 47, 49, 51, 52, 56, 58, 68, 83, 88, 91, 135; urban 60; visual 53; *see also* interior design; Performance Design; scene/scenic design

design dramaturgy 24, 55, 60, 68

designers 3, 5, 7, 15, 32, 42, 43, 44, 46, 48, 51, 52, 53, 56, 57, 135, 136; British 56–7; as dramaturges 60; German 39, 59; performance 7, 124; scenic 42, 109; set 14, 41, 49, 52, 71, 79; sound 47; stage 13, 39, 56, 123; theatre 108–9

determinism 86, 95

Diaghilev, Serge 60

Diamond, Elin 58

Dixon, Steve 88

Dolan, Jill 10

Doležel, Lubomír 79

double negatives: of acting 12, 89; epistemological 32, 36, 107, 110; of surrogacy 36, 110; of theatricality 36; of theatrical representation 33

dramaturgy/dramaturgies 5, 9, 58, 70, 72, 75, 99; design 24; expanded 59, 62, 63; methods of 60; in Norway 59; and scenography 58–61; visual 59

The Drowned Man 108

Duncan, Isadora 69

Dundjerovic, Alexander 53–4

earthworks 62–3

Eckersall, Peter 59, 61–2, 63

ecology/ies: of material circumstances 83; performance 20; scenographic 20; theatrical 72; of theatrical realism 33

editing 61, 134

Eiffel Tower 121

Eliot, T. S. 87

El-Tayeb, Fatima 34

Emin, Tracey 30

empathy, kinesthetic 20

The Empty Space (Brook) 85

Endless House (Kiesler) 105

ensemble effects 108

Entwistle, Joanne 47

environmental aesthetics 108, 110

environments 6–7, 19, 21, 26, 37, 77, 80, 85, 86; architectural 120; choreographed 61; composed and designed 134; fantasy 105; felt 46; 'found' 13; imagined 109; immersive 47, 111; and interior design 104–7; material 28; narrative 45; perceptual 108; physical 48, 73, 75, 108; private vs. public 104; 'real fake' 105; scenographic 77, 106, 111, 113; sound 91; stage/theatrical 13, 39, 41, 47, 49, 53, 58, 60, 63, 68, 71, 72, 76, 77, 83, 86, 91, 99; temporary 45, 120; visual 41

Essin, Christin 19, 100, 113

ethnoscénologie 46

European Scenography Centers 44

event-space 19–20, 127

Ex Machina 52, 136

Expanded Cinema (Youngblood) 62

expanded field 3, 7, 61, 62–3, 73, 121; modeling of *62*

extra-daily techniques 9, 10, 12, 25, 26, 30, 36, 69, 70, 83, 96, 103, 107, 109

façade 119

feedback loop 10, 11, *11*, 24, 99

filmic 61, 70

film scenographies 134

firstspace 23

folding 20, 59, 88–9

Foreman, Richard 44

Forsythe, William 61

Foster, Hal 108

Foucault, Michel 23, 37, 81, 89

frames 33, 53; conceptual 53; illusionary 116; physical 12, 73, 74–5; play- 52; *see also* frameworks; framing

frameworks 3, 10, 15–16, 23, 64, 94, 101, 114, 133, 134; conceptual 26; critical 5, 6, 8, 28, 29, 123, 135; of the curatorial 111; ideological 23, 84; ontological 76; of performance theory 136; relational 135; theoretical 15, 51; traditional 58; *see also* frames; framing

framing 1, 2, 4, 8, 9, 10, 11, 20, 32, 33, 55, 63, 90, 91, 94, 116, 124; metaphorical 87; *see also* frames; frameworks

Frampton, Kenneth 119, 120, 124, 125, 129
Fried, Michel 30–1, 133–4
Fuller, Loie 48

Garber, Megan 109
gardening 16; and scenographic curation 111–13; scenographics of 93
Gecko Physical Theatre 16, 67–8; *MISSING* set 73–7
geography/geographies: architectural 85; distant 89; human 15; lived 85; material 24, 83; normative 126; power 82; psycho- 64, 79; situational/situated 47, 82, 94–5, 122, 125; social 64, 124; socio-political 86; theological 81; *see also* stage geography
Gesamtkunstwerk 43, 57, 72, 74, 83
gestalt theory 107, 109
Ghost Train 35–6
Giannachi, Gabriella 88
Gibson, J. J. 33, 37, 94
Gob Squad 87–8
Goffman, Erving 9
Gough, Richard 6–7, 58, 72
Grafton Architects 12
Graham, Martha 48
graphos 6, 68–9
Grayson, Kent 108, 109
Greenberg, Clement 30
Grotowski, J. 43, 74, 86, 91
Guattari, Felix 85
Gwilt, Joseph 40

Hailey, Charlie 114, 122
Hall, Edward T. 33
Hall, Peter 56, 57, 90
Hannah, Dorita 7, 13, 19–20, 58, 71, 76, 85, 87, 114–15, 124
haptics: experience 33; proxemics 2, 15; response 88; systems 33, 93; visuality 88, 94
Hare, David 56, 57
Harman, Graham 83
harmony: atmospheric 108; of scenography 72, 75
Harsløf, Olav 7, 13, 58, 71, 87
Harvey, David 81, 128–129
Harvie, Jen 39
Hegarty, Brendan 126
Heidegger, Martin 2, 79, 80, 84, 112, 124, 127
Henry 8: A Sexual Sermon (Hannah) 124
Herrmann, Max 31

heteronormativity 33, 34
heterotopias 37, 81, 87
hierarchies: of authorship 46, 58; of collaboration 58, 71; conventional 31, 32; disciplinary 123; professional 3, 5, 13, 15, 56, 58, 71; of recognition 34; of scenography 15; social 81
high modernism 85; *see also* modernism
Hoggard, Liz 90
homonormativity 34
Hopkins, Arthur 32–3
Horswell, John 25
Hotel Pro Forma 70
house interiors *see* interior design
Howard, Pamela 39, 45, 59, 60, 92
Hsieh, Tehching 69–70
Husserl, Edmund 101–2

ideologies *see* stage ideologies
I'd Hide You (Blast Theory) 88, 89–90, 96, 136
If anyone wonders why rocks breakdown (Shearing) 102–3
immersive theatre 83, 90
Imponderabilia (Ulay and Abramović) 90
installation art 12, 16, 100, 122–3; mirrored 62–3; and scenographic scale 101–4
Inszenierung 29, 45–6
interior design 3, 16, 17, 28, 31, 99, 100, 113, 135, 136; and scenographic behaviors 104–8; and scenography 111
'International Scenography' (Kirby) 44
International Theatre Institute (ITI) 42, 43
Irwin, Kathleen 13

Jacobs, Jane M. 106–7
Janin, Jules 53
Jarman, Rhys 74
Jays, David 79, 82
Jones, Inigo 40, 125
Jones, Robert Edmond 7, 24–5
Journée des Barricades ('Day of the Barricades') 114–15
Joy, Jenn 28, 61
Jubb, David 74
Junction City, USA 128, 129

Kafka, Franz 79
Kant, Immanuel 26, 31, 93, 100, 112, 121
Kantor, Tadeusz 7–8, 61
Kaplan, Rachel 107, 110

Kaplan, Stephen 107, 110
Kaprow, Allan 30, 54
Kennedy, Dennis 14, 72
Kershaw, Baz 20, 99
Khan, Omar 90
Kiesler, Frederick 1, *1*, 2, 105, 135
kinesthetics 5, 20, 23, 59
Kirby, Michael 43, 44
Kirshenblatt-Gimblett, Barbara 13
Klotz, Heinrich 45
Kolarevic, Branko 123
Krauss, Rosalind 62–3, 121

Lahav, Amit 74
land-*scape* 47
landscape: scenographic 27; and theatre scenery 27
landscape architecture 22–3, 134
landscape painting 26–7, 125
Laterna Magika 42–3
Lavender, Andy 10–11, 54–5, 71, 72
Lavin, Sylvia 122–3
Lefebvre, Henri 23, 24, 68, 70, 77, 85, 99
Lehmann, Hans-Thies 1, 10–11, 54, 59, 72, 83, 92
Lepage, Robert 44, 52, 53–4
Lessing, G. E. 26, 31, 101
A Letter for Queen Victoria (Wilson) 58
Levin, Laura 25, 109, 133, 134
lighting 4, 25, 49, 73; and marketing 108
Lion King production 20, 108
Lippard, Lucy 87
literalism 30
living art 83, 95
Loos, Adolf 119, 125
Lotker, Sodja Zupanc 6–7, 58, 72, 87
Loutherbourg, Philip de 41
Loxley, James 29

Macgowan, Kenneth 7, 32
Machon, Josephine 83
Mackey, Sally 22
management theory 108
Manovich, Lev 128
marketing, and scenographic seduction 108–11
marketing psychology 108
Marks, L. C. 88, 94
Martinon, Jean-Paul 81
Massey, Doreen 22, 24

materiality 34, 37, 82, 115, 115, 120; affective 70, 77; assemblages of 76; lived 134; physical 54; of the theatre 8, 23, 25, 53, 54, 57, 60, 70, 72, 77, 94–5
Mayakovsky, Vladimir 43
McAuley, Gay 81
McCall, Anthony 30
McCormack, D. 70, 84
McEvilley, Thomas 81, 82, 83
McKinney, Joslin 47, 53, 57, 69, 72, 75, 77, 135
McLuhan, Marshall 94, 96
McNamara, Brooks 43
media projection 122–3
merchandising, visual 107
Merleau-Ponty, Marcel 94
Meyerhold, Vsevolod 75
Miller, Daniel 117
miniaturization 103
minimalism 30
mise en événement 55, 72
mise en abyme 71
mise en scène 2, 4, 15, 24, 27, 31, 45, 51, 68, 70, 71, 72, 76, 95, 110, 134; as a form of design dramaturgy 55; and scenography 52–6, 75
mise en sensibilité 55
Miss, Mary 62–3
MISSING UNPLUGGED (Gecko) 67–8; set of 73–7
modernism 125; in art 63; in dance 61; high 85
Monk, Meredith 43, 58
Monks, Aoife 48
montage 61
monumentality 120–2, 125, 129
Moore, Charles W. 37, 94
Morgan, Morris Hicky 40
Morris, Kelly 43
Morris, Robert 62–3

Nancy, Jean-Luc 16
Naturalism 31
Needles and Opium 52, 136
Neher, Caspar 24, 43, 45–6, 60, 94, 133
Neri, Giancarlo 101–2, 103
New Stagecraft 14, 19, 42, 56, 70, 71, 84, 100
Nield, Sophie 89
normativity 106, 117, 124–5, 135

Occupy movement 113–14, 115
O'Connell, Michael 86

O'Connor, Alan 25–6
O'Doherty, Brian 70, 85
OISTAT 42
One Year Performance (Hsieh) 69
optical machine 92
orientation 33, 37, 133; *see also* place orientation
Orr, Jake 73
othering 99, 100; of place 32–7; queer 36; of scenographics 133
Ove Arntzen, Knut 59

Pallasmaa, Juhani 119, 121, 129
Palmer, Scott 61, 135
Panchenko, Aleksandr 127
Panofsky, Erwin 40
Pavelka, Michael 45, 56
Pavis, Patrice 52, 53–4, 68
Perella, Stephen 88
Pérez-Gómez, Alberto 40
performance 9, 10, 11, 12, 13, 32, 107, 110, 111, 113, 116, 124, 129, 136; authenticity of 10; cultural 46; distributed 134; ecology of 20; of home 107; mediated 89; mixed reality 88, 89; participatory 55; vs. performativity 4; scenography in/as 135; site-specific 92; telepresent 63; vs. theatre 9, 10; theatrical 19, 55, 59; in the United States 58
performance art 9, 12–13, 28, 30, 46, 58, 123; as scenography 43
Performance Design 3, 7, 12–13, 14, 31, 32, 45, 58, 61–2, 64, 71, 72
performance installation 6, 61, 84
performance-making 6, 60, 69, 90
performance practices 46, 55, 72
Performance Studies 7, 8, 10, 13, 28, 31, 32, 44, 45, 46, 64, 68, 136
Performance Studios international (PSi) 102
performance text 43, 54, 68
performance theory 5, 8, 15, 136
performative artwork 29
performatives and performativity 5, 10; and performativity 30; spatial 19; as speech acts 29
perspective 40–1, 92, 112
Phelan, Peggy 122
phenomenology 75; queer 5, 33, 34
picturesque 26–7
'Picturesque' (Townsend) 26
place: vs. space 22–4; special 81, 82, 92, 109; *see also* place orientation; stage places

placemaking: defined 127; and the Potemkin Village 127; scenographic 127–30
place orientation 2, 15, 19–21, 37, 76, 77, 100, 119, 133; crafted 104–5; and installation art 101; interventional 135; and landscape 22–3; and scenographics 28; scenography as 23–4
Planchon, Roger 68
plastic arts 121; *see also* architecture; sculpture
Plato 35, 119, 125
playframe 52
Polieri, Jacques 43
politics: aesthetic 116, 129, 133; of authenticity 36; scenic 15, 24–8; of stage-scenes 134–5; of theatricality 9, 11, 31
Pollock Jackson 29
Ponjavic, Monika 90
Postdramatic Theatre (Lehmann) 59
Postlewait, Thomas 29
postmodernism 10, 63, 119
Potemkin, Grigory 127
Potemkin villages 17, 120, 127–30
power 34, 53, 55, 82, 83, 91, 99, 109, 113, 117, 121–2, 129–30; of alliance 115–16; of images 94; political 121, 129; of scale 103; social 116; and space 23, 114–15; systems of 10, 23, 81
power geography 82
power-geometries 22
Pradier, Jean-Marie 46, 53
Prague Quadrennial (PQ) 3, 43–4, 46, 56, 61, 87, 90, 96
Příhodová, Barbara 5
propaganda, scenographic 125–6
protest, and scenographic activism 17, 100, 113–17
psycho-geography 64, 79
Punchdrunk 16, 90, 91, 92, 108

quantification 27
queering 15, 34, 36
queer phenomenology 5, 33, 34

Raben, Jonathan 128–9
Radulj, Marina 90
Rancière, J. 92
Raumenempfindung 83
Read, Alan 9
Read, Gray 124
realism 9, 10, 81, 85, 92, 94, 103; encrypted 23; felt 134; of illusion 116; vs. illusion 29; material 103; mixed

16, 63, 87, 88, 89, 90, 134; optical 135; production of 10; theatrical 32–3, 84; *see also* us-reality
reality, virtual/augmented 134
Rebentisch, Juliane 101
recorded media 88
refrain 70, 84
Reid Payne, Darwin 4, 42, 44
Reitveld, Gerrit 105
Rewa, Natalie 60
Rist, Pipilotti 122–3
Romanticism 106, 116–17, 119, 125
Roth, Martin 45
Rousseau, Jean-Jacques 30
Roy, Sanjoy 73, 74
Rufford, J. 124

Said, Edward 34
Salter, Chris 121, 122
scaffolding 16, 122–3, 130
scale, scenographic 101–4
Scamozzi, Vincenzo 40
scene-painting 40, 41
scenery/sets 71, 72; designers of 14, 41, 49, 52, 71, 79; *see also* design
scenes 2, 25; natural 27; and scenic politics 24–8; scenographic 27
scene/scenic design 7, 14, 39, 41, 42, 48, 109; expanded 61–5
scene study 27
scenic concept 9, 26
scenic designers 42, 109
scenic politics 15, 24–8
scenographers 13, 51–2, 56, 56–8; in Anglophone theatres 51; in France 58; in Germany 58
scenographic behaviors 104, 106, 113
scenographic revolution 14
scenographics 14, 15, 16, 17, 28–32, 64, 71, 83, 84, 100, 124, 133; critical potential of 31; ecology of 20; and gardening 93, 112–13; interventional tactics of 28, 100; ontological indeterminism of 130; othering qualities of 100; and place orientation 136; potentialities of 95; practice of 96; and scale 101–4; and situational othering 36
scenographic studies 64
scenographic traits 4, 29, 31, 133; as orientating 4
scénographie 51, 52, 62
scenography: as act of place orientation 67; affordances of 77; American 44; in ancient Greece 2; in Anglophone theatres 3, 15, 39–41; as anti-spatial 119; as atmospheric 91; beyond set 71–3; beyond stages 86–92; connotation of the term 39, 42; continental differences pre-1960 41–2; as a crafting 4; as crafting of atmospheres 21; craft of 31; Czech approach to 14, 15, 43, 48, 51, 57, 64, 67; Czech influence in 41–2; in Denmark 41; and designers 3; and dramaturgy 58–61; expanded 3–4, 13, 31, 61–4; as fast architecture 122; filmic 134; first adoption of 64; French 46, 52, 52–3, 56, 62; future of 136; and gardening 111–13; German 45–6, 54; hierarchies of 15; holistic approach to 3, 5, 15, 42, 47–9, 51, 63, 72, 73, 91, 119; and installation art 101–4; and interior design 104–8, 111; in Italy 41; liberation of 13; and marketing 108–11; methods of 60; and *mise en scène* 52–6, 75; as painterly perspective 112; performance art as 43; pervasive 116; as place orientation 19–21, 23–4, 37, 119; post-disciplinary positioning of 4; post-stage 87; and protest 113–17; as 'psycho-plasticity' 14; reappraisal of 1; and scale 101–4; vs. scenographics 14, 17; second adoption of 42–6, 63–4; sound and costume as 46–9; in Spain 41; as 'the spatial' 31; as temporal assemblage 2; as theatre-making 8; time of 65, 67–71, 72, 77; as transformation 105; travelling 48; in the United States 42; West German 44
scénologie 46
Schechner, Richard 10, 11, *11*, 12, 24, 31, 43, 68, 81, 82, 83–4, 89, 91, 92, 116
Schiller, Friedrich 12
Schlemmer, Oskar 95
Schneekloth, Lynda H. 127
Schröder House (Rietveld) 105
Schwarz, Hans Peter 7, 46, 72, 87
sculpture 62–3, 94, 121; architecture and 62, 121
secondspace 23, 25
self-fashioning 105–6
sensing, five perceptual systems of 33
'Sensing Spaces: Architecture Reimagined' exhibit 11–12, 32
Serlio, Sebantiano 40, 125
sets *see* scenery/sets
shared scenic principle 72
Shearing, David 23, 27, 102–3
Shibley, Robert G. 127
Singleton, Brian 52, 56, 57
skēnē 2, 3, 21, 25, 46, 114, 115, 119

skene houses 2–3, 21, 25
skenographia 3, 14, 17, 21, 39–42, 46, 64, 112
Smith, Susan J. 105
social dramas 10, *11*
social hierarchies 81
social status 104, 105
Soft City (Raben) 128–9
Soja, Edward 23–4, 36–7, 105, 129
Sophocles 21, 40
sound 4, 73; non-verbal 48; as scenography 46–9
sound design 41, 47, 75
sound-*scape* 47
soundscape 108, 109
Southern, Richard 85
space: conceived 23; dimensional 23; event 127; heterogeneous 23; and human agency 22; hybrid 88; inbetweenness of 89; lived 23; vs. place 22–4; and power 23; representations of 23; rural 112; social 23, 70; and spatiality 23; visual 94
Sparke, Penny 104–5
spatial imaginary 23–4, 24, 77, 129
stage: as fold 88–9; as liminoid 91–2; origin of concept 2–3; positioning of 85; as transactional border 89
stage design 2, 6, 7, 12, 14, 39, 41, 42, 47, 49, 61, 91; vs. architecture 12; British 56; expanded 63; Restoration-influenced 41
stage designers 13, 39, 56, 113, 123
stage geography 4, 81–4, 96
stage ideologies 84–6
stage image 24, 45, 46, 47, 49, 94, 133
stage places 22, 46, 52, 72, 83–4, 85, 86, 95, 102, 104
stage-scene(s): architectural 124; beyond vision 92–6; politics of 134–5; of scenographic architecture 120
stage-scene symbiosis 2–3, 9, 16, 80
staging 2, 4, 5, 6, 8, 9, 10, 11, 12, 14, 68, 120, 126, 128; as affective orientation 71; art of 4; as basic feature of society 99, 109; contemporary 15, 71; Czech 51, 54; extra-daily forms of 9, 12; French 51–2; German 45–6; history of 2, 21; interior design as 107; kinetic 70; mixed reality 87; and the 'othering' of place 32, 34; of place orientation 40, 64; scenography as 2, 4, 8, 15, 19, 21, 29, 30, 32, 42–3, 45, 47, 53, 59, 68, 69, 76, 84, 90, 92, 95; situational acts of 4, 5, 9–10, 11, 12, 95, 101; techniques of 5, 11, 14, 19, 25; use of term 8, 11; of the vanishing point 41

Stanger, Arabella 77
Stewart, Kathleen 2, 9, 79, 80, 92, 100
still point 87, 96
surrogacy 15, 34–5, 36, 110; material 120
Svoboda, Josef 42–3, 44, 47, 51, 57, 68, 72, 84–5
Swain, Chris 74
Szenenbild 45
Szenografie 45, 46
Szenologie 46

Taper, Bernard 60
Taylor, Diane 9, 30
Taymor, Julie 20
TDR: The Drama Review 43
Teatro Olimpico 40, 101
techne 82
tectonics 124, 129
Thaikhun (restaurant) 109–10
Thames Town (China) 128, 129
theatre: activist 113; affective qualities of 10; ancient Greek 81, 84; as art time 106; as a condition of humanity 83–4; dramatic 48; environmental 91; European innovations in 60; as extra-daily event 30; as historic 10; as 'hypertrophy' 9; immersive 83, 90; institutional 11; as measure of sociometric process 31; medieval Cornish 85; monumental 121; Naturalist 31; operational 11; and performance 8–14; performerless 8; postdramatic 1; post-stage 91; Roman 80, 81, 86; scenographic 59; as situation 55; spatial qualities of 31; as 'special place' 81, 82, 92, 109; studio 91
Theatre and Performance Research Association (TaPRA) 28
theatre design 7, 13, 14, 39, 44, 45, 68; *see also* theatrical design
theatre dramaturgy 9, 60
Theatre in the Expanded Field (Read) 9
theatre-making 3, 15, 16, 22, 41, 43, 51, 53, 58, 60, 61, 63, 64, 84, 86, 90, 99, 125, 133, 135, 136; scenography as 5–8
theatrical design 2, 6, 7, 13, 14, 19, 31, 39, 40, 41, 42, 49, 51, 52, 56, 58, 63, 68, 73, 77, 91, 135; *see also* theatre design
theatricality 4, 30, 104, 107, 108, 116–17; anti- 31, 123; and art theory 30; duality of 10; in ordinary life 31; politics of 9, 11, 26, 31
theatring 11, 12, 45, 134

theatron 121, 134
Theatrum Mundi 81
The Empty Space (Brooks) 8
'The Theatre is Dead' (Kiesler) 1, *1*, 135
thirding 23–4, 37, 61, 129
thirdspace 23–4, 37, 129, 134–5
timeframes 83, 93, 103, 123
Tokumitsu, Mika 111
topiary 112
Towards a Poor Theatre (Grotowski) 43, 74
Townsend, Dabney 26, 27
trompe l'oeil 17, 120, 125–6, 128
Tschumi, Bernard 19–20, 95, 119, 127, 129
Tuan, Y.-F. 81
Tulane Drama Review 43
Turner, Cathy 9, 59, 61, 83, 91, 99
Turner, Victor 9, 10

ultra-space 81, 82, 83
United States: performance in 58; scenography in 42
un-reality 33
Unruh, Delbert 48
urban planning 127

Vacková, Růžena 5
vanishing point 40–1, 101
Vatican City 82
Vessel (Monk) 58

video 42, 56, 75, 87, 88
virtual reality 134
vision, augmented 134
visuality 67, 74, 88, 94
Vitruvius 35, 40–1, 112, 122, 125
Voltaire 121
von Arx, S. 69
von Hantelmann, Dorothea 4, 30, 123

Wagner, Richard 57, 72, 74
Wallen, Lawrence 40
What is Scenography? (Howard) 51
Wickham, Glynne 85
Wiles, David 80, 125
Wilson, Robert 44, 58, 70, 74
withness 79–80
Woodroffe, Simon 105
Wooster Group 87
world concepts 80, 81
worlding 2, 9, 16, 26, 34, 37, 82, 99, 103, 135, 136; anti-spatial 'fictive' 125; and fast architecture 120; of power 113; questions of scale 82–3; scenographic 79–80, 84; and visual space 94
wrights 69

Yo! Home 105
Youngblood, Gene 62
You've Never Had It So Good (Gob Squad) 87